The Letters of
PETER PLYMLEY

To his Brother Abraham
who lives in the country

TOGETHER WITH
Selected Writings, Sermons, and Speeches.

BY

SYDNEY SMITH
Canon Residentiary of St. Paul's, London

WITH AN INTRODUCTION BY
G. C. HESELTINE

LONDON & TORONTO
J. M. DENT & SONS LTD.
NEW YORK: E. P. DUTTON & CO. INC.

FIRST PUBLISHED IN THIS EDITION . . 1929

PRINTED IN GREAT BRITAIN

INTRODUCTION

IT would be as unjust to regard Sydney Smith as a mere man of letters as it would to regard him as a mere wit. The fame that has come to him as such is accidental, as is also the literary quality of his writing. Neither was essential in the man or his work. He did not write for literary fame or artistic expression, nor was he a deliberate wit. His writing and his wit were always either spontaneous expressions of his principles or just fine careless fun. He wrote in 1840: "I printed my reviews to show, if I could, that I had not passed my life merely in making jokes, but that I had used what little powers of pleasantry I might be endowed with to discountenance bad and to encourage wise and liberal principles." He wrote because he must; not for money, since he was never more than comparatively poor, although he thought himself very poor. He had a profession by which to live, and he lived by it. He became a clergyman, despite his inclination to law, because that course suited his father, who had dissipated the family fortunes on some nineteen estates and expended the dregs on providing careers for Sydney's brothers.

Born of a Huguenot-bred mother and schooled at Winchester in the hard days, he was well prepared for the penny-plain frame of mind so acceptable to the Establishment, which then demanded nothing more. His younger contemporary, John Henry Newman, developed the twopence-coloured mind, which Sydney Smith called Newmania, though he too was reared by a Huguenot mother. Some of the vast difference between the two men of similar breeding and circumstances may be due to the fact that Newman escaped the barbarity of the public school. It is certain that the great passion for truth which they possessed in common was expressed very differently, though its inspiration was Christian and its subject matter Catholicism. Both wrote only to give expression to that passion as it was moulded in their minds: Newman metaphysically and mystically in the *Apologia* and *Gerontius*, Sydney Smith logically and practically with the *argumentum ad hominem*, in the Letters to his "Brother Abraham" and his speeches and sermons. Both rendered inestimable service to the cause in which they fought, and Newman directly but Sydney Smith incidentally to Catholicism.

For Sydney Smith never ceased to insist that he hated "the Catholic nonsense," by which he meant the very things that Newman loved. Very likely he meant the nonsense generally and traditionally imputed to Catholics in his day without agreeing for a moment that it was part of Catholic dogma. He was careful to urge, as in the sermon to the Bumbles of Bristol on Guy Fawkes Day, that a religion or sect should not be judged by what its opponents say of it or by how its adherents behave, but by what its responsible exponents confess. Even so, he certainly would have rejected without hesitation very many of the authentic dogmas of Catholicism.

He was not concerned to defend or plead for Catholics, but to oppose tyranny and oppression. This he did in every other sphere, as well as the religious, wherever he found them. His particular fight for toleration was not, however, noticeably extended to Protestant Dissenters— partly no doubt because they were not being specially oppressed, but also because he appeared to see in their tenets, or at any rate in their practice, a rigidity and narrowness that amounted to an oppression of the spirit which was a very different thing from the dogmatic discipline of the Catholic Church. His essays on *Methodism* and *Foreign Missions* are savage in their denunciation of hypocrisy and fanaticism. He had a vast loathing of fanaticism in religion and repeatedly insisted on its dangers. His case for toleration in religion, though professedly general, concerned Catholics only. As a Wykehamist he followed the example of his benefactor William of Wykeham, who had pleaded, nearly five centuries earlier, for toleration without condonation of John Wycliffe.

The *Letters of Peter Plymley*, like all Sydney Smith's writings, derive their literary excellence not from literary craftsmanship, which is so often no more than the trick of making half-baked ideas readable, but from the fact that the writer felt keenly, thought clearly, and expressed his thoughts as directly and forcibly as he could. Fine prose is the natural result of such a proceeding. That explains also why Sydney Smith's writing was never immature: his first essays in the *Edinburgh Review* did not differ in quality from the last, written a quarter of a century later. He wrote very little after his appointment to a prebendal stall at Bristol early in 1828. He did not think it proper in a church dignitary to engage in controversial journalism, and he was not interested in any other sort. The press of a century ago had no prospect of becoming a lucrative pulpit in which lay and clerical theologians could preach side by side. Sydney Smith was jealous of the honour of his profession. Having accepted the profession, albeit from necessity rather than choice, he never repudiated it. His ambitions were centred in it, and any hopes of success or fame he cherished were to be success or fame as a Churchman, not as a writer or even a wit.

Though his facetiously declared motto was "*Faber fortunæ meæ,*" his real motto was "*Volo Episcopari.*" He desired preferment and, ultimately, a bishopric, and he pulled all the wires within his reach to get one—no doubt having in mind the words of St. Paul to Timothy, "If a man desire the office of a bishop, he desireth a good work." He frequently expressed his disappointment when he was passed over for less intelligent and less eligible men than himself. He never got more than the mock-title of Bishop of Mickleham, *in partibus*, conferred by his friend Francis Horner, "the Knight of the Shaggy-Eyebrows," but he seemed satisfied with the canonry at St. Paul's, "a snug thing," as his patron assured him, "worth at least two thousand pounds a year," and by that time he was passing rich on legacies from his aunt and his brother Courtenay. He had reached the age, too, when he did not need to amuse himself with the ambition, and he had fame enough as a wit which no mitre or title could advance. Moreover, he had come to love London and the society of the rich and the intelligent. A bishopric might have meant his removal to the isolation and responsibilities of a diocese. Sydney Smith could not refuse the responsibilities if he took the office and the pay. He was distinguished amongst the canons of St. Paul's for the way in which he discharged his duties, and the efficient manner in which he dealt with the administrative and business side of his office. There is abundant evidence of the important economies and practical improvements he effected, though it is true that he refused to consider seriously the idea of warming the Cathedral, because, he said, "you might as well try to warm the county of Middlesex." The point of view was not unreasonable.

The rather silly suggestion that Sydney Smith was "an indifferent clergyman" has been repeated with parrotic monotony by his successive biographers. It really amounts to saying that he was a different clergyman. Clergymen, for some esoteric reason, were (and are) expected to conform to a pattern even when they do not conform to a

church. Sydney Smith did not conform to the pattern
of the eighteenth-century parson, as a Yorkshire farmer
found in the course of an argument with him. Sydney
had been railing him for not thinking for himself, and the
farmer having exhausted argument sought to clinch the
unequal discussion by saying that if he had a son who was
a damned fool he would make him a parson; and Sydney
retorted that at least he did not get that idea from his
father. But though he did not conform to the pattern of
the parson he certainly did conform to the tenets of his
Church as he understood them. His sermons show that
without question. He had his jokes about the Thirty-
nine Articles, but having subscribed to them he did accept
them. His work as a clergyman was conscientiously done,
and it was a direct interpretation of plain Christianity as
accepted by the Church of England. He did not venture
at all beyond what was common ground. It has been
said in depreciation of his work that he disliked the study
of metaphysics and speculative theology. What he really
disliked was the pedantry and the jargon that were, and
still are, supposed to be inseparable from such studies.
As a young man he gave a famous series of lectures on
"Moral Philosophy" at the Royal Institution. He often
said he was ashamed of them, and regarded them as
catch-penny, having no written qualifications to be considered an authority on the subject. The fact that all
fashionable London fought to hear him did not, naturally,
alter his opinion, for at the age of thirty-three he had
acquired a good sense of proportion. He knew that his
knowledge was a mere smattering; he also knew that even
less passed for profound learning in professional pedants,
and therefore, though a scrupulously honest man, he had
little hesitation in delivering the lectures and taking the
very welcome cash. But he refused to set any value on
the lectures as expositions of moral philosophy himself.

He destroyed most of them and objected to their publication. It remained a perpetual mystery to him that it should be necessary to teach people the plain rudiments of common sense; to do other people's simplest thinking for them. He said so twenty-five years later when he was asked to publish his Bristol sermon on toleration.

It was common sense rather than safety that made Sydney Smith stick to the main and "agreed" dogmas of Christianity and refuse to touch anything that might drag him into the morass of theological speculation in a country which forbade him any footholds. It is ridiculous to call him a liberal Churchman in the sense of one, as we now interpret the phrase, who is free to think and teach anything he likes and set up himself or his particular clique for infallible interpreters of Christianity; liberal teachers who are not even free to accept any truth or interpretation accepted by an earlier age, because it is out of date. Far from being liberal he was exceptionally conservative and restricted in his theological opinions, so that they were such that the fewest possible number of his Christian fellow-men could disagree with him. Hence he could fight bishops, railway companies, and governments on anything offending against Christian charity or justice, and remain immune from attack in his professional capacity. He could keep every controversy free from the complications which must have resulted from such an attack had he been vulnerable to it. So he was able to fight the anti-Catholic oppression and the fear and ignorance that were the mainstay of it without being accused of professional dishonesty —a charge that, even partially sustained, would have proved fatal to his case. So secure was his position that not only was he immune from counter-attack but the case was practically undefended. The Government flew into a panic and was at great pains, he tells us, to discover the author of *Peter Plymley's Letters*; but from that day religious oppression fought a hopeless rearguard action. Peter Plymley's logic, backed by some of the most excellent and well-founded ridicule in the world, was completely effective. Catholic Emancipation might be delayed, but it could no longer be denied.

Almost every sort of oppression that was attacked by Sydney Smith succumbed to the attack. The effect on public opinion of his advocacy of the Reform Bill was enormous. The Game Laws, Poor Laws, Botany Bay, Climbing Boys, Locking-in on Railroads were all subject to correction during his lifetime. The two exceptions to this generalisation were the Ballot and the Society for the Suppression of Vice. The ballot, he said, should be open and not secret: men should have the courage of their convictions and men with courage should not be forced to secretive voting to save the faces of cowards. He was convinced that an insistence on the right to vote freely and openly was more dignified than the secretive protection of men who, if they had not courage enough, were not fit to vote. He stood for the sound principle against the furtive expedient. The furtive expedient still persists. Nothing brought forth Sydney Smith's contempt more than the nepotism and nummary corruption of the politics of his day. He felt that openness all round would reduce this. He may yet be justified.

The Society for the Suppression of Vice called forth one of his most invincible arguments—that an organisation of common informers is a menace to the administration of justice, and usurps the proper functions of the machinery of the law. Such organisations still flourish and they exhibit all the serious defects which Sydney Smith said were inherent in them. Amongst other bad principles on which they are founded is the assumption that individuals, and particularly the poor, need the moral correction of the self-righteous, and particularly the rich, for the good of

society. These societies have survived, not because they
are justified: the arguments against them are as unanswer-
able as they were a century ago, but because prosperity
makes prigs; and it is no part of a plutocracy's business to
unmake them by making the law effective without them.

Sydney Smith's instincts in this matter were perfectly
sound. He had no illusions about the virtues of democracy as we understand it; but he did not on that account
detest plutocracy less. He was very well aware of the
incapacities of the common people and their need for
government from above. But he was not blind to the
dangers of class legislation and class arrogance. A curate
of twenty-three going from New College to the bleak and
destitute village of Netheravon on Salisbury Plain could
hardly be expected to see the hidden beauties of human
nature in the samples he found there. He has left us a
catalogue of the samples, and a more pitiable collection
of human beings it would be difficult to find. A few
centuries of dispossession and the recent incidence of
industrial prosperity were too much for an emasculated
Christianity to cope with. The degradation was wellnigh
complete. Sydney Smith never recovered from the shock
he received from contact with it.

When the patron of the living sent him as tutor with
his son to Edinburgh, he was glad to escape from the
prison and poverty of the country curacy to the society
of his fellows. Thenceforward he never lacked the society
of the plutocracy, or "plousiocracy" as he preferred to call
it, and the aristocracy. He was reasonably well paid for
his tutoring and he did a little preaching at Edinburgh.
When he went to London and married Miss Katherine
Pybus of Cheam, he had difficulty in making ends meet in
the society in which he moved, but he was never destitute
or likely to be so. Yet in his sermons, lectures, and
reviews he is constantly referring to farm labourers and

living conditions amongst the propertyless serfs. He never concealed his poor opinion of them—their weakness of intellect and morals; but he never made any mistake about the responsibility for their condition. He blamed those who had money, power, and culture for the condition of those who had not. He may have suffered from considerable class-consciousness himself and behaved in a domineering and even at times arrogant fashion towards his social inferiors, but he never gave them a word of blame and they loved him. His parishioners, and especially his servants at Foston and Combe Florey, were devoted to him. Many of his servants followed him from Yorkshire to Somerset when his promotion to the prebendal stall at Bristol came in 1828, and that was a considerable sacrifice for Yorkshire folk to make in the days before it was so easy to return.

Few pastors can have lived for their flocks more industriously than Sydney Smith. As a spiritual father he fed them with the facts of Christianity in simple, direct, and interesting language, as they had not been fed for many a day. The first time he thumped the plush top of the pulpit at Foston, he tells us, the dust of 150 years rose and obscured his congregation. With that reasonable appreciation of the interdependence of body and soul which distinguishes true Christianity from the neo-Manichean variety, Sydney Smith was as careful of the bodies of his flock as of their souls. He had acquired a smattering of medicine at Edinburgh, and amateur doctoring was his great hobby. He always kept a well-stocked medicine-chest for the benefit of the parish, and rarely went abroad without pills for somebody in one pocket and sugar-plums for the youngsters in another. His animals came in for their share of his physic too; and sometimes, as when his horse swallowed a complete box of opium pills, rather more.

Then, to complete his public usefulness, he was a Justice of the Peace. And a pretty unconventional Justice he must have been when the rest of his fellow-magistrates held poaching and stealing to deserve transportation and hanging, for he administered the Game Laws with great reluctance, not to say leniency. The juvenile offender who appeared before the stern parson was usually terrified by his manner and the threat of the parson's "private gallows,"—but he was not sent to prison.

For nearly a quarter of a century at Foston and another seventeen years at Combe Florey this pastor served his people by ministering to them at home and fighting for their better government in high places. His popularity with neighbouring gentry and his hospitality assured him a sufficiency of the sort of company he liked, and he never lacked old friends. He was continually gaining and never losing them till in his Pauline days he had as big a circle (with Holland House for its centre) as the most sociable of men could wish for.

In the true tradition of the bon-vivants, Sydney Smith loved good food and good drink, good clothes, and comfort, which he held with his prototype of Chinon to be "indeed the true diet prescribed by the art of good and sound Physick, although a rabble of loggerheaded Physicians, nuzzeled in the brabbling shop of Sophistes, counsel the contrary." Foston Rectory, the "Rector's Head," built under his own supervision to his own plan, was a model of combined architectural economy and comfort. He built a house to live in, and could not afford to build one to look at. Everywhere he invented labour-saving and comfort-promoting devices, and had the routine of the house carefully regulated to suit his comfort rather than convention.

From devising catapults for turkey-snatching at school to the "Universal Scratcher" for his farm animals, the fire-iron holder for his study, the suit of "rheumatic-armour" for the afflicted, and the "Tantalus" accelerator for his mare "Calamity," he turned to nicknames for all and sundry. His servant was Bunch, and his draught oxen Tug and Lug (who required buckets of sal volatile), and Haul and Crawl. He described his friend Jeffrey, when he met him astride "Bitty" the donkey, as

> Witty as Horatius Flaccus,
> As great a Jacobin as Gracchus,
> Short, though not as fat, as Bacchus
> Riding on a little jackass.

He was himself one of the great company of fat men, "of the family of Falstaff," and never walked where he could ride, and never rode a horse where he could get a carriage. Spiritual and mental health, he insisted, depended very much on environment, so he had his house lighted "like a town celebrating a naval victory," and he kept his company, even when it was no more than his own household, in perpetual good humour. The wit who can always rise to the occasion in public is well enough and tolerable, in some exceptional cases, even to a facetious old age, but Sydney Smith could keep his own household in roars of laughter to his dying day. When a man can make his own family appreciate his wit after forty years, there is probably something in it. Tom Moore said that Sydney's wit always involved a thought worth remembering for its own sake, and that, considering wits at large, must have struck people as rather funny.

In London ten o'clock breakfasts for his friends were the rule, and since they were affairs of "muffins and metaphysics, crumpets and contradictions," they had indefinite periods. As probably the greatest diner-out of his day he had the pick of the dinners of London. He enjoyed his wine and so flung all his weight against interference with the poor man's drink. He was fond of clubs. The

B

Friday Club at Edinburgh, the King of Clubs in London, and even the Athenæum (but in the pre-morgue days of John Wilson Croker and Byron) were his favourite haunts. The modern silent clubman may be thankful that Sydney Smith is no longer likely to apply for membership.

Sydney's love of society, and the particular kind of society which was led by Lord and Lady Holland, made him come to like London inordinately and regard the country as a "healthy grave," a sort of limbo to recuperate in but not to live in. Yet his chosen association with the wealthy and the nobility whose darling he was, never blinded him to the dangers of plutocratic patronage of the arts, though he accepted that patronage in spirit if not in kind. He often spoke vehemently against it, just before going to dine with a plutocrat. He did not hesitate to make unto himself friends of the mammon of iniquity, but he would never call it anything else or bend his mind or his pen in submission to it. When he had anything to say he said it without counting the cost or considering the reaction against himself. For that he suffered lack of preferment in his profession; but he would not have taken back a word, though it cost him his living or his liberty. He never concealed his opinions whatever the company. Therefore he could safely hate the plutocracy and yet dine with it. He saw no reason, as he says, for any puritanical feeling against eating Tory dinners because he was an inveterate Whig

> Tory and Whig in turns shall be my host,
> I taste no politics in boiled and roast.

Gout is a penalty of good living. Sydney paid that penalty heavily and cheerfully. But God knows why he should have been afflicted with asthma and hay fever all his life, each separately enough to kill the spirit in any man. In 1820 he wrote, "Nobody has suffered more from low spirits than I have done," and he was then only fifty. He suffered as do all sensitive men at the sight of misery and destitution, oppression and corruption. The effect on his very sensitive, very humane mind, which was begun at Winchester College and confirmed fiercely at Netheravon, was sufficiently intense to have unbalanced a less stable mind. As it was, he craved the counteraction of ease and comfort and high spirits. "I love liberty," he says at sixty, "but hope it can be so managed that I shall have soft beds, good dinners, and fine linen for the rest of my life. I am too old to fight or to suffer."

It was so managed. But that did not relieve him of the extreme depression of spirits of which he tells us he had full comprehension. Nor did the accidents of this our mortality spare him occasions for depression. The death of his eldest and very promising son synchronised with the passing of the Catholic Emancipation Act. He was ultimately rich enough, however, to indulge his natural generosity in alleviating the sufferings of others which were a source of his depression. Once he took a whole family down to Somerset and sent them back "corpulent and desiring no better Paradise hereafter than Combe Florey." There was nothing smug about his kindness and manly benevolence. He could not even bestow a living on a poverty-stricken curate, facing starvation with his family, without making it the occasion of a practical joke, the touch of cruelty in which enhanced the ultimate joy of the recipient. There is a very Franciscan air about the light-hearted virtue of this comfort-loving parson, thanking God who had made him poor, that he had made him merry. He was in the true line of the Mountebanks of God.

As for his fine indignation, his scorn and contempt for mean and paltry men, his command of fighting words, his broad views and his wisdom, his vigorous and vituperative English, you may read it for yourselves.

The best of his incomparable wit he has taken with him to the company of his fat friends Socrates, François Rabelais, Samuel Johnson, and Horace, and no doubt the Dumb Ox also. For his wit does not bear repetition. Surprise was in the essence of it; and his own personality and delivery made it live as it can never live again in printers' ink. He has left us an example of patriotism and courage, honesty and humanity which it is hard to match in English letters and harder still in English politics.

G. C. HESELTINE.

BIOGRAPHICAL DATA

1771. Born at Woodford, Essex, the son of Robert Smith and his wife Marie Olier.

1777–82. At a private school kept by Mr. Marsh at Southampton.

1782–8. Scholar of Winchester College.

1789–94. Scholar and later Fellow of New College, Oxford.

1794. Ordained. Curate at Netheravon.

1797. To Edinburgh as tutor to Michael Hicks-Beach.

1801. Founded the *Edinburgh Review* with Francis Jeffrey, Brougham, Horner, Lord Webb Seymour, and others, and edited first number.

1803. To London, and Holland House (1805).

1804–6. Delivered lectures on "Moral Philosophy" at the Royal Institution. Preacher at the Foundling Hospital, Berkeley Chapel, and Fitzroy Chapel.

1806. Presented to the living of Foston in Yorkshire by the influence of Lord and Lady Holland.

1807. Wrote the *Letters of Peter Plymley*.

1809. To Yorkshire.

1828. Canon of Bristol Cathedral and rector of Combe Florey.

1831. Canon residentiary of St. Paul's, London.

1839. Published *Collected Works*.

1845. Died at 56 Green Street, Grosvenor Square. Buried at Kensal Green.

CONTENTS

WHAT IS A PUSEYITE?

"At a recent trial Lord Justice Knight Bruce asked if any of the learned counsel could define a Puseyite, but none of the learned gentlemen attempted a definition."—*Morning Herald.*

PRAY tell me what's a Puseyite? 'tis puzzling to describe
This ecclesiastic genus of a pious, hybrid tribe.
At Lambeth and the Vatican, he's equally at home
Altho' 'tis said, he rather gives the preference to Rome.

Voracious as a bookworm is his antiquarian maw,
The "Fathers" are his text-book, the "Canons" are his law,
He's mighty in the Rubrics, and well up in the Creeds,
But he only quotes the "Articles" just as they suit his needs.

The Bible is to him almost a sealed book,
Reserve is on his lips and mystery in his look;
The sacramental system is the torch to illume his night,
He loves the earthly candlestick more than the heavenly light.

He's great in punctilios, where he bows and where he stands,
In the cutting of his surplice and the hemming of his bands,
Each saint upon the Calendar he knows by heart at least,
He always dates his letters on a "Vigil" or a "Feast."

But hark! With what a nasal twang, betwixt a whine and groan,
He doth our noble liturgy most murderously intone;
Cold are his prayers and praises, his preaching colder still,
Inanimate and passionless; his very look does chill.

He talketh much of discipline, yet when the shoe doth pinch,
This most obedient, duteous son will not give way an inch;
Pliant and obstinate by turns, whate'er may be the whim,
He's only for the Bishop when the Bishop is for him.

Others as weak but more sincere, who rather feel than think,
Encouraging he leads to Popery's dizzy brink,
And when they take the final plunge, he walks back quite content
To his snug berth in Mother Church, and wonders why they went.

Such, and much worse, aye, worse! had I time to write,
Is a faint sketch, your worship, of a thorough Puseyite,
Whom even Rome repudiates, as she laughs within her sleeve,
At the sacerdotal mimic, the solemn Would-Believe.

S. S.

THE
LETTERS OF PETER PLYMLEY

July 14th, 1807.

MY DEAR LADY HOLLAND,

Mr. Allen has mentioned to me the letters of a Mr. Plymley, which I have obtained from the adjacent market-town, and read with some entertainment. My conjecture lies between three persons, Sir Samuel Romilly, Sir Arthur Piggott, or Mr. Horner, for the name is evidently fictitious. I shall be very happy to hear your conjectures on this subject on Saturday, when I hope you will let me dine with you at Holland House. . . .

SYDNEY SMITH.

I wish I could write as well as Plymley; but if I could, where is such a case to be found? When had any lawyer such a brief?

LETTER FROM SYDNEY SMITH TO EARL GREY.

The Government of that day took great pains to find out the author; all that they *could* find was, that they were brought to Mr. Budd, the publisher, by the Earl of Lauderdale. Somehow or another, it came to be conjectured that I was the author. I have always denied it; but finding that I deny it in vain . . .

SYDNEY SMITH'S PREFACE TO *Collected Works*, 1839.

LETTER I

DEAR ABRAHAM,

A worthier and better man than yourself does not exist;
but I have always told you from the time of our boyhood,
that you were a bit of a goose. Your parochial affairs
are governed with exemplary order and regularity; you
are as powerful in the vestry as Mr. Perceval[1] is in the
House of Commons,—and, I must say, with much more
reason; nor do I know any church where the faces and
smock-frocks of the congregation are so clean, or their
eyes so uniformly directed to the preacher. There is
another point, upon which I will do you ample justice;
and that is, that the eyes so directed towards you are
wide open; for the rustic has, in general, good principles,
though he cannot control his animal habits; and, however
loud he may snore, his face is perpetually turned toward
the fountain of orthodoxy.

Having done you this act of justice, I shall proceed,
according to our ancient intimacy and familiarity, to
explain to you my opinions about the Catholics, and to
reply to yours.

In the first place, my sweet Abraham, the Pope is not
landed—nor are there any curates sent out after him—
nor has he been hid at St. Alban's by the Dowager Lady
Spencer—nor dined privately at Holland House[2]—nor been
seen near Dropmore. If these fears exist (which I do
not believe), they exist only in the mind of the Chancellor
of the Exchequer[3]; they emanate from his zeal for the
Protestant interest; and, though they reflect the highest
honour upon the delicate irritability of his faith, must
certainly be considered as more ambiguous proofs of the
sanity and vigour of his understanding. By this time,
however, the best informed clergy in the neighbourhood
of the metropolis are convinced that the rumour is without
foundation: and, though the Pope is probably hovering
about our coast in a fishing-smack, it is most likely he will

[1] See p. 291.   [2] See p. 291.   [3] See p. 291.

C   I

fall a prey to the vigilance of our cruisers; and it is certain
he has not yet polluted the Protestantism of our soil.

Exactly in the same manner, the story of the wooden
gods seized at Charing Cross, by an order from the Foreign
Office, turns out to be without the shadow of a foundation:
instead of the angels and archangels, mentioned by the
informer, nothing was discovered but a wooden image of
Lord Mulgrave,[1] going down to Chatham, as a head-piece
for the Spanker gun-vessel: it was an exact resemblance
of his Lordship in his military uniform; and *therefore* as
little like a god as can well be imagined.

Having set your fears at rest, as to the extent of the
conspiracy formed against the Protestant religion, I will
now come to the argument itself.

You say these men interpret the Scriptures in an un-
orthodox manner, and that they eat their god.—Very
likely. All this may seem very important to you, who live
fourteen miles from a market town, and, from long residence
upon your living, are become a kind of holy vegetable; and,
in a theological sense, it is highly important. But I want
soldiers and sailors for the state; I want to make a greater
use than I now can do of a poor country full of men; I
want to render the military service popular among the
Irish; to check the power of France; to make every possible
exertion for the safety of Europe, which in twenty years'
time will be nothing but a mass of French slaves: and then
you, and ten other such boobies as you, call out—"For
God's sake, do not think of raising cavalry and infantry
in Ireland! . . . They interpret the Epistle to Timothy
in a different manner from what we do! . . . They eat a
bit of wafer every Sunday, which they call their God!"
. . . I wish to my soul they would eat you, and such
reasoners as you are. What! when Turk, Jew, Heretic,
Infidel, Catholic, Protestant, are all combined against this
country; when men of every religious persuasion, and no
religious persuasion; when the population of half the globe
is up in arms against us; are we to stand examining our
generals and armies as a bishop examines a candidate for
holy orders? and to suffer no one to bleed for England who
does not agree with you about the 2nd of Timothy? You
talk about Catholics! If you and your brotherhood have

[1] See p. 291.

been able to persuade the country into a continuation of
this grossest of all absurdities, you have ten times the
power which the Catholic clergy ever had in their best days.
Louis XIV, when he revoked the Edict of Nantes, never
thought of preventing the Protestants from fighting his
battles; and gained accordingly some of his most splendid
victories by the talents of his Protestant generals. No
power in Europe, but yourselves, has ever thought for
these hundred years past, of asking whether a bayonet is
Catholic, or Presbyterian, or Lutheran; but whether it is
sharp and well-tempered. A bigot delights in public
ridicule; for he begins to think he is a martyr. I can
promise you the full enjoyment of this pleasure, from one
extremity of Europe to the other.

I am as disgusted with the nonsense of the Roman
Catholic religion as you can be: and no man who talks
such nonsense shall ever tithe the product of the earth,
nor meddle with the ecclesiastical establishment in any
shape;—but what have I to do with the speculative nonsense of his theology, when the object is to elect the
mayor of a county town, or to appoint a colonel of a
marching regiment? Will a man discharge the solemn
impertinences of the one office with less zeal, or shrink
from the bloody boldness of the other with greater timidity,
because the blockhead believes in all the Catholic nonsense
of the real presence? I am sorry there should be such
impious folly in the world, but I should be ten times a
greater fool than he is, if I refused, in consequence of his
folly, to lead him out against the enemies of the state.
Your whole argument is wrong: the state has nothing
whatever to do with theological errors which do not
violate the common rules of morality, and militate against
the fair power of the ruler: it leaves all these errors to you,
and to such as you. You have every tenth porker in your
parish for refuting them; and take care that you are
vigilant, and logical in the task.

I love the Church as well as you do; but you totally
mistake the nature of an establishment, when you contend
that it ought to be connected with the military and civil
career of every individual in the state. It is quite right
that there should be one clergyman to every parish interpreting the Scriptures after a particular manner, ruled

by a regular hierarchy, and paid with a rich proportion of haycocks and wheat-sheafs. When I have laid this foundation for a rational religion in the state—when I have placed ten thousand well-educated men in different parts of the kingdom to preach it up, and compelled everybody to pay them, whether they hear them or not—I have taken such measures as I know must always procure an immense majority in favour of the Established Church; but I can go no farther. I cannot set up a civil inquisition, and say to one, you shall not be a butcher, because you are not orthodox; and prohibit another from brewing, and a third from administering the law, and a fourth from defending the country. If common justice did not prohibit me from such a conduct, common sense would. The advantage to be gained by quitting the heresy would make it shameful to abandon it; and men who had once left the Church would continue in such a state of alienation from a point of honour, and transmit that spirit to the latest posterity. This is just the effect your disqualifying laws have produced. They have fed Dr. Rees,[1] and Dr. Kippis[2]; crowded the congregation of the Old Jewry to suffocation; and enabled every sublapsarian, and superlapsarian, and semi-pelagian clergyman, to build himself a neat brick chapel, and live with some distant resemblance to the state of a gentleman.

You say the King's coronation oath will not allow him to consent to any relaxation of the Catholic laws.—Why not relax the Catholic laws as well as the laws against Protestant dissenters? If one is contrary to his oath, the other must be so too; for the spirit of the oath is, to defend the Church establishment, which the Quaker and the Presbyterian differ from as much or more than the Catholic; and yet his Majesty has repealed the Corporation and Test Act in Ireland, and done more for the Catholics of both kingdoms than had been done for them since the Reformation. In 1778, the ministers said nothing about the royal conscience; in 1793 * no conscience; in 1804 no conscience; the common feeling of humanity and justice then seem to have had their fullest influence upon the

---

[1] See p. 291.   [2] See p. 291.
* These feelings of humanity and justice were at some periods a little quickened by the representations of 40,000 armed volunteers.

advisers of the Crown: but in 1807—a year, I suppose,
eminently fruitful in moral and religious scruples (as some
years are fruitful in apples, some in hops)—it is contended
by the well-paid John Bowles, and by Mr. Perceval (who
tried to be well paid), that that is now perjury which we
had hitherto called policy and benevolence! Religious
liberty has never made such a stride as under the reign of
his present Majesty; nor is there any instance in the annals
of our history, where so many infamous and damnable
laws have been repealed as those against the Catholics
which have been put an end to by him: and then, at the
close of this useful policy, his advisers discover that the
very measures of concession and indulgence, or (to use my
own language) the measures of justice, which he has been
pursuing through the whole of his reign, are contrary to
the oath he takes at its commencement! That oath binds
his Majesty not to consent to any measure contrary to the
interest of the Established Church: but who is to judge of
the tendency of each particular measure? Not the King
alone: it can never be the intention of this law that the
King, who listens to the advice of his Parliament upon a
road bill, should reject it upon the most important of all
measures. Whatever be his own private judgment of the
tendency of any ecclesiastical bill, he complies most strictly
with his oath, if he is guided in that particular point by the
advice of his Parliament, who may be presumed to understand its tendency better than the King, or any other
individual. You say, if Parliament had been unanimous
in their opinion of the absolute necessity for Lord Howick's
bill, and the King had thought it pernicious, he would have
been perjured if he had not rejected it. I say, on the
contrary, his Majesty would have acted in the most conscientious manner, and have complied most scrupulously
with his oath, if he had sacrificed his own opinion to the
opinion of the great council of the nation; because the
probability was that such opinion was better than his
own; and upon the same principle, in common life, you
give up your opinion to your physician, your lawyer,
and your builder.

You admit this bill did not compel the King to elect
Catholic officers, but only gave him the option of doing
so if he pleased; but you add, that the King was right in

not trusting such dangerous power to himself or his successors. Now you are either to suppose that the King for the time being has a zeal for the Catholic establishment, or that he has not. If he has not, where is the danger of giving such an option? If you suppose that he may be influenced by such an admiration of the Catholic religion, why did his present Majesty,[1] in the year 1804, consent to that bill which empowered the Crown to station ten thousand Catholic soldiers in any part of the kingdom, and placed them absolutely at the disposal of the Crown? If the King of England for the time being is a good Protestant, there can be no danger in making the Catholic *eligible* to anything: if he is not, no power can possibly be so dangerous as that conveyed by the bill last quoted; to which, in point of peril, Lord Howick's[2] bill is a mere joke. But the real fact is, one bill opened a door to his Majesty's advisers for trick, jobbing, and intrigue; the other did not.

Besides, what folly to talk to me of an oath, which, under all possible circumstances, is to prevent the relaxation of the Catholic laws! for such a solemn appeal to God sets all conditions and contingencies at defiance. Suppose Bonaparte was to retrieve the only very great blunder he has made, and were to succeed, after repeated trials, in making an impression upon Ireland, do you think we should hear any thing of the impediment of a coronation oath? or would the spirit of this country tolerate for an hour such ministers, and such unheard-of nonsense, if the most distant prospect existed of conciliating the Catholics by every species even of the most abject concession? And yet, if your argument is good for any thing, the coronation oath ought to reject, at such a moment, every tendency to conciliation, and to bind Ireland for ever to the crown of France.

I found in your letter the usual remarks about fire, fagot, and bloody Mary. Are you aware, my dear Priest, that there were as many persons put to death for religious opinions under the mild Elizabeth as under the bloody Mary? The reign of the former was, to be sure, ten times as long, but I only mention the fact, merely to show you that something depends upon the age in which men live,

[1] See p. 291.   [2] See p. 291.

as well as on their religious opinions. Three hundred
years ago, men burnt and hanged each other for these
opinions. Time has softened Catholic as well as Protestant; they both required it; though each perceives only
his own improvement, and is blind to that of the other.
We are all the creatures of circumstances. I know not a
kinder and better man than yourself; but you (if you had
lived in those times) would certainly have roasted your
Catholic: and I promise you, if the first exciter of this
religious mob had been as powerful then as he is now, you
would soon have been elevated to the mitre. I do not go
to the length of saying that the world has suffered as much
from Protestant as from Catholic persecution; far from it:
but you should remember the Catholics had all the power,
when the idea first started up in the world that there
could be two modes of faith; and that it was much more
natural they should attempt to crush this diversity of
opinion by great and cruel efforts, than that the Protestants
should rage against those who differed from them, when
the very basis of their system was complete freedom in
all spiritual matters.

I cannot extend my letter any further at present, but
you shall soon hear from me again. You tell me I am a
party man. I hope I shall always be so, when I see my
country in the hands of a pert London joker[1] and a second-
rate lawyer.[2] Of the first, no other good is known than
that he makes pretty Latin verses; the second seems
to me to have the head of a country parson, and the tongue
of an Old Bailey lawyer.

If I could see good measures pursued, I care not a farthing
who is in power; but I have a passionate love for common
justice, and for common sense, and I abhor and despise
every man who builds up his political fortune upon their
ruin.

God bless you, reverend Abraham, and defend you
from the Pope, and all of us from that administration who
seek power by opposing a measure which Burke, Pitt, and
Fox all considered as absolutely necessary to the existence
of the country.

[1] See p. 291.   [2] See p. 291.

LETTER II

DEAR ABRAHAM,

The Catholic not respect an oath! why not? What upon earth has kept him out of Parliament, or excluded him from all the offices whence he is excluded, but his respect for oaths? There is no law which prohibits a Catholic to sit in Parliament. There could be no such law; because it is impossible to find out what passes in the interior of any man's mind. Suppose it were in contemplation to exclude all men from certain offices who contended for the legality of taking tithes: the only mode of discovering that fervid love of decimation which I know you to possess would be to tender you an oath against that damnable doctrine, that it is lawful for a spiritual man to take, abstract, appropriate, subduct, or lead away the tenth calf, sheep, lamb, ox, pigeon, duck, etc. etc. etc., and every other animal that ever existed, which of course the lawyers would take care to enumerate. Now this oath I am sure you would rather die than take; and so the Catholic is excluded from Parliament because he will not swear that he disbelieves the leading doctrines of his religion! The Catholic asks you to abolish some oaths which oppress him; your answer is, that he does not respect oaths. Then why subject him to the test of oaths? The oaths keep him out of Parliament; why, then, he respects them. Turn which way you will, either your laws are nugatory, or the Catholic is bound by religious obligations as you are: but no eel in the well-sanded fist of a cook-maid, upon the eve of being skinned, ever twisted and writhed as an orthodox parson does when he is compelled by the gripe of reason to admit anything in favour of a Dissenter.

I will not dispute with you whether the Pope be or be not the Scarlet Lady of Babylon. I hope it is not so; because I am afraid it will induce his Majesty's Chancellor of the Exchequer to introduce several severe bills against popery, if that is the case; and though he will have the decency to appoint a previous committee of inquiry as to the fact, the committee will be garbled and the report inflammatory. Leaving this to be settled as he pleases to settle it, I wish to inform you, that previously to the bill last passed in favour of the Catholics, at the suggestion of Mr. Pitt, and for his satisfaction, the opinions of six of the most celebrated of the foreign Catholic universities were taken as to the right of the Pope to interfere in the temporal concerns of any country. The answer cannot possibly leave the shadow of a doubt, even in the mind of Baron Maseres[1]; and Dr. Rennel[2] would be compelled to admit it, if three Bishops lay dead at the very moment the question were put to him. To this answer might be added also the solemn declaration and signature of all the Catholics in Great Britain.

I should perfectly agree with you, if the Catholics admitted such a dangerous dispensing power in the hands of the Pope; but they all deny it, and laugh at it, and are ready to abjure it in the most decided manner you can devise. They obey the Pope as the spiritual head of their church; but are you really so foolish as to be imposed upon by mere names?—What matters it the seven thousandth part of a farthing who is the spiritual head of any church? Is not Mr. Wilberforce[3] at the head of the church of Clapham? Is not Dr. Letsom[4] at the head of the Quaker church? Is not the General Assembly at the head of the church of Scotland? How is the government disturbed by these many-headed churches? or in what way is the power of the Crown augmented by this almost nominal dignity?

The King appoints a fast day once a year, and he makes the Bishops: and if the government would take half the pains to keep the Catholics out of the arms of France that it does to widen Temple Bar, or improve Snow Hill, the King would get into his hands the appointments of the titular Bishops of Ireland.—Both Mr. C——'s[5] sisters enjoy pensions more than sufficient to place the two greatest dignitaries of the Irish Catholic Church entirely at the disposal of the Crown.—Every body who knows Ireland knows perfectly well, that nothing would be easier, with the expenditure of a little money, than to preserve enough of the ostensible appointment in the hands of the Pope to satisfy the scruples of the Catholics, while the real nomination remained with the Crown. But, as I have before said, the moment the very name of Ireland is mentioned, the English seem to bid adieu to common feeling, common

[1] See p. 292. [2] See p. 292. [3] See p. 292. [4] See p. 292. [5] See p. 292.

prudence, and common sense, and to act with the barbarity of tyrants, and the fatuity of idiots.

Whatever your opinion may be of the follies of the Roman Catholic religion, remember they are the follies of four millions of human beings,[1] increasing rapidly in numbers, wealth, and intelligence, who, if firmly united with this country, would set at defiance the power of France, and if once wrested from their alliance with England, would in three years render its existence as an independent nation absolutely impossible. You speak of danger to the Establishment: I request to know when the Establishment was ever so much in danger as when Hoche was in Bantry Bay, and whether all the books of Bossuet, or the arts of the Jesuits, were half so terrible? Mr. Perceval and his parsons forgot all this, in their horror lest twelve or fourteen old women may be converted to holy water, and Catholic nonsense. They never see that, while they are saving these venerable ladies from perdition, Ireland may be lost, England broken down, and the Protestant Church, with all its deans, prebendaries, Percevals and Rennels, be swept into the vortex of oblivion.

Do not, I beseech you, ever mention to me again the name of Dr. Duigenan.[2] I have been in every corner of Ireland, and have studied its present strength and condition with no common labour. Be assured Ireland does not contain at this moment less than five millions of people. There were returned in the year 1791 to the hearth tax 701,000 houses, and there is no kind of question that there were about 50,000 houses omitted in that return. Taking, however, only the number returned for the tax, and allowing the average of six to a house (a very small average for a potato-fed people), this brings the population to 4,200,000 people in the year 1791: and it can be shown from the clearest evidence (and Mr. Newenham[3] in his book shows it), that Ireland for the last fifty years has increased in its population at the rate of 50,000 or 60,000 per annum; which leaves the present population of Ireland at about five millions, after every possible deduction for *existing circumstances, just and necessary wars, monstrous and unnatural rebellions,* and all other sources of human destruction. Of this population, two out of ten are

[1] See p. 292.   [2] See p. 292.   [3] See p. 292.

Protestants; and the half of the Protestant population are Dissenters, and as inimical to the Church as the Catholics themselves.   In this state of things, thumbscrews and whipping—admirable engines of policy, as they must be considered to be—will not ultimately avail.   The Catholics will hang over you; they will watch for the moment, and compel you hereafter to give them ten times as much, against your will, as they would now be contented with, if it were voluntarily surrendered.   Remember what happened in the American war; when Ireland compelled you to give her every thing she asked, and to renounce, in the most explicit manner, your claim of sovereignty over her. God Almighty grant the folly of these present men may not bring on such another crisis of public affairs!

What are your dangers which threaten the Establishment?—Reduce this declamation to a point, and let us understand what you mean.   The most ample allowance does not calculate that there would be more than twenty members who were Roman Catholics in one house, and ten in the other, if the Catholic emancipation were carried into effect.   Do you mean that these thirty members would bring in a bill to take away the tithes from the Protestant, and to pay them to the Catholic clergy?   Do you mean that a Catholic general would march his army into the House of Commons and purge it of Mr. Perceval and Dr. Duigenan? or, that the theological writers would become all of a sudden more acute and more learned, if the present civil incapacities were removed?   Do you fear for your tithes, or your doctrines, or your person, or the English Constitution?   Every fear, taken separately, is so glaringly absurd, that no man has the folly or the boldness to state it.   Every one conceals his ignorance, or his baseness, in a stupid general panic, which, when called on, he is utterly incapable of explaining.   Whatever you think of the Catholics, there they are—you cannot get rid of them; your alternative is, to give them a lawful place for stating their grievances, or an unlawful one: if you do not admit them to the House of Commons, they will hold their parliament in Potato-place, Dublin, and be ten times as violent and inflammatory as they would be in Westminster.   Nothing would give me such an idea of security, as to see twenty or thirty Catholic gentlemen in Parliament,

looked upon by all the Catholics as the fair and proper
organ of their party. I should have thought it the height
of good fortune that such a wish existed on their part,
and the very essence of madness and ignorance to reject
it. Can you murder the Catholics?—Can you neglect
them? They are too numerous for both these expedients.
What remains to be done is obvious to every human
being—but to that man [1] who, instead of being a Methodist
preacher, is, for the curse of us and our children, and for
the ruin of Troy, and the misery of good old Priam and his
sons, become a legislator and a politician.

A distinction, I perceive, is taken, by one of the most
feeble noblemen in Great Britain, between persecution and
the deprivation of political power; whereas there is no more
distinction between these two things than there is between
him who makes the distinction and a booby. If I strip
off the relic-covered jacket of a Catholic, and give him
twenty stripes . . . I persecute: if I say, Every body in
the town where you live shall be a candidate for lucrative
and honourable offices but you, who are a Catholic . . .
I do not persecute!—What barbarous nonsense is this! as
if degradation was not as great an evil as bodily pain, or
as severe poverty: as if I could not be as great a tyrant by
saying, You shall not enjoy—as by saying, You shall
suffer. The English, I believe, are as truly religious as
any nation in Europe; I know no greater blessing: but it
carries with it this evil in its train—that any villain who
will bawl out *"The Church is in danger!"* may get a place
and a good pension; and that any administration who will
do the same thing may bring a set of men into power who,
at a moment of stationary and passive piety, would be
hooted by the very boys in the streets. But it is not all
religion; it is, in great part, the narrow and exclusive spirit
which delights to keep the common blessings of sun, and
air, and freedom, from other human beings. "Your religion has always been degraded; you are in the dust, and
I will take care you never rise again. I should enjoy less
the possession of an earthly good, by every additional
person to whom it was extended." You may not be
aware of it yourself, most reverend Abraham, but you
deny their freedom to the Catholics upon the same

[1] See p. 292.

principle that Sarah your wife refuses to give the receipt for
a ham or a gooseberry dumpling: she values her receipts,
not because they secure to her a certain flavour, but
because they remind her that her neighbours want it:—a
feeling laughable in a priestess, shameful in a priest; venial
when it withholds the blessings of a ham, tyrannical and
execrable when it narrows the boon of religious freedom.

You spend a great deal of ink about the character of the
present prime minister. Grant you all that you write—
I say, I fear he will ruin Ireland, and pursue a line of policy
destructive to the true interest of his country: and then
you tell me, he is faithful to Mrs. Perceval, and kind to the
Master Percevals! These are, undoubtedly, the first qualifications to be looked to in a time of the most serious public
danger; but somehow or another (if public and private
virtues must always be incompatible), I should prefer that
he destroyed the domestic happiness of Wood or Cockell,
owed for the veal of the preceding year, whipped his boys,
and saved his country.

The late administration did not do right; they did not
build their measures upon the solid basis of facts. They
should have caused several Catholics to have been dis-
sected after death by surgeons of either religion, and the
report to have been published with accompanying plates.
If the viscera, and other organs of life, had been found to
be the same as in Protestant bodies; if the provisions of
nerves, arteries, cerebrum, and cerebellum, had been the
same as we are provided with, or as the Dissenters are now
known to possess; then, indeed, they might have met
Mr. Perceval upon a proud eminence, and convinced the
country at large of the strong probability that the Catholics
are really human creatures, endowed with the feelings of
men, and entitled to all their rights. But instead of this
wise and prudent measure, Lord Howick, with his usual
precipitation, brings forward a bill in their favour, without
offering the slightest proof to the country that they were
any thing more than horses and oxen. The person who
shows the lama at the corner of Piccadilly has the precaution to write up—*Allowed by Sir Joseph Banks to be a
real quadruped*: so his Lordship might have said—*Allowed
by the Bench of Bishops to be real human creatures*. . . .
I could write you twenty letters upon this subject; but I am

tired, and so I suppose are you.   Our friendship is now of
forty years' standing: you know me to be a truly religious
man; but I shudder to see religion treated like a cockade,
or a pint of beer, and made the instrument of a party.
I love the King, but I love the people as well as the King;
and if I am sorry to see his old age molested, I am much
more sorry to see four millions of Catholics baffled in their
just expectations.   If I love Lord Grenville [1] and Lord
Howick, it is because they love their country: if I abhor
* * * * * *, it is because I know there is but one man among
them who is not laughing at the enormous folly and
credulity of the country, and that he is an ignorant and
mischievous bigot.   As for the light and frivolous jester
of whom it is your misfortune to think so highly—learn,
my dear Abraham, that this political Killigrew,[2] just before
the breaking-up of the last administration, was in actual
treaty with them for a place; and if they had survived
twenty-four hours longer, he would have been now declaim-
ing against the cry of No Popery! instead of inflaming it.—
With this practical comment on the baseness of human
nature, I bid you adieu!

LETTER III

ALL that I have so often told you, Mr. Abraham Plymley,
is now come to pass.   The Scythians, in whom you and the
neighbouring country gentlemen placed such confidence,
are smitten hip and thigh; their Benningsen put to open
shame; their magazines of train oil intercepted—and we
are waking from our disgraceful drunkenness to all the
horrors of Mr. Perceval and Mr. Canning. . . . We shall
now see if a nation is to be saved by school-boy jokes and
doggerel rhymes, by affronting petulance, and by the tones
and gesticulations of Mr. Pitt.[3]   But these are not all the
auxiliaries on which we have to depend; to these his
colleague will add the strictest attention to the smaller
parts of ecclesiastical government—to hassocks, to psalters,
and to surplices; in the last agonies of England, he will
bring in a bill to regulate Easter-offerings; and he will

[1] See p. 292.   [2] See p. 292.   [3] See p. 292.

adjust the stipends of curates * when the flag of France is unfurled on the hills of Kent.   Whatever can be done by very mistaken notions of the piety of a Christian, and by very wretched imitation of the eloquence of Mr. Pitt, will be done by these two gentlemen.   After all, if they both really were what they both either wish to be or wish to be thought; if the one were an enlightened Christian, who drew from the Gospel the toleration, the charity, and the sweetness which it contains; and if the other really possessed any portion of the great understanding of his Nisus who guarded him from the weapons of the Whigs; I should still doubt if they could save us.   But I am sure, we are not to be saved by religious hatred and by religious trifling; by any psalmody, however sweet; or by any persecution, however sharp: I am certain the sounds of Mr. Pitt's voice, and the measure of his tones, and the movement of his arms, will do nothing for us; when these tones, and movements, and voice bring us always declamation without sense or knowledge, and ridicule without good humour or conciliation.   Oh, Mr. Plymley, Mr. Plymley! this never will do.   Mrs. Abraham Plymley, my sister, will be led away captive by an amorous Gaul; and Joel Plymley, your first-born, will be a French drummer.

"Out of sight, out of mind," seems to be a proverb which applies to enemies as well as friends.   Because the French army was no longer seen from the cliffs of Dover; because the sound of cannon was no longer heard by the debauched London bathers on the Sussex coast; because the *Morning Post* no longer fixed the invasion sometimes for Monday, sometimes for Tuesday, sometimes (positively for the last time of invading) on Saturday; because all these causes of terror were suspended, you conceived the power of Bonaparte to be at an end, and were setting off for Paris, with Lord Hawkesbury [1] the conqueror.—This is precisely the method in which the English have acted during the whole of the revolutionary war.   If Austria or Prussia armed, doctors of divinity immediately printed those passages out of Habakkuk in which the destruction

---

* The Reverend the Chancellor of the Exchequer has, since this was written, found time in the heat of the session to write a book on the Stipends of Curates.

[1] See p. 292.

of the Usurper by General Mack and the Duke of Brunswick
is so clearly predicted. If Bonaparte halted, there was a
mutiny, or a dysentery. If any one of his generals were
eaten up by the light troops of Russia, and picked (as their
manner is) to the bone, the sanguine spirit of this country
displayed itself in all its glory. What scenes of infamy
did the Society for the Suppression of Vice lay open to
our astonished eyes! tradesmen's daughters dancing; pots
of beer carried out between the first and second lesson;
and dark and distant rumours of indecent prints. Clouds
of Mr. Canning's cousins arrived by the waggon; all the
contractors left their cards with Mr. Rose [1]; and every
plunderer of the public crawled out of his hole, like slugs,
and grubs, and worms, after a shower of rain.

If my voice could have been heard at the late changes,
I should have said, "Gently; patience; stop a little; the
time is not yet come; the mud of Poland will harden, and
the bowels of the French grenadiers will recover their
tone. When honesty, good sense, and liberality have
extricated you out of your present embarrassment, then
dismiss them as a matter of course; but you cannot spare
them just now. Don't be in too great a hurry, or there
will be no monarch to flatter and no country to pillage.
Only submit for a little time to be respected abroad; overlook the painful absence of the tax-gatherer for a few
years; bear up nobly under the increase of freedom and of
liberal policy for a little time, and I promise you, at the
expiration of that period, you shall be plundered, insulted,
disgraced, and restrained to your heart's content. Do not
imagine I have any intention of putting servility and cant-
ing hypocrisy permanently out of place, or of filling up
with courage and sense those offices which naturally devolve
upon decorous imbecility and flexible cunning: give us only
a little time to keep off the hussars of France, and then the
jobbers and jesters shall return to their birthright, and
public virtue be called by its own name of fanaticism." *

[1] See p. 292.

* This is Mr. Canning's term for the detection of public abuses;
a term invented by him, and adopted by that simious parasite
who is always grinning at his heels. Nature descends down to
infinite smallness. Mr. Canning has his parasites; and if you take
a large buzzing blue-bottle fly, and look at it in a microscope, you
may see twenty or thirty little ugly insects crawling about it, which

Such is the advice I would have offered to my infatuated countrymen; but it rained very hard in November, Brother Abraham, and the bowels of our enemies were loosened, and we put our trust in white fluxes and wet mud; and there is nothing now to oppose to the conqueror of the world but a small table wit, and the sallow Surveyor of the Meltings.[1]

You ask me, if I think it possible for this country to survive the recent misfortunes of Europe?—I answer you, without the slightest degree of hesitation: that if Bonaparte lives, and a great deal is not immediately done for the conciliation of the Catholics, it does seem to me absolutely impossible but that we must perish; and take this with you, that we shall perish without exciting the slightest feeling of present or future compassion, but fall amidst the hootings and revilings of Europe, as a nation of block-heads, Methodists, and old women. If there were any great scenery, any heroic feelings, any blaze of ancient virtue, any exalted death, any termination of England that would be ever remembered, ever honoured in that western world, where liberty is now retiring, conquest would be more tolerable, and ruin more sweet; but it is doubly miserable to become slaves abroad, because we would be tyrants at home; to persecute, when we are contending against persecution; and to perish, because we have raised up worse enemies within, from our own bigotry, than we are exposed to without, from the unprincipled ambition of France. It is, indeed, a most silly and affecting spectacle to rage at such a moment against our own kindred and our own blood; to tell them they cannot be honourable in war, because they are conscientious in religion; to stipulate (at the very moment when we should buy their hearts and swords at any price) that they must hold up the right hand in prayer, and not the left; and adore one common God, by turning to the east rather than to the west.

What is it the Catholics ask of you? Do not exclude us from the honours and emoluments of the state, because we

doubtless think their fly to be the bluest, grandest, merriest, most important animal in the universe, and are convinced the world would be at an end if it ceased to buzz.

[1] See p. 293.

D

worship God in one way, and you worship him in another.
In a period of the deepest peace, and the fattest prosperity,
this would be a fair request: it should be granted, if
Lord Hawkesbury had reached Paris, if Mr. Canning's [1]
interpreter had threatened the Senate in an opening Speech,
or Mr. Perceval explained to them the improvements he
meant to introduce into the Catholic religion; but to deny
the Irish this justice now, in the present state of Europe,
and in the summer months, just as the season for destroying
kingdoms is coming on, is (beloved Abraham), whatever
you may think of it, little short of positive insanity.

Here is a frigate attacked by a corsair of immense
strength and size, rigging cut, masts in danger of coming
by the board, four foot water in the hold, men dropping
off very fast; in this dreadful situation how do you think
the Captain acts (whose name shall be Perceval)?   He
calls all hands upon deck; talks to them of King, country,
glory, sweethearts, gin, French prison, wooden shoes, Old
England, and hearts of oak: they give three cheers, rush
to their guns, and, after a tremendous conflict, succeed in
beating off the enemy.   Not a syllable of all this: this is
not the manner in which the honourable Commander goes
to work: the first thing he does is to secure twenty or
thirty of his prime sailors who happen to be Catholics, to
clap them in irons, and set over them a guard of as many
Protestants; having taken this admirable method of
defending himself against his infidel opponents, he goes
upon deck, reminds the sailors, in a very bitter harangue,
that they are of different religions; exhorts the Episcopal
gunner not to trust to the Presbyterian quarter-master;
issues positive orders that the Catholics should be fired at
upon the first appearance of discontent; rushes through
blood and brains, examining his men in the Catechism and
Thirty-nine Articles, and positively forbids every one to
sponge or ram who has not taken the Sacrament according
to the Church of England.   Was it right to take out a
captain made of excellent British stuff, and to put in such
a man as this?   Is not he more like a parson, or a talking
lawyer, than a thorough-bred seaman?   And built as she is
of heart of oak, and admirably manned, is it possible with
such a captain, to save this ship from going to the bottom?

[1] See p. 293.

You have an argument, I perceive, in common with many others, against the Catholics, that their demands complied with would only lead to further exactions, and that it is better to resist them now, before any thing is conceded, than hereafter, when it is found that all concessions are in vain. I wish the Chancellor of the Exchequer, who uses this reasoning to exclude others from their just rights, had tried its efficacy, not by his understanding, but by (what are full of much better things) his pockets. Suppose the person to whom he applied for the Meltings had withstood every plea of wife and fourteen children, no business, and good character, and refused him this paltry little office, because he might hereafter attempt to get hold of the revenues of the Duchy of Lancaster for life; would not Mr. Perceval have contended eagerly against the injustice of refusing moderate requests, because immoderate ones may hereafter be made? Would he not have said (and said truly), Leave such exorbitant attempts as these to the general indignation of the Commons, who will take care to defeat them when they do occur; but do not refuse me the Irons and the Meltings now, because I may totally lose sight of all moderation hereafter? Leave hereafter to the spirit and the wisdom of hereafter; and do not be niggardly now, from the apprehension that men as wise as you should be profuse in times to come.

You forget, Brother Abraham, that it is a vast art (where quarrels cannot be avoided) to turn the public opinion in your favour and to the prejudice of your enemy; a vast privilege to feel that you are in the right, and to make him feel that he is in the wrong: a privilege which makes you more than a man, and your antagonist less; and often secures victory, by convincing him who contends, that he must submit to injustice if he submits to defeat. Open every rank in the army and the navy to the Catholic; let him purchase at the same price as the Protestant (if either Catholic or Protestant can purchase such refined pleasures) the privilege of hearing Lord Castlereagh [1] speak for three hours; keep his clergy from starving, soften some of the most odious powers of the tything-man, and you will for ever lay this formidable question to rest. But if I am wrong, and you must quarrel at last, quarrel upon just

[1] See p. 293.

rather than unjust grounds; divide the Catholic, and unite the Protestant; be just, and your own exertions will be more formidable and their exertions less formidable; be just, and you will take away from their party all the best and wisest understandings of both persuasions, and knit them firmly to your own cause. "Thrice is he armed who has his quarrel just"; and ten times as much may he be taxed. In the beginning of any war, however destitute of common sense, every mob will roar, and every Lord of the Bed-chamber address; but if you are engaged in a war that is to last for years, and to require important sacrifices, take care to make the justice of your case so clear and so obvious, that it cannot be mistaken by the most illiterate country gentleman who rides the earth. Nothing, in fact, can be so grossly absurd as the argument which says, I will deny justice to you now, because I suspect future injustice from you. At this rate, you may lock a man up in your stable, and refuse to let him out, because you suspect that he has an intention, at some future period, of robbing your hen-roost. You may horsewhip him at Lady-day, because you believe he will affront you at Midsummer. You may commit a greater evil, to guard against a less which is merely contingent, and may never happen. You may do what you have done a century ago in Ireland, made the Catholics worse than Helots, because you suspected that they might hereafter aspire to be more than fellow-citizens; rendering their sufferings certain from your jealousy, while yours were only doubtful from their ambition; an ambition sure to be excited by the very measures which were taken to prevent it.

The physical strength of the Catholics will not be greater because you give them a share of political power. You may by these means turn rebels into friends; but I do not see how you make rebels more formidable. If they taste of the honey of lawful power, they will love the hive from whence they procure it; if they will struggle with us like men in the same state for civil influence, we are safe. All that I dread is, the physical strength of four millions of men combined with an invading French army. If you are to quarrel at last with this enormous population, still put it off as long as you can; you must gain, and cannot lose, by the delay. The state of Europe cannot be worse; the conviction which the Catholics entertain of your tyranny and injustice cannot be more alarming, nor the opinions of your own people more divided. Time, which produces such effect upon brass and marble, may inspire one Minister with modesty, and another with compassion; every circumstance may be better; some certainly will be so, none can be worse; and, after all, the evil may never happen.

You have got hold, I perceive, of all the vulgar English stories respecting the hereditary transmission of forfeited property, and seriously believe that every Catholic beggar wears the terriers [1] of his father's land next his skin, and is only waiting for better times to cut the throat of the Protestant possessor, and get drunk in the hall of his ancestors. There is one irresistible answer to this mistake, and that is, that the forfeited lands are purchased indiscriminately by Catholic and Protestant, and that the Catholic purchaser never objects to such a title. Now the land (so purchased by a Catholic) is either his own family estate, or it is not. If it is, you suppose him so desirous of coming into possession, that he resorts to the double method of rebellion and purchase; if it is not his own family estate of which he becomes the purchaser, you suppose him first to purchase, then to rebel, in order to defeat the purchase. These things may happen in Ireland; but it is totally impossible they can happen any where else. In fact, what land can any man of any sect purchase in Ireland, but forfeited property? In all other oppressed countries which I have ever heard of, the rapacity of the conqueror was bounded by the territorial limits in which the objects of his avarice were contained; but Ireland has been actually confiscated twice over, as a cat is twice killed by a wicked parish boy.

I admit there is a vast luxury in selecting a particular set of Christians, and in worrying them as a boy worries a puppy dog; it is an amusement in which all the young English are brought up from their earliest days. I like the idea of saying to men who use a different hassock from me, that till they change their hassock, they shall never be Colonels, Aldermen, or Parliament-men. While I am gratifying my personal insolence respecting religious forms,

[1] See p. 293.

I fondle myself into an idea that I am religious, and that
I am doing my duty in the most exemplary (as I certainly
am in the most easy) way. But then, my good Abraham,
this sport, admirable as it is, is become, with respect to the
Catholics, a little dangerous; and if we are not extremely
careful in taking the amusement, we shall tumble into the
holy water, and be drowned. As it seems necessary to
your idea of an established Church to have somebody to
worry and torment, suppose we were to select for this
purpose William Wilberforce, Esq., and the patent Christians
of Clapham. We shall by this expedient enjoy the same
opportunity for cruelty and injustice, without being
exposed to the same risks: we will compel them to abjure
vital clergymen by a public test, to deny that the said
William Wilberforce has any power of working miracles,
touching for barrenness or any other infirmity, or that he
is endowed with any preternatural gift whatever. We
will swear them to the doctrine of good works, compel
them to preach common sense, and to hear it; to frequent
Bishops, Deans, and other high Churchmen; and to appear
(once in the quarter at the least) at some melodrame, opera,
pantomime, or other light scenical representation; in short,
we will gratify the love of insolence and power: we will
enjoy the old orthodox sport of witnessing the impotent
anger of men compelled to submit to civil degradation, or
to sacrifice their notions of truth to ours. And all this
we may do without the slightest risk, because their numbers
are (as yet) not very considerable. Cruelty and injustice
must, of course, exist: but why connect them with danger?
Why torture a bull-dog, when you can get a frog or a rabbit?
I am sure my proposal will meet with the most universal
approbation. Do not be apprehensive of any opposition
from ministers. If it is a case of hatred, we are sure that
one man will defend it by the Gospel: if it abridges human
freedom, we know that another will find precedents for
it in the Revolution.

In the name of Heaven, what are we to gain by suffering
Ireland to be rode by that faction which now predominates
over it? Why are we to endanger our own Church and
State, not for five hundred thousand Episcopalians, but
for ten or twelve great Orange families, who have been
sucking the blood of that country for these hundred years

last past? and the folly of the Orangemen * in playing this game themselves, is almost as absurd as ours in playing it for them. They ought to have the sense to see that their business now is to keep quietly the lands and beeves of which the fathers of the Catholics were robbed in days of yore; they must give to their descendants the sop of political power: by contending with them for names, they will lose realities, and be compelled to beg their potatoes in a foreign land, abhorred equally by the English, who have witnessed their oppression, and by the Catholic Irish, who have smarted under them.

LETTER IV

THEN comes Mr. Isaac Hawkins Brown (the gentleman who danced † so badly at the Court of Naples), and asks if it is not an anomaly to educate men in another religion than your own? It certainly is our duty to get rid of error, and above all of religious error; but this is not to be done *per saltum*, or the measure will miscarry, like the Queen. It may be very easy to dance away the royal embryo of a great kingdom; but Mr. Hawkins Brown must look before he leaps, when his object is to crush an opposite sect in religion; false steps aid the one effect, as much as they are fatal to the other: it will require not only the lapse of Mr. Hawkins Brown, but the lapse of centuries, before the absurdities of the Catholic religion are laughed at as much as they deserve to be; but surely, in the mean time, the Catholic religion is better than none; four millions of Catholics are better than four millions of wild beasts; two hundred priests educated by our own government are better than the same number educated by the man who means to destroy us.

* This remark begins to be sensibly felt in Ireland. The Protestants in Ireland are fast coming over to the Catholic cause.

† In the third year of his present Majesty, and in the 30th of his own age, Mr. Isaac Hawkins Brown, then upon his travels, danced one evening at the Court of Naples. His dress was a volcano silk with lava buttons. Whether (as the Neapolitan wits said) he had studied dancing under St. Vitus, or whether David, dancing in a linen vest, was his model, is not known; but Mr. Brown danced with such inconceivable alacrity and vigour, that he threw the Queen of Naples into convulsions of laughter, which terminated in a miscarriage, and changed the dynasty of the Neapolitan throne.

The whole sum now appropriated by Government to the religious education of four millions of Christians is £13,000; a sum about one hundred times as large being appropriated in the same country to about one eighth part of this number of Protestants.   When it was proposed to raise this grant from £8000 to £13,000, its present amount, this sum was objected to by that most indulgent of Christians, Mr. Spencer Perceval, as enormous; he himself having secured for his own eating and drinking, and the eating and drinking of the Master and Miss Percevals, the reversionary sum of £21,000 a year of the public money, and having just failed in a desperate and rapacious attempt to secure to himself for life the revenues of the Duchy of Lancaster: and the best of it is, that this Minister, after abusing his predecessors for their impious bounty to the Catholics, has found himself compelled, from the apprehension of immediate danger, to grant the sum in question; thus dissolving his pearl * in vinegar, and destroying all the value of the gift by the virulence and reluctance with which it was granted.

I hear from some persons in Parliament, and from others in the sixpenny societies for debate, a great deal about unalterable laws passed at the Revolution.   When I hear any man talk of an unalterable law, the only effect it produces upon me is to convince me that he is an unalterable fool.   A law passed when there was Germany, Spain, Russia, Sweden, Holland, Portugal, and Turkey; when there was a disputed succession: when four or five hundred acres were won and lost after ten years' hard fighting; when armies were commanded by the sons of kings, and campaigns passed in an interchange of civil letters and ripe fruit; and for these laws, when the whole state of the world is completely changed, we are now, according to my Lord Hawkesbury, to hold ourselves ready to perish. It is no mean misfortune, in times like these, to be forced to say any thing about such men as Lord Hawkesbury, and to be reminded that we are governed by them; but as I am driven to it, I must take the liberty of observing, that the wisdom and liberality of my Lord Hawkesbury are of that complexion which always shrinks from the

* Perfectly ready at the same time to follow the other half o Cleopatra's example, and to swallow the solution himself.

present exercise of these virtues, by praising the splendid examples of them in ages past. If he had lived at such periods, he would have opposed the Revolution by praising the Reformation, and the Reformation by speaking handsomely of the Crusades. He gratifies his natural antipathy to great and courageous measures, by playing off the wisdom and courage which have ceased to influence human affairs against that wisdom and courage which living men would employ for present happiness. Besides, it happens unfortunately for the Warden of the Cinque Ports, that to the principal incapacities under which the Irish suffer, they were subjected after that great and glorious Revolution, to which we are indebted for so many blessings, and his Lordship for the termination of so many periods. The Catholics were not excluded from the Irish House of Commons, or military commands, before the 3d and 4th of William and Mary, and the 1st and 2d of Queen Anne.

If the great mass of the people, environed as they are on every side with Jenkinsons,[1] Percevals, Melvilles,[2] and other perils, were to pray for divine illumination and aid, what more could Providence in its mercy do than send them the example of Scotland? For what a length of years was it attempted to compel the Scotch to change their religion: horse, foot, artillery, and armed Prebendaries, were sent out after the Presbyterian parsons and their congregations. The Percevals of those days called for blood: this call is never made in vain, and blood was shed; but to the astonishment and horror of the Percevals of those days, they could not introduce the Book of Common Prayer, nor prevent that metaphysical people from going to heaven their true way, instead of our true way. With a little oatmeal for food, and a little sulphur for friction, allaying cutaneous irritation with the one hand, and holding his Calvinistical creed in the other, Sawney ran away to his flinty hills, sung his psalm out of tune his own way, and listened to his sermon of two hours long, amid the rough and imposing melancholy of the tallest thistles. But Sawney brought up his unbreeched offspring in a cordial hatred of his oppressors; and Scotland was as much a part of the weakness of England then, as Ireland is at this moment. The true and the only remedy was applied;

[1] See p. 293.   [2] See p. 293.

the Scotch were suffered to worship God after their own
tiresome manner, without pain, penalty, and privation.
No lightning descended from heaven; the country was not
ruined; the world is not yet come to an end; the dignitaries,
who foretold all these consequences, are utterly forgotten,
and Scotland has ever since been an increasing source of
strength to Great Britain.   In the six hundredth year of
our empire over Ireland, we are making laws to transport
a man, if he is found out of his house after eight o'clock at
night.   That this is necessary, I know too well; but tell
me why it is necessary?   It is not necessary in Greece,
where the Turks are masters.

Are you aware that there is at this moment a universal
clamour throughout the whole of Ireland against the
Union?   It is now one month since I returned from that
country; I have never seen so extraordinary, so alarming,
and so rapid a change in the sentiments of any people.
Those who disliked the Union before are quite furious
against it now; those who doubted doubt no more: those
who were friendly to it have exchanged that friendship
for the most rooted aversion: in the midst of all this
(which is by far the most alarming symptom), there is the
strongest disposition on the part of the Northern Dissenters
to unite with the Catholics, irritated by the faithless injustice with which they have been treated.   If this combination does take place (mark what I say to you), you will
have meetings all over Ireland for the cry of *No Union*;
that cry will spread like wild-fire, and blaze over every
opposition; and if this be the case, there is no use in mincing
the matter, Ireland is gone, and the death-blow of England
is struck; and this event may happen *instantly*—before
Mr. Canning and Mr. Hookham Frere[1] have turned Lord
Howick's last speech into doggerel rhyme; before "*the near
and dear relations*" have received another quarter of their
pension, or Mr. Perceval conducted the Curates' Salary
Bill safely to a third reading.—If the mind of the English
people, cursed as they now are with that madness of
religious dissension which has been breathed into them
for the purposes of private ambition, can be alarmed by
any remembrances, and warned by any events, they should
never forget how nearly Ireland was lost to this country

[1] See p. 293.

during the American war; that it was saved merely by the jealousy of the Protestant Irish towards the Catholics, then a much more insignificant and powerless body than they now are. The Catholic and the Dissenter have since combined together against you. Last war, the winds, those ancient and unsubsidised allies of England, the winds, upon which English ministers depend as much for saving kingdoms as washerwomen do for drying clothes; the winds stood your friends: the French could only get into Ireland in small numbers, and the rebels were defeated. Since then, all the remaining kingdoms of Europe have been destroyed; and the Irish see that their national independence is gone, without having received any single one of those advantages which they were taught to expect from the sacrifice. All good things were to flow from the Union; they have none of them gained any thing. Every man's pride is wounded by it; no man's interest is promoted. In the seventh year of that Union, four million Catholics, lured by all kinds of promises to yield up the separate dignity and sovereignty of their country, are forced to squabble with such a man as Mr. Spencer Perceval for five thousand pounds with which to educate their children in their own mode of worship; he, the same Mr. Spencer, having secured to his own Protestant self a reversionary portion of the public money amounting to four times that sum. A senior Proctor of the University of Oxford, the head of a house, or the examining Chaplain to a Bishop, may believe these things can last: but every man of the world, whose understanding has been exercised in the business of life, must see (and see with a breaking heart) that they will soon come to a fearful termination.

Our conduct to Ireland, during the whole of this war, has been that of a man who subscribes to hospitals, weeps at charity sermons, carries out broth and blankets to beggars, and then comes home and beats his wife and children. We had compassion for the victims of all other oppression and injustice, except our own. If Switzerland was threatened, away went a Treasury Clerk with a hundred thousand pounds for Switzerland; large bags of money were kept constantly under sailing orders; upon the slightest demonstration towards Naples, down went Sir

William Hamilton [1] upon his knees, and begged for the love of St. Januarius [2] they would help us off with a little money; all the arts of Machiavel were resorted to, to persuade Europe to borrow; troops were sent off in all directions to save the Catholic and Protestant world; the Pope himself was guarded by a regiment of English dragoons; if the Grand Lama had been at hand, he would have had another; every Catholic Clergyman who had the good fortune to be neither English nor Irish was immediately provided with lodging, soap, crucifix, missal, chapel-beads, relics, and holy water; if Turks had landed, Turks would have received an order from the Treasury for coffee, opium, korans, and seraglios. In the midst of all this fury of saving and defending this crusade, for conscience and Christianity, there was a universal agreement among all descriptions of people to continue every species of internal persecution; to deny at home every just right that had been denied before; to pummel poor Dr. Abraham Rees and his Dissenters; and to treat the unhappy Catholics of Ireland as if their tongues were mute, their heels cloven, their nature brutal, and designedly subjected by Providence to their Orange masters.

How would my admirable brother, the Rev. Abraham Plymley, like to be marched to a Catholic chapel, to be sprinkled with the sanctified contents of a pump, to hear a number of false quantities in the Latin tongue, and to see a number of persons occupied in making right angles upon the breast and forehead? And if all this would give you so much pain, what right have you to march Catholic soldiers to a place of worship, where there is no aspersion, no rectangular gestures, and where they understand every word they hear, having first, in order to get him to enlist, made a solemn promise to the contrary? Can you wonder, after this, that the Catholic priest stops the recruiting in Ireland, as he is now doing to a most alarming degree?

The late question concerning military rank did not individually affect the lowest persons of the Catholic persuasion; but do you imagine they do not sympathise with the honour and disgrace of their superiors? Do you think that satisfaction and dissatisfaction do not travel down

[1] See p. 293.   [2] See p. 293.

from Lord Fingal to the most potatoless Catholic in Ireland, and that the glory or shame of the sect is not felt by many more than these conditions personally and corporeally affect? Do you suppose that the detection of Sir H. M. and the disappointment of Mr. Perceval *in the matter* of the Duchy of Lancaster, did not affect every dabbler in public property? Depend upon it these things were felt through all the gradations of small plunderers, down to him who filches a pound of tobacco from the King's warehouses; while, on the contrary, the acquittal of any noble and official thief would not fail to diffuse the most heartfelt satisfaction over the larcenous and burglarious world. Observe, I do not say because the lower Catholics are affected by what concerns their superiors, that they are not affected by what concerns themselves. There is no disguising the horrid truth; *there must be some relaxation with respect to tithe*: this is the cruel and heart-rending price which must be paid for national preservation. I feel how little existence will be worth having, if any alteration, however slight, is made in the property of Irish rectors; I am conscious how much such changes must affect the daily and hourly comforts of every Englishman; I shall feel too happy if they leave Europe untouched, and are not ultimately fatal to the destinies of America; but I am madly bent upon keeping foreign enemies out of the British Empire, and my limited understanding presents me with no other means of effecting my object.

You talk of waiting till another reign before any alteration is made; a proposal full of good sense and good nature, if the measure in question were to pull down St. James's Palace, or to alter Kew Gardens. Will Bonaparte agree to put off his intrigues, and his invasion of Ireland? If so, I will overlook the question of justice, and finding the danger suspended, agree to the delay. I sincerely hope this reign may last many years, yet the delay of a single session of Parliament may be fatal; but if another year elapse without some serious concession made to the Catholics, I believe, before God, that all future pledges and concessions will be made in vain. I do not think that peace will do you any good under such circumstances: if Bonaparte give you a respite, it will only be to get ready the gallows on which he means to hang you. The Catholic

and the Dissenter can unite in peace as well as war.   If
they do, the gallows is ready; and your executioner, in
spite of the most solemn promises, will turn you off the
next hour.

With every disposition to please (where to please within
fair and rational limits is a high duty), it is impossible for
public men to be long silent about the Catholics; pressing
evils are not got rid of, because they are not talked of.   A
man may command his family to say nothing more about
the stone, and surgical operations: but the ponderous
malice still lies upon the nerve, and gets so big, that the
patient breaks his own law of silence, clamours for the
knife, and expires under its late operation.   Believe me,
you talk folly, when you talk of suppressing the Catholic
question.   I wish to God the case admitted of such a
remedy: bad as it is, it does not admit of it.   If the wants
of the Catholics are not heard in the manly tones of Lord
Grenville, or the servile drawl of Lord Castlereagh, they
will be heard ere long in the madness of mobs, and the
conflicts of armed men.

I observe, it is now universally the fashion to speak of
the first personage in the state as the great obstacle to the
measure.   In the first place, I am not bound to believe
such rumours because I hear them; and in the next place,
I object to such language, as unconstitutional.   Whoever
retains his situation in the ministry, while the incapacities
of the Catholics remain, is the advocate for those incapacities; and to him, and to him only, am I to look for responsibility.   But waive this question of the Catholics, and
put a general case:—How is a minister of this country to
act when the conscientious scruples of his Sovereign prevent
the execution of a measure deemed by him absolutely
necessary to the safety of the country?   His conduct
is quite clear—he should resign.   But what is his successor
to do?—Resign.   But is the King to be left without
ministers, and is he in this manner to be compelled to act
against his own conscience?   Before I answer this, pray
tell me in my turn, what better defence is there against
the machinations of a wicked, or the errors of a weak,
Monarch, than the impossibility of finding a minister who
will lend himself to vice and folly?   Every English Monarch,
in such a predicament, would sacrifice his opinions and

views to such a clear expression of the public will; and it is one method in which the Constitution aims at bringing about such a sacrifice. You may say, if you please, the ruler of a state is forced to give up his object, when the natural love of place and power will tempt no one to assist him in its attainment. This may be force; but it is force without injury, and therefore without blame. I am not to be beat out of these obvious reasonings, and ancient constitutional provisions, by the term conscience. There is no fantasy, however wild, that a man may not persuade himself that he cherishes from motives of conscience; eternal war against impious France, or rebellious America, or Catholic Spain, may in times to come be scruples of conscience. One English Monarch may, from scruples of conscience, wish to abolish every trait of religious persecution; another Monarch may deem it his absolute and indispensable duty to make a slight provision for Dissenters out of the revenues of the Church of England. So that you see, Brother Abraham, there are cases where it would be the duty of the best and most loyal subjects to oppose the conscientious scruples of their Sovereign, still taking care that their actions were constitutional, and their modes respectful. Then you come upon me with personal questions, and say that no such dangers are to be apprehended now under our present gracious Sovereign, of whose good qualities we must be all so well convinced. All these sorts of discussions I beg leave to decline; what I have said upon constitutional topics, I mean of course for general, not for particular application. I agree with you in all the good you have said of the powers that be, and I avail myself of the opportunity of pointing out general dangers to the Constitution, at a moment when we are so completely exempted from their present influence. I cannot finish this letter without expressing my surprise and pleasure at your abuse of the servile addresses poured in upon the Throne; nor can I conceive a greater disgust to a Monarch, with a true English heart, than to see such a question as that of Catholic Emancipation argued, not with a reference to its justice or importance, but universally considered to be of no further consequence than as it affects his own private feelings. That these sentiments should be mine, is not wonderful; but how they came to be yours, does, I confess, fill me with surprise. Are you moved by the arrival of the Irish Brigade at Antwerp, and the amorous violence which awaits Mrs. Plymley?

LETTER V

DEAR ABRAHAM,

I never met a parson in my life, who did not consider the Corporation and Test Acts as the great bulwarks of the Church; and yet it is now just sixty-four years since bills of indemnity to destroy their penal effects, or, in other words, to repeal them, have been passed annually as a matter of course.

Heu vatum ignaræ mentes.

These bulwarks, without which no clergyman thinks he could sleep with his accustomed soundness, have actually not been in existence since any man now living has taken holy orders. Every year the Indemnity Act pardons past breaches of these two laws, and prevents any fresh actions of informers from coming to a conclusion before the period for the next indemnity bill arrives; so that these penalties, by which alone the Church remains in existence, have not had one moment's operation for sixty-four years. You will say the legislature, during the whole of this period, has reserved to itself the discretion of suspending, or not suspending. But had not the legislature the right of re-enacting, if it was necessary? And now when you have kept the rod over these people (with the most scandalous abuse of all principle) for sixty-four years, and not found it necessary to strike once, is not that the best of all reasons why the rod should be laid aside? You talk to me of a very valuable hedge running across your fields which you would not part with on any account. I go down, expecting to find a limit impervious to cattle, and highly useful for the preservation of property; but, to my utter astonishment, I find that the hedge was cut down half a century ago, and that every year the shoots are clipped the moment they appear above ground: it appears, upon further inquiry, that the hedge never ought to have existed at all; that it originated in the malice of antiquated quarrels, and was cut down because it subjected you to vast inconvenience, and broke up your intercourse with a country absolutely necessary to your existence. If the remains of this hedge serve only to keep up an irritation in your neighbours, and to remind them of the feuds of former times, good nature and good sense teach you that you ought to grub it up, and cast it into the oven. This is the exact state of these two laws; and yet it is made a great argument against concession to the Catholics, that it involves their repeal; which is to say, Do not make me relinquish a folly that will lead to my ruin; because, if you do, I must give up other follies ten times greater than this.

I confess, with all our bulwarks and hedges, it mortifies me to the very quick, to contrast with our matchless stupidity, and inimitable folly, the conduct of Bonaparte upon the subject of religious persecution. At the moment when we are tearing the crucifixes from the necks of the Catholics, and washing pious mud from the foreheads of the Hindoos; at that moment this man is assembling the very Jews at Paris, and endeavouring to give them stability and importance. I shall never be reconciled to mending shoes in America; but I see it must be my lot, and I will then take a dreadful revenge upon Mr. Perceval, if I catch him preaching within ten miles of me. I cannot for the soul of me conceive whence this man has gained his notions of Christianity: he has the most evangelical charity for errors in arithmetic, and the most inveterate malice against errors in conscience. While he rages against those whom in the true spirit of the Gospel he ought to indulge, he forgets the only instance of severity which that Gospel contains, and leaves the jobbers, and contractors, and money-changers at their seats, without a single stripe.

You cannot imagine, you say, that England will ever be ruined and conquered; and for no other reason that I can find, but because it seems so very odd it should be ruined and conquered. Alas! so reasoned, in their time, the Austrian, Russian, and Prussian Plymleys. But the English are brave: so were all these nations. You might get together a hundred thousand men individually brave; but without generals capable of commanding such a machine, it would be as useless as a first-rate man of war manned by Oxford clergymen, or Parisian shopkeepers.

E

I do not say this to the disparagement of English officers:
they have had no means of acquiring experience; but I
do say it to create alarm; for we do not appear to me to
be half alarmed enough, or to entertain that sense of our
danger which leads to the most obvious means of self-
defence. As for the spirit of the peasantry in making a
gallant defence behind hedge-rows, and through plate-
racks and hen-coops, highly as I think of their bravery,
I do not know any nation in Europe so likely to be struck
with the panic as the English; and this from their total
unacquaintance with the science of war. Old wheat and
beans blazing for twenty miles round; cart mares shot;
sows of Lord Somerville's breed running wild over the
country; the minister of the parish wounded sorely in his
hinder parts; Mrs. Plymley in fits; all these scenes of war
an Austrian or a Russian has seen three or four times over;
but it is now three centuries since an English pig has fallen
in a fair battle upon English ground, or a farm-house been
rifled, or a clergyman's wife been subjected to any other
proposals of love than the connubial endearments of her
sleek and orthodox mate. The old edition of Plutarch's
Lives, which lies in the corner of your parlour window, has
contributed to work you up to the most romantic expectations of our Roman behaviour. You are persuaded that
Lord Amherst [1] will defend Kew Bridge like Cocles; that
some maid of honour will break away from her captivity,
and swim over the Thames; that the Duke of York will
burn his capitulating hand; and little Mr. Sturges Bourne *
give forty years' purchase for Moulsham Hall, while the
French are encamped upon it. I hope we shall witness all
this, if the French do come; but in the mean time I am so
enchanted with the ordinary English behaviour of these
invaluable persons, that I earnestly pray no opportunity
may be given them for Roman valour, and for those very
un-Roman pensions which they would all, of course, take
especial care to claim in consequence. But whatever
was our conduct, if every ploughman was as great a hero

[1] See p. 293.
* There is nothing more objectionable in Plymley's Letters than
the abuse of Mr. Sturges Bourne, who is an honourable, able, and
excellent person; but such are the malevolent effects of party spirit.
See p. 293.

as he who was called from his oxen to save Rome from her enemies, I should still say, that at such a crisis you want the affections of all your subjects, in both islands: there is no spirit which you must alienate, no art you must avert, every man must feel he has a country, and that there is an urgent and pressing cause why he should expose himself to death.

The effects of penal laws, in matters of religion, are never confined to those limits in which the legislature intended they should be placed: it is not only that I am excluded from certain offices and dignities because I am a Catholic, but the exclusion carries with it a certain stigma, which degrades me in the eyes of the monopolising sect, and the very name of my religion becomes odious. These effects are so very striking in England, that I solemnly believe blue and red baboons to be more popular here than Catholics and Presbyterians; they are more understood, and there is a greater disposition to do something for them. When a country squire hears of an ape, his first feeling is to give it nuts and apples; when he hears of a Dissenter, his immediate impulse is to commit it to the county jail, to shave its head, to alter its customary food, and to have it privately whipped. This is no caricature, but an accurate picture of national feelings, as they degrade and endanger us at this very moment. The Irish Catholic gentleman would bear his legal disabilities with greater temper, if these were all he had to bear—if they did not enable every Protestant cheesemonger and tide-waiter to treat him with contempt. He is branded on the forehead with a red-hot iron, and treated like a spiritual felon, because, in the highest of all considerations he is led by the noblest of all guides, his own disinterested conscience.

Why are nonsense and cruelty a bit the better because they are enacted? If Providence, which gives wine and oil, had blessed us with that tolerant spirit which makes the countenance more pleasant and the heart more glad than these can do; if our Statute book had never been defiled with such infamous laws, the sepulchral Spencer Perceval would have been hauled through the dirtiest horse-pond in Hampstead, had he ventured to propose them. But now persecution is good, because it exists; every law which originated in ignorance and malice, and gratifies the passions from whence it sprang, we call the wisdom of our ancestors: when such laws are repealed, they will be cruelty and madness; till they are repealed, they are policy and caution.

I was somewhat amused with the imputation brought against the Catholics by the University of Oxford, that they are enemies to liberty. I immediately turned to my History of England, and marked as an historical error that passage in which it is recorded that, in the reign of Queen Anne, the famous decree of the University of Oxford, respecting passive obedience, was ordered, by the House of Lords, to be burnt by the hands of the common hangman, as contrary to the liberty of the subject, and the law of the land. Nevertheless, I wish, whatever be the modesty of those who impute, that the imputation was a little more true, the Catholic cause would not be quite so desperate with the present Administration. I fear, however, that the hatred to liberty in these poor devoted wretches may ere long appear more doubtful than it is at present to the Vice-Chancellor and his Clergy, inflamed, as they doubtless are, with classical examples of republican virtue, and panting, as they always have been, to reduce the power of the Crown within narrower and safer limits. What mistaken zeal, to attempt to connect one religion with freedom and another with slavery! Who laid the foundations of English liberty? What was the mixed religion of Switzerland? What has the Protestant religion done for liberty in Denmark, in Sweden, throughout the North of Germany, and in Prussia? The purest religion in the world, in my humble opinion, is the religion of the Church of England: for its preservation (so far as it is exercised without intruding upon the liberties of others) I am ready at this moment to venture my present life, and but through that religion I have no hopes of any other; yet I am not forced to be silly because I am pious; nor will I ever join in eulogiums on my faith, which every man of common reading and common sense can so easily refute.

You have either done too much for the Catholics (worthy Abraham), or too little; if you had intended to refuse them political power, you should have refused them civil rights. After you had enabled them to acquire property, after you had conceded to them all that you did concede in '78 and

'93, the rest is wholly out of your power: you may choose whether you will give the rest in an honourable or a disgraceful mode, but it is utterly out of your power to withhold it.

In the last year, land to the amount of *eight hundred thousand pounds* was purchased by the Catholics in Ireland. Do you think it possible to be-Perceval, and be-Canning, and be-Castlereagh, such a body of men as this out of their common rights, and their common sense? Mr. George Canning may laugh and joke at the idea of Protestant bailiffs ravishing Catholic ladies, under the 9th clause of the Sunset Bill; but if some better remedy be not applied to the distractions of Ireland than the jocularity of Mr. Canning, they will soon put an end to his pension, and to the pension of those "near and dear relatives," for whose eating, drinking, washing, and clothing, every man in the United Kingdoms now pays his two-pence or three-pence a year. You may call these observations coarse, if you please; but I have no idea that the Sophias and Carolines of any man breathing are to eat national veal, to drink public tea, to wear Treasury ribands, and then that we are to be told that it is coarse to animadvert upon this pitiful and eleemosynary splendour. If this is right, why not mention it? If it is wrong, why should not he who enjoys the ease of supporting his sisters in this manner bear the shame of it? Every body seems hitherto to have spared a man who never spares any body.

As for the enormous wax candles, and superstitious mummeries, and painted jackets of the Catholic priests, I fear them not. Tell me that the world will return again under the influence of the smallpox; that Lord Castlereagh will hereafter oppose the power of the Court; that Lord Howick and Mr. Grattan [1] will do each of them a mean and dishonourable action; that any body who has heard Lord Redesdale [2] speak once will knowingly and willingly hear him again; that Lord Eldon [3] has assented to the fact of two and two making four, without shedding tears, or expressing the smallest doubt or scruple; tell me any other thing absurd or incredible, but, for the love of common sense, let me hear no more of the danger to be apprehended from the general diffusion of Popery. It is too absurd to

[1] See p. 293.   [2] See p. 293.   [3] See p. 293.

be reasoned upon; every man feels it is nonsense when he hears it stated, and so does every man while he is stating it.

I cannot imagine why the friends to the Church Establishment should entertain such a horror of seeing the doors of Parliament flung open to the Catholics, and view so passively the enjoyment of that right by the Presbyterians and by every other species of Dissenter.   In their tenets, in their Church government, in the nature of their endowments, the Dissenters are infinitely more distant from the Church of England than the Catholics are; yet the Dissenters have never been excluded from Parliament.   There are forty-five members in one House, and sixteen in the other, who always are Dissenters.   There is no law which would prevent every member of the Lords and Commons from being Dissenters.   The Catholics could not bring into Parliament half the number of the Scotch members; and yet one exclusion is of such immense importance, because it has taken place; and the other no human being thinks of, because no one is accustomed to it.   I have often thought, if the *wisdom of our ancestors* had excluded all persons with red hair from the House of Commons, of the throes and convulsions it would occasion to restore them to their natural rights.   What mobs and riots would it produce!   To what infinite abuse and obloquy would the capillary patriot be exposed; what wormwood would distil from Mr. Perceval, what froth would drop from Mr. Canning; how (I will not say *my*, but *our* Lord Hawkesbury, for he belongs to us all)—how our Lord Hawkesbury would work away about the hair of King William and Lord Somers, and the authors of the great and glorious Revolution; how Lord Eldon would appeal to the Deity and his own virtues, and to the hair of his children: some would say that red-haired men were superstitious; some would prove they were atheists; they would be petitioned against as the friends of slavery, and the advocates for revolt; in short, such a corruptor of the heart and the understanding is the spirit of persecution, that these unfortunate people (conspired against by their fellow-subjects of every complexion), if they did not emigrate to countries where hair of another colour was persecuted, would be driven to the falsehood of perukes, or the hypocrisy of the Tricosian fluid.

As for the dangers of the Church (in spite of the staggering events which have lately taken place), I have not yet entirely lost my confidence in the power of common sense, and I believe the Church to be in no danger at all; but if it is, that danger is not from the Catholics, but from the Methodists, and from that patent Christianity which has been for some time manufacturing at Clapham, to the prejudice of the old and admirable article prepared by the Church. I would counsel my lords the Bishops to keep their eyes upon that holy village, and its hallowed vicinity: they will find there a zeal in making converts far superior to any thing which exists among the Catholics; a contempt for the great mass of English clergy, much more rooted and profound; and a regular fund to purchase livings for those groaning and garrulous gentlemen, whom they denominate (by a standing sarcasm against the regular Church) Gospel preachers, and vital clergymen. I am too firm a believer in the general propriety and respectability of the English clergy, to believe they have much to fear either from old nonsense, or from new; but if the Church must be supposed to be in danger, I prefer that nonsense which is grown half venerable from time, the force of which I have already tried and baffled, which at least has some excuse in the dark and ignorant ages in which it originated. The religious enthusiasm manufactured by living men before my own eyes disgusts my understanding as much, influences my imagination not at all, and excites my apprehensions much more.

I may have seemed to you to treat the situation of public affairs with some degree of levity; but I feel it deeply, and with nightly and daily anguish; because I know Ireland; I have known it all my life; I love it, and I foresee the crisis to which it will soon be exposed. Who can doubt but that Ireland will experience ultimately from France a treatment to which the conduct they have experienced from England is the love of a parent, or a brother? Who can doubt but that five years after he has got hold of the country, Ireland will be tossed away by Bonaparte as a present to some one of his ruffian generals, who will knock the head of Mr. Keogh [1] against the head of Cardinal Troy,[2] shoot twenty of the most noisy block-

[1] See p. 293.　　　　　　　　　　[2] See p. 294.

heads of the Roman persuasion, wash his pug-dogs in holy water, and confiscate the salt butter of the Milesian Republic to the last tub? But what matters this? or who is wise enough in Ireland to heed it? or when had common sense much influence with my poor dear Irish? Mr. Perceval does not know the Irish; but I know them, and I know that at every rash and mad hazard, they will break the Union, revenge their wounded pride and their insulted religion, and fling themselves into the open arms of France, sure of dying in the embrace. And now what means have you of guarding against this coming evil, upon which the future happiness or misery of every Englishman depends? Have you a single ally in the whole world? Is there a vulnerable point in the French Empire where the astonishing resources of that people can be attracted and employed? Have you a ministry wise enough to comprehend the danger, manly enough to believe unpleasant intelligence, honest enough to state their apprehensions at the peril of their places? Is there any where the slightest disposition to join any measure of love, or conciliation, or hope, with that dreadful bill which the distractions of Ireland have rendered necessary? At the very moment that the last Monarchy in Europe has fallen, are we not governed by a man of pleasantry, and a man of theology? In the six hundredth year of our empire over Ireland, have we any memorial of ancient kindness to refer to? any people, any zeal, any country on which we can depend? Have we any hope, but in the winds of heaven, and the tides of the sea? any prayer to prefer to the Irish, but that they should forget and forgive their oppressors, who, in the very moment that they are calling upon them for their exertions, solemnly assure them that the oppression shall still remain.

Abraham, farewell! If I have tired you, remember how often you have tired me and others. I do not think we really differ in politics so much as you suppose; or, at least, if we do, that difference is in the means, and not in the end. We both love the Constitution, respect the King, and abhor the French. But though you love the Constitution, you would perpetuate the abuses which have been engrafted upon it; though you respect the King, you would confirm his scruples against the Catholics;

though you abhor the French, you would open to them the conquest of Ireland. My method of respecting my Sovereign is by protecting his honour, his empire, and his lasting happiness; I evince my love of the Constitution, by making it the guardian of all men's rights and the source of their freedom; and I prove my abhorrence of the French, by uniting against them the disciples of every church in the only remaining nation in Europe. As for the men of whom I have been compelled in this age of mediocrity to say so much, they cannot of themselves be worth a moment's consideration, to you, to me, or to any body. In a year after their death, they will be forgotten as completely as if they had never been; and are now of no further importance, than as they are the mere vehicles of carrying into effect the commonplace and mischievous prejudices of the times in which they live.

LETTER VI

Dear Abraham,

What amuses me the most is to hear of the *indulgences* which the Catholics have received, and their exorbitance in not being satisfied with those indulgences: now if you complain to me that a man is obtrusive and shameless in his requests, and that it is impossible to bring him to reason, I must first of all hear the whole of your conduct towards him; for you may have taken from him so much in the first instance, that, in spite of a long series of restitution, a vast latitude for petition may still remain behind.

There is a village (no matter where) in which the inhabitants, on one day in the year, sit down to a dinner prepared at the common expense: by an extraordinary piece of tyranny (which Lord Hawkesbury would call the wisdom of the village ancestors), the inhabitants of three of the streets, about a hundred years ago, seized upon the inhabitants of the fourth street, bound them hand and foot, laid them upon their backs, and compelled them to look on while the rest were stuffing themselves with beef and beer: the next year the inhabitants of the persecuted street (though they contributed an equal quota of the expense) were treated precisely in the same manner. The tyranny grew into a custom; and (as the manner of our

nature is) it was considered as the most sacred of all duties
to keep these poor fellows without their annual dinner:
the village was so tenacious of this practice, that nothing
could induce them to resign it; every enemy to it was looked
upon as a disbeliever in Divine Providence, and any
nefarious churchwarden who wished to succeed in his
election had nothing to do but to represent his antagonist
as an abolitionist, in order to frustrate his ambition,
endanger his life, and throw the village into a state of the
most dreadful commotion. By degrees, however, the
obnoxious street grew to be so well peopled, and its inhabitants so firmly united, that their oppressors, more
afraid of injustice, were more disposed to be just. At the
next dinner they are unbound, the year after allowed to
sit upright, then a bit of bread and a glass of water; till
at last, after a long series of concessions, they are embold-
ened to ask, in pretty plain terms, that they may be
allowed to sit down at the bottom of the table, and to fill
their bellies as well as the rest. Forthwith a general cry
of shame and scandal: "Ten years ago, were you not laid
upon your backs? Don't you remember what a great
thing you thought it to get a piece of bread? How thankful you were for cheese-parings? Have you forgotten
that memorable era when the lord of the manor interfered
to obtain for you a slice of the public pudding? And now,
with an audacity only equalled by your ingratitude, you
have the impudence to ask for knives and forks, and to
request, in terms too plain to be mistaken, that you may
sit down to table with the rest, and be indulged even with
beef and beer: there are not more than half a dozen dishes
which we have reserved for ourselves; the rest has been
thrown open to you in the utmost profusion; you have
potatoes, and carrots, suet dumplings, sops in the pan, and
delicious toast and water, in incredible quantities. Beef,
mutton, lamb, pork, and veal are ours; and if you were not
the most restless and dissatisfied of human beings, you
would never think of aspiring to enjoy them."

Is not this, my dainty Abraham, the very nonsense and
the very insult which is talked to and practised upon the
Catholics? You are surprised that men who have tasted
of partial justice should ask for perfect justice; that he
who has been robbed of coat and cloak will not be con-

tented with the restitution of one of his garments. He would be a very lazy blockhead if he were content, and I (who, though an inhabitant of the village, have preserved, thank God, some sense of justice) most earnestly counsel these half-fed claimants to persevere in their just demands, till they are admitted to a more complete share of a dinner for which they pay as much as the others; and if they see a little attenuated lawyer squabbling at the head of their opponents, let them desire him to empty his pockets, and to pull out all the pieces of duck, fowl, and pudding, which he has filched from the public feast, to carry home to his wife and children.

You parade a great deal upon the vast concessions made by this country to the Irish before the Union. I deny that any voluntary concession was ever made by England to Ireland. What did Ireland ever ask that was granted? What did she ever demand that was not refused? How did she get her Mutiny Bill—a limited parliament—a repeal of Poynings's Law[1]—a constitution? Not by the concessions of England, but by her fears. When Ireland asked for all these things upon her knees, her petitions were rejected with Percevalism and contempt; when she demanded them with the voice of sixty thousand armed men, they were granted with every mark of consternation and dismay. Ask of Lord Auckland[2] the fatal consequences of trifling with such a people as the Irish. He himself was the organ of these refusals. As secretary to the Lord Lieutenant, the insolence and the tyranny of this country passed through his hands. Ask him if he remembers the consequences. Ask him if he has forgotten that memorable evening, when he came down booted and mantled to the House of Commons, when he told the House he was about to set off for Ireland that night, and declared before God, if he did not carry with him a compliance with all their demands, Ireland was for ever lost to this country. The present generation have forgotten this; but I have not forgotten it; and I know, hasty and undignified as the submission of England then was, that Lord Auckland was right, that the delay of a single day might very probably have separated the two people for ever. The terms submission and fear are galling terms,

[1] See p. 294.   [2] See p. 294.

when applied from the lesser nation to the greater; but it
is the plain historical truth, it is the natural consequence
of injustice, it is the predicament in which every country
places itself which leaves such a mass of hatred and discontent by its side. No empire is powerful enough to
endure it; it would exhaust the strength of China, and sink
it with all its mandarins and tea-kettles to the bottom of
the deep. By refusing them justice, now when you are
strong enough to refuse them any thing more than justice,
you will act over again, with the Catholics, the same scene
of mean and precipitate submission which disgraced you
before America, and before the volunteers of Ireland.
We shall live to hear the Hampstead Protestant [1] pro-
nouncing such extravagant panegyrics upon holy water,
and paying such fulsome compliments to the thumbs and
offals of departed saints, that parties will change sentiments, and Lord Henry Petty [2] and Sam Whitbread [3]
take a spell at No Popery. The wisdom of Mr. Fox was
alike employed in teaching his country justice when
Ireland was weak, and dignity when Ireland was strong.
We are fast pacing round the same miserable circle of ruin
and imbecility. Alas! where is our guide?

You say that Ireland is a millstone about our necks;
that it would be better for us if Ireland were sunk at the
bottom of the sea; that the Irish are a nation of irre-
claimable savages and barbarians. How often have I
heard these sentiments fall from the plump and thoughtless
squire, and from the thriving English shopkeeper, who has
never felt the rod of an Orange master upon his back.
Ireland a millstone about your neck! Why is it not a
stone of Ajax in your hand? I agree with you most
cordially, that, governed as Ireland now is, it would be a
vast accession of strength if the waves of the sea were to
rise and engulf her to-morrow. At this moment, opposed
as we are to all the world, the annihilation of one of the
most fertile islands on the face of the globe, containing
five millions of human creatures, would be one of the most
solid advantages which could happen to this country.
I doubt very much, in spite of all the just abuse which has
been lavished upon Bonaparte, whether there is any one
of his conquered countries the blotting out of which would

[1] See p. 294.   [2] See p. 294.   [3] See p. 294.

be as beneficial to him as the destruction of Ireland would
be to us: of countries I speak differing in language from
the French, little habituated to their intercourse, and
inflamed with all the resentments of a recently conquered
people. Why will you attribute the turbulence of our
people to any cause but the right—to any cause but your
own scandalous oppression?   If you tie your horse up to a
gate, and beat him cruelly, is he vicious because he kicks
you?   If you have plagued and worried a mastiff dog for
years, is he mad because he flies at you whenever he sees
you?   Hatred is an active, troublesome passion.   Depend
upon it, whole nations have always some reason for their
hatred.   Before you refer the turbulence of the Irish to
incurable defects in their character, tell me if you have
treated them as friends and equals?   Have you protected
their commerce?   Have you respected their religion?
Have you been as anxious for their freedom as your own?
Nothing of all this.   What then?   Why you have confiscated the territorial surface of the country twice over:
you have massacred and exported her inhabitants: you
have deprived four-fifths of them of every civil privilege:
you have at every period made her commerce and manufactures slavishly subordinate to your own: and yet the
hatred which the Irish bear to you is the result of an original
turbulence of character, and of a primitive, obdurate wild-
ness, utterly incapable of civilisation.   The embroidered
inanities and the sixth-form effusions of Mr. Canning are
really not powerful enough to make me believe this; nor
is there any authority on earth (always excepting the Dean
of Christ Church) which could make it credible to me.
I am sick of Mr. Canning.   There is not a "ha'p'orth of
bread to all this sugar and sack."   I love not the cretaceous
and incredible countenance of his colleague.   The only
opinion in which I agree with these two gentlemen is that
which they entertain of each other; I am sure that the
insolence of Mr. Pitt, and the unbalanced accounts
of Melville, were far better than the perils of this new
ignorance:

> Nonne fuit satius tristes Amaryllidis iras
> Atque superba pati fastidia—nonne Menalcam
> Quamvis ille *niger*?

In the midst of the most profound peace, the secret

articles of the Treaty of Tilsit, in which the destruction of
Ireland is resolved upon, induce you to rob the Danes of
their fleet. After the expedition sailed comes the Treaty
of Tilsit, containing no article,* public or private, alluding
to Ireland. The state of the world, you tell me, justified
us in doing this. Just God! do we think only of the state
of the world when there is an opportunity for robbery,
for murder, and for plunder; and do we forget the state
of the world when we are called upon to be wise, and good,
and just? Does the state of the world never remind us,
that we have four millions of subjects whose injuries we
ought to atone for, and whose affections we ought to
conciliate? Does the state of the world never warn us to
lay aside our infernal bigotry, and to arm every man who
acknowledges a God and can grasp a sword? Did it never
occur to this administration that they might virtuously
get hold of a force ten times greater than the force of the
Danish fleet? Was there no other way of protecting
Ireland, but by bringing eternal shame upon Great Britain,
and by making the earth a den of robbers? See what the
men whom you have supplanted would have done. They
would have rendered the invasion of Ireland impossible,
by restoring to the Catholics their long-lost rights: they
would have acted in such a manner that the French would
neither have wished for invasion, nor dared to attempt it:
they would have increased the permanent strength of the
country while they preserved its reputation unsullied.
Nothing of this kind your friends have done, because they
are solemnly pledged to do nothing of this kind; because
to tolerate all religions, and to equalise civil rights to all
sects, is to oppose some of the worst passions of our nature
—to plunder and to oppress is to gratify them all. They
wanted the huzzas of mobs, and they have for ever blasted
the fame of England to obtain them. Were the fleets of
Holland, France, and Spain destroyed by larceny? You
resisted the power of one hundred and fifty sail of the line
by sheer courage, and violated every principle of morals
from the dread of fifteen hulks, while the expedition itself
cost you three times more than the value of the larcenous
matter brought away. The French trample upon the
laws of God and man, not for old cordage, but for kingdoms,

* This is now completely confessed to be the case by ministers.

and always take care to be well paid for their crimes. We
contrive, under the present administration, to unite moral
with intellectual deficiency, and to grow weaker and worse
by the same action. If they had any evidence of the
intended hostility of the Danes, why was it not produced?
Why have the nations of Europe been allowed to feel an
indignation against this country beyond the reach of all
subsequent information?   Are these times, do you imagine,
when we can trifle with a year of universal hatred, dally
with the curses of Europe, and then regain a lost character
at pleasure, by the parliamentary perspirations of the
Foreign Secretary, or the solemn asseverations of the
pecuniary Rose?   Believe me, Abraham, it is not under
such ministers as these that the dexterity of honest Englishmen will ever equal the dexterity of French knaves; it is
not in their presence that the serpent of Moses will ever
swallow up the serpents of the magician.

Lord Hawkesbury says that nothing is to be granted to
the Catholics from fear. What! not even justice? Why
not?   There are four millions of disaffected people within
twenty miles of your own coast. I fairly confess, that the
dread which I have of their physical power, is with me a
very strong motive for listening to their claims. To talk
of not acting from fear is mere parliamentary cant. From
what motive but fear, I should be glad to know, have all
the improvements in our constitution proceeded? I
question if any justice has ever been done to large masses
of mankind from any other motive. By what other motives
can the plunderers of the Baltic suppose nations to be
governed in their intercourse *with each other*? If I say,
give this people what they ask because it is just, do you
think I should get ten people to listen to me? Would not
the lesser of the two Jenkinsons [1] be the first to treat me
with contempt? the only true way to make the mass of
mankind see the beauty of justice, is by showing to them
in pretty plain terms the consequences of injustice. If
any body of French troops land in Ireland, the whole
population of that country will rise against you to a man,
and you could not possibly survive such an event three
years. Such, from the bottom of my soul, do I believe to
be the present state of that country; and so far does it

[1] See p. 294.

appear to me to be impolitic and unstatesmanlike to concede
any thing to such a danger, that if the Catholics, in addition
to their present just demands, were to petition for the
perpetual removal of the said Lord Hawkesbury from his
Majesty's councils, I think, whatever might be the effect
upon the destinies of Europe, and however it might retard
our own individual destruction, that the prayer of the
petition should be instantly complied with. Canning's
crocodile tears should not move me; the hoops of the
maids of honour should not hide him. I would tear him
from the banisters of the back stairs, and plunge him in
the fishy fumes of the dirtiest of all his Cinque Ports.

LETTER VII

DEAR ABRAHAM,

In the correspondence which is passing between us you
are perpetually alluding to the Foreign Secretary; and in
answer to the dangers of Ireland, which I am pressing upon
your notice, you have nothing to urge but the confidence
which you repose in the discretion and sound sense of this
gentleman.* I can only say, that I have listened to him
long and often, with the greatest attention; I have used
every exertion in my power to take a fair measure of him,
and it appears to me impossible to hear him upon any
arduous topic without perceiving that he is eminently
deficient in those solid and serious qualities upon which,
and upon which alone, the confidence of a great country
can properly repose. He sweats, and labours, and works
for sense, and Mr. Ellis [1] seems always to think it is coming,
but it does not come; the machine can't draw up what is
not to be found in the spring; Providence has made him a
light, jesting, paragraph-writing man, and that he will
remain to his dying day. When he is jocular he is strong,
when he is serious he is like Samson in a wig: any ordinary

* The attack upon virtue and morals in the debate upon Copen-
hagen is brought forward with great ostentation by this gentleman's
friends. But is Harlequin less Harlequin because he acts well?
I was present: he leaped about, touched facts with his wand, turned
yes into no, and no into yes: it was a pantomime well played, but a
pantomime: Harlequin deserves higher wages than he did two years
ago: is he therefore fit for serious parts?

[1] See p. 294.

person is a match for him: a song, an ironical letter, a
burlesque ode, an attack in the Newspaper upon Nicoll's
eye, a smart speech of twenty minutes, full of gross misrepresentations and clever turns, excellent language, a
spirited manner, lucky quotation, success in provoking
dull men, some half information picked up in Pall Mall
in the morning: these are your friend's natural weapons;
all these things he can do; here I allow him to be truly
great: nay, I will be just, and go still further, if he would
confine himself to these things, and consider the *facete*
and the playful to be the basis of his character, he would
for that species of man, be universally regarded as a person
of a very good understanding; call him a legislator, a
reasoner, and the conductor of the affairs of a great nation,
and it seems to me as absurd as if a butterfly were to teach
bees to make honey.   That he is an extraordinary writer
of small poetry, and a diner out of the highest lustre, I
do most readily admit.   After George Selwyn,[1] and
perhaps Tickell,[2] there has been no such man for this half
century.   The Foreign Secretary is a gentleman, a respectable as well as a highly agreeable man in private life; but
you may as well feed me with decayed potatoes as console
me for the miseries of Ireland by the resources of his *sense*
and his *discretion*.   It is only the public situation which
this gentleman holds which entitles me or induces me to
say so much about him.   He is a fly in amber, nobody
cares about the fly: the only question is, How the devil
did it get there?   Nor do I attack him for the love of glory,
but from the love of utility, as a burgomaster hunts a rat
in a Dutch dyke, for fear it should flood a province.

The friends of the Catholic question are, I observe,
extremely embarrassed in arguing when they come to the
loyalty of the Irish Catholics.   As for me, I shall go
straight forward to my object, and state what I have no
manner of doubt, from an intimate knowledge of Ireland,
to be the plain truth.   Of the great Roman Catholic
proprietors, and of the Catholic prelates, there may be a
few, and but a few, who would follow the fortunes of
England at all events: there is another set of men who,
thoroughly detesting this country, have too much property
and too much character to lose, not to wait for some very

[1] See p. 294.   [2] See p. 294.

F

favourable event before they show themselves; but the
great mass of Catholic population, upon the slightest
appearance of a French force in that country, would rise
upon you to a man.   It is the most mistaken policy to
conceal the plain truth.   There is no loyalty among the
Catholics: they detest you as their worst oppressors, and
they will continue to detest you till you remove the cause
of their hatred.   It is in your power in six months' time
to produce a total revolution of opinions among this
people; and in some future letter I will show you that this
is clearly the case.   At present, see what a dreadful state
Ireland is in.   The common toast among the low Irish is,
the feast of the *passover*.   Some allusion to *Bonaparte*,
in a play lately acted at Dublin, produced thunders of
applause from the pit and the galleries; and a politician
should not be inattentive to the public feelings expressed
in theatres.   Mr. Perceval thinks he has disarmed the
Irish: he has no more disarmed the Irish than he has
resigned a shilling of his own public emoluments.   An
Irish * peasant fills the barrel of his gun full of tow dipped
in oil, butters up the lock, buries it in a bog, and allows
the Orange bloodhound to ransack his cottage at pleasure.
Be just and kind to the Irish, and you will indeed disarm
them; rescue them from the degraded servitude in which
they are held by a handful of their own countrymen, and
you will add four millions of brave and affectionate men
to your strength.   Nightly visits, Protestant inspectors,
licences to possess a pistol, or a knife and fork, the odious
vigour of the *evangelical* Perceval—acts of Parliament,
drawn up by some English attorney, to save you from the
hatred of four millions of people—the guarding yourselves
from universal disaffection by a police; a confidence in the
little cunning of Bow Street, when you might rest your
security upon the eternal basis of the best feelings: this is
the meanness and madness to which nations are reduced
when they lose sight of the first elements of justice, without
which a country can be no more secure than it can be
healthy without air.   I sicken at such policy and such men.
The fact is, the Ministers know nothing about the present

* No man who is not intimately acquainted with the Irish, can
tell to what a curious extent this concealment of arms is carried.
I have stated the exact mode in which it is done.

state of Ireland; Mr. Perceval sees a few clergymen, Lord
Castlereagh a few general officers, who take care, of course,
to report what is pleasant rather than what is true.   As
for the joyous and lepid consul, he jokes upon neutral flags
and frauds, jokes upon Irish rebels, jokes upon northern,
and western, and southern foes, and gives himself no trouble
upon any subject; nor is the mediocrity of the idolatrous
deputy of the slightest use.   Dissolved in grins, he reads
no memorials upon the state of Ireland, listens to no
reports, asks no questions, and is the

"*Bourn* from whom no traveller returns."

The danger of an immediate insurrection is now, I
believe,* blown over.   You have so strong an army in
Ireland, and the Irish are become so much more cunning
from the last insurrection, that you may perhaps be
tolerably secure just at present from that evil: but are you
secure from the efforts which the French may make to
throw a body of troops into Ireland? and do you consider
that event to be difficult and improbable?   From Brest
Harbour to Cape St. Vincent, you have above three thousand miles of hostile sea coast, and twelve or fourteen
harbours quite capable of containing a sufficient force for
the powerful invasion of Ireland.   The nearest of these
harbours is not two days' sail from the southern coast
of Ireland, with a fair leading wind; and the furthest not
ten.   Five ships of the line, for so very short a passage,
might carry five or six thousand troops with cannon and
ammunition; and Ireland presents to their attack a southern
coast of more than five hundred miles, abounding in deep
bays, admirable harbours, and disaffected inhabitants.
Your blockading ships may be forced to come home for
provisions and repairs, or they may be blown off in a gale
of wind and compelled to bear away for their own coast!
—and you will observe, that the very same wind which
locks you up in the British Channel when you are got
there, is evidently favourable for the invasion of Ireland.
And yet this is called Government, and the people huzza
Mr. Perceval for continuing to expose his country day
after day to such tremendous perils as these; cursing the

* I know too much, however, of the state of Ireland, not to speak
tremblingly about this.   I hope to God I am right.

men who would have given up a question in theology to have saved us from such a risk. The British Empire at this moment is in the state of a peach-blossom—if the wind blows gently from one quarter, it survives, if furiously from the other, it perishes. A stiff breeze may set in from the north, the Rochefort squadron will be taken, and the Minister will be the most holy of men: if it comes from some other point, Ireland is gone; we curse ourselves as a set of monastic madmen, and call out for the unavailing satisfaction of Mr. Perceval's head. Such a state of political existence is scarcely credible; it is the action of a mad young fool standing upon one foot, and peeping down the crater of Mount Ætna, not the conduct of a wise and sober people deciding upon their best and dearest interests: and in the name, the much-injured name, of Heaven, what is it all for that we expose ourselves to these dangers? Is it that we may sell more muslin? Is it that we may acquire more territory? Is it that we may strengthen what we have already acquired? No: nothing of all this; but that one set of Irishmen may torture another set of Irishmen—that Sir Phelim O'Callaghan may continue to whip Sir Toby M'Tackle, his next door neighbour, and continue to ravish his Catholic daughters; and these are the measures which the honest and consistent Secretary supports; and this is the Secretary, whose genius in the estimation of Brother Abraham is to extinguish the genius of Bonaparte. Pompey was killed by a slave, Goliath smitten by a stripling, Pyrrhus died by the hand of a woman; tremble, thou great Gaul, from whose head an armed Minerva leaps forth in the hour of danger; tremble, thou scourge of God, a pleasant man is come out against thee, and thou shalt be laid low by a joker of jokes, and he shall talk his pleasant talk against thee, and thou shalt be no more!

You tell me, in spite of all this parade of sea coast, Bonaparte has neither ships nor sailors: but this is a mistake. He has not ships and sailors to contest the empire of the seas with Great Britain, but there remains quite sufficient of the navies of France, Spain, Holland, and Denmark, for these short excursions and invasions. Do you think, too, that Bonaparte does not add to his navy every year? Do you suppose, with all Europe at his feet, that he can find any difficulty in obtaining timber, and that money will not procure for him any quantity of naval stores he may want? The mere machine, the empty ship, he can build as well, and as quickly, as you can; and though he may not find enough of practised sailors to man large fighting fleets—it is not possible to conceive that he can want sailors for such sort of purposes as I have stated. He is at present the despotic monarch of above twenty thousand miles of sea coast, and yet you suppose he cannot procure sailors for the invasion of Ireland. Believe, if you please, that such a fleet met at sea by any number of our ships at all comparable to them in point of force, would be immediately taken, let it be so; I count nothing upon their power of resistance, only upon their power of escaping unobserved. If experience has taught us any thing, it is the impossibility of perpetual blockades. The instances are innumerable, during the course of this war, where whole fleets have sailed in and out of harbour in spite of every vigilance used to prevent it. I shall only mention those cases where Ireland is concerned. In December, 1796, seven ships of the line, and ten transports, reached Bantry Bay from Brest, without having seen an English ship in their passage. It blew a storm when they were off shore, and therefore England still continues to be an independent kingdom. You will observe that at the very time the French fleet sailed out of Brest Harbour, Admiral Colpoys was cruising off there with a powerful squadron, and still, from the particular circumstances of the weather, found it impossible to prevent the French from coming out. During the time that Admiral Colpoys was cruising off Brest, Admiral Richery, with six ships of the line, passed him, and got safe into the harbour. At the very moment when the French squadron was lying in Bantry Bay, Lord Bridport with his fleet was locked up by a foul wind in the Channel, and for several days could not stir to the assistance of Ireland. Admiral Colpoys, totally unable to find the French fleet, came home. Lord Bridport, at the change of the wind, cruised for them in vain, and they got safe back to Brest, without having seen a single one of those floating bulwarks, the possession of which we believe will enable us with impunity to set justice and common sense at defiance. Such is the miserable and precarious state of an anemocracy, of a people who put their trust in hurricanes, and are governed by wind. In August, 1798, three forty-gun frigates landed 1100 men under Humbert, making the passage from Rochelle to Killala without seeing any English ship. In October of the same year, four French frigates anchored in Killala Bay with 2000 troops; and though they did not land their troops, they returned to France in safety. In the same month, a line-of-battle ship, eight stout frigates, and a brig, all full of troops and stores, reached the coast of Ireland, and were fortunately, in sight of land, destroyed, after an obstinate engagement, by Sir John Warren.

If you despise the little troop which, in these numerous experiments, did make good its landing, take with you, if you please, this *précis* of its exploits: 1100 men, commanded by a soldier raised from the ranks, put to rout a select army of 6000 men, commanded by General Lake, seized their ordnance, ammunition, and stores, advanced 150 miles into a country containing an armed force of 150,000 men, and at last surrendered to the Viceroy, an experienced general, gravely and cautiously advancing, at the head of all his chivalry and of an immense army, to oppose him. You must excuse these details about Ireland; but it appears to me to be of all other subjects the most important. If we conciliate Ireland, we can do nothing amiss; if we do not, we can do nothing well. If Ireland was friendly, we might equally set at defiance the talents of Bonaparte, and the blunders of his rival, Mr. Canning; we could then support the ruinous and silly bustle of our useless expeditions, and the almost incredible ignorance of our commercial Orders in Council. Let the present administration give up but this one point, and there is nothing which I would not consent to grant them. Mr. Perceval shall have full liberty to insult the tomb of Mr. Fox, and to torment every eminent Dissenter in Great Britain; Lord Camden shall have large boxes of plums; Mr. Rose receive permission to prefix to his name the appellative of virtuous; and to the Viscount Castlereagh * a round sum of ready money shall be well and truly paid into his hand. Lastly, what remains to Mr. George Canning, but that he ride up and down Pall Mall glorious

* This is a very unjust imputation on Lord Castlereagh.

upon a white horse, and that they cry out before him, Thus shall it be done to the statesman who hath written *The Needy Knife-Grinder*, and the German play? Adieu only for the present; you shall soon hear from me again; it is a subject upon which I cannot long be silent.

LETTER VIII

NOTHING can be more erroneous than to suppose that Ireland is not bigger than the Isle of Wight, or of more consequence than Guernsey or Jersey; and yet I am almost inclined to believe, from the general supineness which prevails here respecting the dangerous state of that country, that such is the rank which it holds in our statistical tables. I have been writing to you a great deal about Ireland, and perhaps it may be of some use to state to you concisely the nature and resources of the country which has been the subject of our long and strange correspondence. There were returned, as I have before observed, to the hearth tax, in 1791, 701,132 * houses, which Mr. Newenham shows, from unquestionable documents, to be nearly 80,000 below the real number of houses in that country. There are 27,457 square English miles in Ireland,† and more than five millions of people.

By the last survey it appears that the inhabited houses in England and Wales amount to 1,574,902; and the population to 9,343,578, which gives an average of 5⅞ to each house, in a country where the density of population is certainly less considerable than in Ireland. It is commonly supposed that two-fifths of the army and navy are Irishmen, at periods when political disaffection does not avert the Catholics from the service. The current value of Irish exports in 1807 was £9,314,854 17s. 7d.; a state of commerce about equal to the commerce of England in the middle of the reign of George II. The tonnage of ships entered inward and cleared outward in the trade of

---

* The checks to population were very trifling from the rebellion. It lasted two months: of his Majesty's Irish forces there perished about 1600: of the rebels 11,000 were killed in the field, and 2000 hanged or exported: 400 loyal persons were assassinated.

† In England 49,450.

Ireland, in 1807, amounted to 1,567,430 tons. The quantity of home spirits exported amounted to 10,284 gallons in 1796, and to 930,800 gallons in 1804. Of the exports which I have stated, provisions amounted to 4,000,000, and linen to about 4,500,000. There was exported from Ireland, upon an average of two years ending in January, 1804, 591,274 barrels of barley, oats, and wheat; and by weight 910,848 cwts. of flour, oatmeal, barley, oats, and wheat. The amount of butter exported in 1804, from Ireland, was worth, in money, £1,704,680 sterling. The importation of ale and beer, from the immense manufactures now carrying on of these articles, was diminished to 3209 barrels, in the year 1804, from 111,920 barrels, which was the average importation per annum, taking from three years ending in 1792; and at present there is an export trade of porter.[1] On an average of the three years ending March, 1783, there were imported into Ireland, of cotton wool, 3326 cwts., of cotton yarn, 5405 lbs.; but on an average of three years, ending January, 1803, there were imported, of the first article, 13,159 cwts., and of the latter, 628,406 lbs. It is impossible to conceive any manufacture more flourishing. The export of linen has increased in Ireland from 17,776,862 yards, the average in 1770, to 43,534,971 yards, the amount in 1805. The tillage of Ireland has more than trebled within the last twenty-one years. The importation of coals has increased from 230,000 tons, in 1783, to 417,030, in 1804; of tobacco, from 3,459,861 lbs. in 1783, to 6,611,543, in 1804; of tea, from 1,703,855 lbs. in 1783, to 3,358,256, in 1804; of sugar, from 143,117 cwts. in 1782, to 309,076, in 1804. Ireland now supports a funded debt of above 64 millions; and it is computed that more than three millions of money are annually remitted to Irish absentees resident in this country. In Mr. Foster's[2] report, of 100 folio pages, presented to the House of Commons in the year 1806, the total expenditure of Ireland is stated at £9,760,013. Ireland has increased about two-thirds in its population within twenty-five years: and yet, and in about the same space of time, its exports of beef, bullocks, cows, pork, swine, butter, wheat, barley, and oats, collectively taken, have doubled; and this in spite of two years' famine,

[1] See p. 294.   [2] See p. 294.

and the presence of an immense army, that is always
at hand to guard the most valuable appanage of our
empire from joining our most inveterate enemies. Ireland
has the greatest possible facilities for carrying on commerce with the whole of Europe. It contains, within
a circuit of 750 miles, 66 secure harbours; and presents
a western frontier against Great Britain, reaching from
the Firth of Clyde, north, to the Bristol Channel, south,
and varying in distance from 20 to 100 miles; so that
the subjugation of Ireland would compel us to guard
with ships and soldiers a new line of coast, certainly
amounting, with all its sinuosities, to more than 700
miles—an addition of polemics, in our present state of
hostility with all the world, which must highly gratify
the vigorists, and give them an ample opportunity of
displaying that foolish energy upon which their claims to
distinction are founded. Such is the country which the
Right Reverend the Chancellor of the Exchequer would
drive into the arms of France; and for the conciliation of
which we are requested to wait, as if it were one of those
sinecure places which were given to Mr. Perceval snarling
at the breast, and which cannot be abolished till his decease.

How sincerely and fervently have I often wished that
the Emperor of the French had thought as Mr. Spencer
Perceval does upon the subject of government; that he
had entertained doubts and scruples upon the propriety
of admitting the Protestants to an equality of rights with
the Catholics, and that he had left in the middle of his
empire these vigorous seeds of hatred and disaffection!
But the world was never yet conquered by a blockhead.
One of the very first measures we saw him recurring to was
the complete establishment of religious liberty: if his
subjects fought and paid as he pleased, he allowed them
to believe as they pleased: the moment I saw this, my
best hopes were lost. I perceived in a moment the kind
of man we had to do with. I was well aware of the
miserable ignorance and folly of this country upon the
subject of toleration; and every year has been adding to
the success of that game which it was clear he had the will
and the ability to play against us.

You say Bonaparte is not in earnest upon the subject
of religion, and that this is the cause of his tolerant spirit;

but is it possible you can intend to give us such dreadful and unamiable notions of religion? Are we to understand that the moment a man is sincere he is narrow-minded; that persecution is the child of belief; and that a desire to leave all men in the quiet and unpunished exercise of their own creed can only exist in the mind of an infidel? Thank God! I know many men whose principles are as firm as they are expanded, who cling tenaciously to their own modification of the Christian faith, without the slightest disposition to force that modification upon other people. If Bonaparte is liberal in subjects of religion because he has no religion, is this a reason why we should be illiberal because we are Christians? If he owes this excellent quality to a vice, is that any reason why we may not owe it to a virtue? Toleration is a great good, and a good to be imitated, let it come from whom it will. If a sceptic is tolerant, it only shows that he is not foolish in practice as well as erroneous in theory. If a religious man is tolerant, it evinces that he is religious from thought and inquiry, because he exhibits in his conduct one of the most beautiful and important consequences of a religious mind, —an inviolable charity to all the honest varieties of human opinion.

Lord Sidmouth,[1] and all the anti-Catholic people, little foresee that they will hereafter be the sport of the anti-quary; that their prophecies of ruin and destruction from Catholic emancipation will be clapped into the notes of some quaint history, and be matter of pleasantry even to the sedulous housewife and the rural dean. There is always a copious supply of Lord Sidmouths in the world; nor is there one single source of human happiness, against which they have not uttered the most lugubrious pre-dictions. Turnpike roads, navigable canals, inoculation, hops, tobacco, the Reformation, the Revolution—there are always a set of worthy and moderately-gifted men, who bawl out death and ruin upon every valuable change which the varying aspect of human affairs absolutely and im-periously requires. I have often thought that it would be extremely useful to make a collection of the hatred and abuse that all those changes have experienced which are now admitted to be marked improvements in our condition.

[1] See p. 294.

Such a history might make folly a little more modest, and suspicious of its own decisions.

Ireland, you say, since the Union is to be considered as a part of the whole kingdom; and therefore, however Catholics may predominate in that particular spot, yet, taking the whole empire together, they are to be considered as a much more insignificant quota of the population. Consider them in what light you please, as part of the whole, or by themselves, or in what manner may be most consentaneous to the devices of your holy mind—I say in a very few words, if you do not relieve these people from the civil incapacities to which they are exposed, you will lose them; or you must employ great strength and much treasure in watching over them. In the present state of the world, you can afford to do neither the one nor the other. Having stated this, I shall leave you to be ruined, Puffendorf in hand (as Mr. Secretary Canning says), and to lose Ireland, just as you have found out what proportion the aggrieved people should bear to the whole population, before their calamities meet with redress. As for your parallel cases, I am no more afraid of deciding upon them than I am upon their prototype. If ever any one heresy should so far spread itself over the principality of Wales that the Established Church were left in a minority of one to four; if you had subjected these heretics to very severe civil privations; if the consequence of such privations were a universal state of disaffection among that caseous and wrathful people; and if at the same time you were at war with all the world, how can you doubt for a moment that I would instantly restore them to a state of the most complete civil liberty? What matters it under what name you put the same case? Common sense is not changed by appellations. I have said how I would act to Ireland, and I would act so to all the world.

I admit that, to a certain degree, the Government will lose the affections of the Orangemen by emancipating the Catholics; much less, however, at present, than three years past. The few men, who have ill-treated the whole crew, live in constant terror that the oppressed people will rise upon them and carry the ship into Brest:—they begin to find that it is a very tiresome thing to sleep every night with cocked pistols under their pillows, and to breakfast,

dine, and sup with drawn hangers.[1]   They suspect that the
privilege of beating and kicking the rest of the sailors is
hardly worth all this anxiety, and that if the ship does ever
fall into the hands of the disaffected, all the cruelties which
they have experienced will be thoroughly remembered
and amply repaid.   To a short period of disaffection among
the Orangemen, I confess I should not much object: my
love of poetical justice does carry me as far as that; one
summer's whipping, only one: the thumb-screw for a
short season; a little light easy torturing between Lady-
day and Michaelmas; a short specimen of Mr. Perceval's
vigour.   I have malice enough to ask this slight atone-
ment for the groans and shrieks of the poor Catholics,
unheard by any human tribunal, but registered by the
Angel of God against their Protestant and enlightened
oppressors.

Besides, if you who count ten so often can count five,
you must perceive that it is better to have four friends and
one enemy than four enemies and one friend; and the more
violent the hatred of the Orangemen, the more certain the
reconciliation of the Catholics.   The disaffection of the
Orangemen will be the Irish rainbow; when I see it, I shall
be sure that the storm is over.

If those incapacities, from which the Catholics ask to
be relieved, were to the mass of them only a mere feeling
of pride, and if the question were respecting the attainment
of privileges which could be of importance only to the
highest of the sect, I should still say, that the pride of the
mass was very naturally wounded by the degradation of
their superiors.   Indignity to George Rose would be felt
by the smallest nummary gentleman in the king's employ;
and Mr. John Bannister [2] could not be indifferent to any
thing which happened to Mr. Canning.   But the truth is,
it is a most egregious mistake to suppose that the Catholics
are contending merely for the fringes and feathers of their
chiefs.   I will give you a list, in my next Letter, of those
privations which are represented to be of no consequence
to any body but Lord Fingal,[3] and some twenty or thirty
of the principal persons of their sect.   In the mean time,
adieu, and be wise.

[1] See p. 294.   [2] See p. 294.   [3] See p. 294.

LETTER IX

Dear Abraham,

No Catholic can be chief Governor or Governor of this
Kingdom, Chancellor or Keeper of the Great Seal, Lord
High Treasurer, Chief of any of the Courts of Justice,
Chancellor of the Exchequer, Puisne Judge, Judge in the
Admiralty, Master of the Rolls, Secretary of State, Keeper
of the Privy Seal, Vice-Treasurer or his Deputy, Teller or
Cashier of Exchequer, Auditor or General, Governor or
Custos Rotulorum of Counties, Chief Governor's Secretary,
Privy Councillor, King's Counsel, Sergeant, Attorney,
Solicitor-General, Master in Chancery, Provost or Fellow
of Trinity College, Dublin, Postmaster-General, Master
and Lieutenant-General of Ordnance, Commander-in-
Chief, General on the Staff, Sheriff, Sub-Sheriff, Mayor,
Bailiff, Recorder, Burgess, or any other officer in a City,
or a Corporation. No Catholic can be guardian to a
Protestant, and no priest guardian at all: no Catholic
can be a gamekeeper, or have for sale, or otherwise, any
arms or warlike stores: no Catholic can present to a living,
unless he choose to turn Jew in order to obtain that privilege; the pecuniary qualification of Catholic jurors is made
higher than that of Protestants, and no relaxation of the
ancient rigorous code is permitted, unless to those who
shall take an oath prescribed by 13 and 14 Geo. III. Now
if this is not picking the plums out of the pudding, and
leaving the mere batter to the Catholics, I know not what
is. If it were merely the Privy Council, it would be (I
allow) nothing but a point of honour for which the mass
of Catholics were contending, the honour of being chief-
mourners or pall-bearers to the country; but surely no
man will contend that every barrister may not speculate
upon the possibility of being a puisne Judge; and that
every shopkeeper must not feel himself injured by his
exclusion from borough offices.

One of the greatest practical evils which the Catholics
suffer in Ireland is their exclusion from the offices of Sheriff
and Deputy Sheriff. Nobody who is unacquainted with
Ireland can conceive the obstacles which this opposes to
the fair administration of justice. The formation of
juries is now entirely in the hands of the Protestants; the

lives, liberties, and properties of the Catholics in the hands
of the juries; and this is the arrangement for the administration of justice in a country where religious prejudices
are inflamed to the greatest degree of animosity!   In this
country, if a man be a foreigner, if he sell slippers, and
sealing-wax, and artificial flowers, we are so tender of
human life that we take care half the number of persons
who are to decide upon his fate should be men of similar
prejudices and feelings with himself: but a poor Catholic
in Ireland may be tried by twelve Percevals, and destroyed
according to the manner of that gentleman in the name of
the Lord, and with all the insulting forms of justice.   I do
not go the length of saying that deliberate and wilful
injustice is done.   I have no doubt that the Orange
Deputy Sheriff thinks it would be a most unpardonable
breach of his duty if he did not summon a Protestant
panel.   I can easily believe that a Protestant panel may
conduct themselves very conscientiously in hanging the
gentlemen of the crucifix; but I blame the law which
does not guard the Catholic against the probable tenor of
those feelings which must unconsciously influence the
judgments of mankind.   I detest that state of society
which extends unequal degrees of protection to different
creeds and persuasions; and I cannot describe to you the
contempt I feel for a man who, calling himself a statesman,
defends a system which fills the heart of every Irishman
with treason, and makes his allegiance prudence, not
choice.

I request to know if the vestry taxes in Ireland are a
mere matter of romantic feeling, which can affect only the
Earl of Fingal?   In a parish where there are four thousand
Catholics and fifty Protestants, the Protestants may meet
together in a vestry meeting, at which no Catholic has the
right to vote, and tax all the lands in the parish 1s. 6d.
per acre, or in the pound, I forget which, for the repairs
of the church—and how has the necessity of these repairs
been ascertained?   A Protestant plumber has discovered
that it wants new leading; a Protestant carpenter is convinced the timbers are not sound, and the glazier who hates
holy water (as an accoucheur hates celibacy because he
gets nothing by it) is employed to put in new sashes.

The grand juries in Ireland are the great scene of jobbing.

They have a power of making a county rate to a considerable extent for roads, bridges, and other objects of general accommodation. "You suffer the road to be brought through my park, and I will have the bridge constructed in a situation where it will make a beautiful object to your house. You do my job, and I will do yours." These are the sweet and interesting subjects which occasionally occupy Milesian gentlemen while they are attendant upon this grand inquest of justice. But there is a religion, it seems, even in jobs; and it will be highly gratifying to Mr. Perceval to learn that no man in Ireland who believes in seven sacraments can carry a public road, or bridge, one yard out of the direction most beneficial to the public, and that nobody can cheat that public who does not expound the Scriptures in the purest and most orthodox manner. This will give pleasure to Mr. Perceval: but, from his unfairness upon these topics, I appeal to the justice and the proper feelings of Mr. Huskisson.[1] I ask him if the human mind can experience a more dreadful sensation than to see its own jobs refused, and the jobs of another religion perpetually succeeding? I ask him his opinion of a jobless faith, of a creed which dooms a man through life to a lean and plunderless integrity. He knows that human nature cannot and will not bear it; and if we were to paint a political Tartarus, it would be an endless series of snug expectations, and cruel disappointments. These are a few of many dreadful inconveniences which the Catholics of all ranks suffer from the laws by which they are at present oppressed. Besides, look at human nature: —what is the history of all professions? Joel is to be brought up to the bar: has Mrs. Plymley the slightest doubt of his being Chancellor? Do not his two shrivelled aunts live in the certainty of seeing him in that situation, and of cutting out with their own hands his equity habiliments? And I could name a certain minister of the Gospel who does not, in the bottom of his heart, much differ from these opinions. Do you think that the fathers and mothers of the holy Catholic Church are not as absurd as Protestant papas and mammas? The probability I admit to be, in each particular case, that the sweet little blockhead will in fact never get a brief;—but I will venture

[1] See p. 294.

to say, there is not a parent from the Giant's Causeway to Bantry Bay who does not conceive that his child is the unfortunate victim of the exclusion, and that nothing short of positive law could prevent his own dear pre-eminent Paddy from rising to the highest honours of the State. So with the army, and parliament; in fact, few are excluded; but, in imagination, all: you keep twenty or thirty Catholics out, and you lose the affections of four millions; and, let me tell you, that recent circumstances have by no means tended to diminish in the minds of men that hope of elevation beyond their own rank which is so congenial to our nature: from pleading for John Roe to taxing John Bull, from jesting for Mr. Pitt and writing in the *Anti-Jacobin*, to managing the affairs of Europe—these are leaps which seem to justify the fondest dreams of mothers and of aunts.

I do not say that the disabilities to which the Catholics are exposed amount to such intolerable grievances, that the strength and industry of a nation are overwhelmed by them: the increasing prosperity of Ireland fully demonstrates to the contrary. But I repeat again, what I have often stated in the course of our correspondence—that your laws against the Catholics are exactly in that state in which you have neither the benefits of rigour nor of liberality: every law which prevented the Catholic from gaining strength and wealth is repealed; every law which can irritate remains; if you were determined to insult the Catholics, you should have kept them weak; if you resolved to give them strength, you should have ceased to insult them;—at present your conduct is pure unadulterated folly.

Lord Hawkesbury says, We heard nothing about the Catholics till we began to mitigate the laws against them; when we relieved them in part from this oppression they began to be disaffected. This is very true; but it proves just what I have said, that you have either done too much or too little; and as there lives not, I hope, upon earth, so depraved a courtier that he would load the Catholics with their ancient chains, what absurdity it is then not to render their dispositions friendly, when you leave their arms and legs free!

You know, and many Englishmen know, what passes in China; but nobody knows or cares what passes in Ireland.

At the beginning of the present reign, no Catholic could realise property, or carry on any business; they were absolutely annihilated, and had no more agency in the country than so many trees. They were like Lord Mulgrave's eloquence and Lord Camden's [1] wit; the legislative bodies did not know of their existence. For these twenty-five years last past, the Catholics have been engaged in commerce; within that period the commerce of Ireland has doubled;—there are four Catholics at work for one Protestant, and eight Catholics at work for one Episcopalian; of course, the proportion which Catholic wealth bears to Protestant wealth is every year altering rapidly in favour of the Catholics. I have already told you what their purchases of land were the last year: since that period, I have been at some pains to find out the actual state of the Catholic wealth: it is impossible, upon such a subject, to arrive at complete accuracy; but I have good reason to believe that there are at present two thousand Catholics in Ireland, possessing an income from £500 upwards, many of these with incomes of one, two, three and four thousand, and some amounting to fifteen and twenty thousand per annum:—and this is the kingdom, and these the people, for whose conciliation we are to wait Heaven knows when, and Lord Hawkesbury why! As for me, I never think of the situation of Ireland without feeling the same necessity for immediate interference as I should do if I saw blood flowing from a great artery. I rush towards it with the instinctive rapidity of a man desirous of preventing death, and have no other feeling but that in a few seconds the patient may be no more.

I could not help smiling in the times of No Popery, to witness the loyal indignation of many persons at the attempt made by the last ministry to do something for the relief of Ireland. The general cry in the country was, that they would not see their beloved Monarch used ill in his old age, and that they would stand by him to the last drop of their blood. I respect good feelings, however erroneous be the occasions on which they display themselves; and therefore I saw in all this as much to admire as to blame. It was a species of affection, however, which reminded me very forcibly of the attachment displayed

[1] See p. 294.

G

by the servants of the Russian ambassador, at the beginning of the last century. His Excellency happened to fall down in a kind of apoplectic fit, when he was paying a morning visit in the house of an acquaintance. The confusion was of course very great, and messengers were despatched, in every direction, to find a surgeon; who, upon his arrival, declared that his Excellency must be immediately blooded, and prepared himself forthwith to perform the operation: the barbarous servants of the embassy, who were there in great numbers, no sooner saw the surgeon prepared to wound the arm of their master with a sharp shining instrument, than they drew their swords, put themselves in an attitude of defence, and swore in pure Sclavonic, "that they would murder any man who attempted to do him the slightest injury: he had been a very good master to them, and they would not desert him in his misfortunes, or suffer his blood to be shed while he was off his guard, and incapable of defending himself." By good fortune, the secretary arrived about this period of the dispute, and his Excellency, relieved from superfluous blood and perilous affection, was, after much difficulty, restored to life.

There is an argument brought forward with some appearance of plausibility in the House of Commons, which certainly merits an answer: You know that the Catholics now vote for members of parliament in Ireland, and that they outnumber the Protestants in a very great proportion; if you allow Catholics to sit in parliament, religion will be found to influence votes more than property, and the greater part of the one hundred Irish members who are returned to parliament will be Catholics.—Add to these the Catholic members who are returned in England, and you will have a phalanx of heretical strength which every minister will be compelled to respect, and occasionally to conciliate by concessions incompatible with the interests of the Protestant Church. The fact is, however, that you are at this moment subjected to every danger of this kind which you can possibly apprehend hereafter. If the spiritual interests of the voters are more powerful than their temporal interests, they can bind down their representatives to support any measures favourable to the Catholic religion, and they can change the objects of their choice till they have found Protestant members (as they easily may do) perfectly obedient to their wishes. If the superior possessions of the Protestants prevent the Catholics from uniting for a common political object, then the danger you fear cannot exist: if zeal, on the contrary, gets the better of acres, then the danger at present exists, from the right of voting already given to the Catholics, and it will not be increased by allowing them to sit in parliament. There are, as nearly as I can recollect, thirty seats in Ireland for cities and counties, where the Protestants are the most numerous, and where the members returned must of course be Protestants. In the other seventy representations, the wealth of the Protestants is opposed to the number of the Catholics; and if all the seventy members returned were of the Catholic persuasion, they must still plot the destruction of our religion in the midst of five hundred and eighty-eight Protestants. Such terrors would disgrace a cook-maid, or a toothless aunt—when they fall from the lips of bearded and senatorial men, they are nauseous, anti-peristaltic, and emetical.

How can you for a moment doubt of the rapid effects which would be produced by the emancipation?—In the first place, to my certain knowledge, the Catholics have long since expressed to his Majesty's Ministers their perfect readiness *to vest in his Majesty, either with the consent of the Pope, or without it if it cannot be obtained, the nomination of the Catholic prelacy.* The Catholic prelacy in Ireland consists of twenty-six bishops and the warden of Galway, a dignitary enjoying Catholic jurisdiction. The number of Roman Catholic priests in Ireland exceeds one thousand. The expenses of his peculiar worship are, to a substantial farmer or mechanic, five shillings per annum; to a labourer (where he is not entirely excused) one shilling per annum; this includes the contribution of the whole family, and for this the priest is bound to attend them when sick, and to confess them when they apply to him: he is also to keep his chapel in order, to celebrate divine service, and to preach on Sundays and holydays. In the northern district a priest gains from £30 to £50; in the other parts of Ireland from £60 to £90 per ann. The best paid Catholic bishops receive about £400 per ann.; the others from £300 to £350. My plan is very simple;

I would have three hundred Catholic parishes at £100 per ann., three hundred at £200 per ann., and four hundred at £300 per ann.; this, for the whole thousand parishes, would amount to £190,000. To the prelacy I would allot £20,000 in unequal proportions, from £1000 to £500; and I would appropriate £40,000 more for the support of Catholic schools, and the repairs of Catholic churches; the whole amount of which sum is £250,000, about the expense of three days of one of our genuine, good, English, *just and necessary wars*. The clergy should all receive their salaries at the Bank of Ireland, and I would place the whole patronage in the hands of the Crown. Now, I appeal to any human being, except Spencer Perceval, Esq., of the parish of Hampstead, what the disaffection of a clergy would amount to, gaping after this graduated bounty of the Crown, and whether Ignatius Loyola himself, if he were a living blockhead, instead of a dead saint, could withstand the temptation of bouncing from £100 a year at Sligo, to £300 in Tipperary? This is the miserable sum of money for which the merchants, and landowners, and nobility of England are exposing themselves to the tremendous peril of losing Ireland. The sinecure places of the Roses and the Percevals, and the "dear and near relations," put up to auction at thirty years' purchase, would almost amount to the money.

I admit that nothing can be more reasonable than to expect that a Catholic priest should starve to death, genteelly and pleasantly, for the good of the Protestant religion; but is it equally reasonable to expect that he should do so for the Protestant pews, and Protestant brick and mortar? On an Irish Sabbath, the bell of a neat parish church often summons to church only the parson and an occasionally conforming clerk; while, two hundred yards off, a thousand Catholics are huddled together in a miserable hovel, and pelted by all the storms of heaven. Can any thing be more distressing than to see a venerable man pouring forth sublime truths in tattered breeches, and depending for his food upon the little offal he gets from his parishioners? I venerate a human being who starves for his principles, let them be what they may; but starving for any thing is not at all to the taste of the honourable flagellants: strict principles, and good pay, is the motto of Mr. Perceval: the one he keeps in great measure for the faults of his enemies, the other for himself.

There are parishes in Connaught in which a Protestant was never settled, nor even seen: in that province, in Munster, and in parts of Leinster, the entire peasantry for sixty miles are Catholics; in these tracts the churches are frequently shut for want of a congregation, or opened to an assemblage of from six to twenty persons. Of what Protestants there are in Ireland, the greatest part are gathered together in Ulster, or they live in towns. In the country of the other three provinces the Catholics see no other religion but their own, and are at the least as fifteen to one Protestant. In the diocese of Tuam they are sixty to one; in the parish of St. Mullins, diocese of Leghlin, there are four thousand Catholics and *one Protestant*; in the town of Grasgenamana, in the county of Kilkenny, there are between four and five hundred Catholic houses, and three Protestant houses. In the parish of Allen, county Kildare, there is no Protestant, though it is very populous. In the parish of Arlesin, Queen's County, the proportion is one hundred to one. In the whole county of Kilkenny, by actual enumeration, it is seventeen to one; in the diocese of Kilmacduagh, province of Connaught, fifty-two to one, by ditto. These I give you as a few specimens of the present state of Ireland;—and yet there are men impudent and ignorant enough to contend that such evils require no remedy, and that mild family man who dwelleth in Hampstead can find none but the cautery and the knife,

> ———omne per ignem
> Excoquitur vitium.

I cannot describe the horror and disgust which I felt at hearing Mr. Perceval call upon the then ministry for measures of vigour in Ireland. If I lived at Hampstead upon stewed meats and claret; if I walked to church every Sunday before eleven young gentlemen of my own begetting, with their faces washed, and their hair pleasingly combed: if the Almighty had blessed me with every earthly comfort—how awfully would I pause before I sent forth the flame and the sword over the cabins of the poor, brave, generous, open-hearted peasants of Ireland! How easy it is to shed human blood—how easy it is to persuade ourselves that it is our duty to do so—and that the decision has cost us a severe struggle—how much in all ages have wounds and shrieks and tears been the cheap and vulgar resources of the rulers of mankind—how difficult and how noble it is to govern in kindness and to found an empire upon the everlasting basis of justice and affection! —But what do men call vigour? To let loose hussars and to bring up artillery, to govern with lighted matches, and to cut, and push, and prime—I call this, not vigour, but the *sloth of cruelty and ignorance*. The vigour I love consists in finding out wherein subjects are aggrieved, in relieving them, in studying the temper and genius of a people, in consulting their prejudices, in selecting proper persons to lead and manage them, in the laborious, watchful, and difficult task of increasing public happiness by allaying each particular discontent. In this way Hoche pacified La Vendée—and in this way only will Ireland ever be subdued. But this, in the eyes of Mr. Perceval—is imbecility and meanness: houses are not broken open— women are not insulted—the people seem all to be happy; they are not rode over by horses, and cut by whips. Do you call this vigour?—Is this government?

LETTER X. AND LAST

You must observe that all I have said of the effects which will be produced by giving salaries to the Catholic Clergy, only proceeds upon the supposition that the emancipation of the laity is effected:—without that, I am sure there is not a clergyman in Ireland who would receive a shilling from government; he could not do so, without an entire loss of credit among the members of his own persuasion.

What you say of the moderation of the Irish Protestant Clergy in collecting tithes, is, I believe, strictly true. Instead of collecting what the law enables them to collect, I believe they seldom or ever collect more than two-thirds; and I entirely agree with you, that the abolition of agistment tithe in Ireland by a vote of the Irish House of Commons, and without any remuneration to the Church, was a most scandalous and Jacobinical measure. I do

not blame the Irish clergy; but I submit to your common
sense—if it be possible to explain to an Irish peasant upon
what principle of justice, or common sense, he is to pay
every tenth potato in his little garden to a clergyman in
whose religion nobody believes for twenty miles around
him, and who has nothing to preach to but bare walls.   It
is true, if the tithes are bought up, the cottager must
pay more rent to his landlord; but the same thing done in
the shape of rent is less odious than when it is done in
the shape of tithe.   I do not want to take a shilling out
of the pockets of the clergy, but to leave the substance of
things, and to change their names.   I cannot see the
slightest reason why the Irish labourer is to be relieved
from the real onus, or from anything else but the name of
tithe.   At present he rents only nine-tenths of the produce
of the land; which is all that belongs to the owner; this he
has at the market price; if the landowner purchase the
other tenth of the Church, of course he has a right to make
a correspondent advance upon his tenant.

I very much doubt, if you were to lay open all civil
offices to the Catholics, and to grant salaries to their
clergy, in the manner I have stated, if the Catholic laity
would give themselves much trouble about the advance
of their Church; for they would pay the same tithes under
one system that they do under another.   If you were to
bring the Catholics into the daylight of the world, to the
high situations of the army, the navy, and the bar, numbers
of them would come over to the Established Church, and
do as other people do; instead of that, you set a mark of
infamy upon them, rouse every passion of our nature in
favour of their creed, and then wonder that men are
blind to the follies of the Catholic religion.   There are
hardly any instances of old and rich families among the
Protestant Dissenters: when a man keeps a coach, and lives
in good company, he comes to church, and gets ashamed
of the meeting-house; if this is not the case with the father,
it is almost always the case with the son.   These things
would never be so, if the Dissenters were in *practice* as
much excluded from all the concerns of civil life, as the
Catholics are.   If a rich young Catholic were in parliament, he would belong to White's and to Brookes's, would
keep race-horses—would walk up and down Pall Mall, be

exonerated of his ready money and his constitution, become as totally devoid of morality, honesty, knowledge, and civility as Protestant loungers in Pall Mall, and return home with a supreme contempt for Father O'Leary and Father O'Callaghan. I am astonished at the madness of the Catholic clergy, in not perceiving that Catholic emancipation is Catholic infidelity; that to entangle their people in the intrigues of a Protestant parliament, and a Protestant court, is to insure the loss of every man of fashion and consequence in their community. The true receipt for preserving their religion, is Mr. Perceval's receipt for destroying it: it is to deprive every rich Catholic of all the objects of secular ambition, to separate him from the Protestant, and to shut him up in his castle with priests and relics.

We are told, in answer to all our arguments, that this is not a fit period,—that a period of universal war is not the proper time for dangerous innovations in the constitution: this is as much as to say, that the worst time for making friends is the period when you have made many enemies; that it is the greatest of all errors to stop when you are breathless, and to lie down when you are fatigued. Of one thing I am quite certain: if the safety of Europe is once completely restored, the Catholics may for ever bid adieu to the slightest probability of effecting their object. Such men as hang about a court not only are deaf to the suggestions of mere justice, but they despise justice; they detest the word *right*; the only word which rouses them is *peril*; where they can oppress with impunity, they oppress for ever, and call it loyalty and wisdom.

I am so far from conceiving the legitimate strength of the Crown would be diminished by those abolitions of civil incapacities in consequence of religious opinions, that my only objection to the increase of religious freedom is, that it would operate as a diminution of political freedom: the power of the Crown is so overbearing at this period, that almost the only steady opposers of its fatal influence are men disgusted by religious intolerance. Our establishments are so enormous, and so utterly disproportioned to our population, that every second or third man you meet in society gains something from the public; my brother the commissioner, — my nephew the police justice, —

purveyor of small beer to the army in Ireland,—clerk of
the mouth,—yeoman to the left hand,—these are the
obstacles which common sense and justice have now to
overcome. Add to this, that the King, old and infirm,
excites a principle of very amiable generosity in his favour;
that he has led a good, moral, and religious life, equally
removed from profligacy and methodistical hypocrisy;
that he has been a good husband, a good father, and a
good master; that he dresses plain, loves hunting and
farming, hates the French, and is, in all his opinions and
habits, quite English:—these feelings are heightened by
the present situation of the world, and the yet unexploded
clamour of Jacobinism. In short, from the various
sources of interest, personal regard, and national taste,
such a tempest of loyalty has set in upon the people that
the 47th proposition in Euclid might now be voted down
with as much ease as any proposition in politics; and
therefore if Lord Hawkesbury hates the abstract truths
of science as much as he hates concrete truth in human
affairs, now is his time for getting rid of the multiplication
table, and passing a vote of censure upon the pretensions
of the *hypothenuse*. Such is the history of English parties
at this moment: you cannot seriously suppose that the
people care for such men as Lord Hawkesbury, Mr. Canning,
and Mr. Perceval, on their own account; you cannot really
believe them to be so degraded as to look to their safety
from a man who proposes to subdue Europe by keeping
it without Jesuits' Bark.[1] The people, at present, have
one passion, and but one—

A Jove principium, Jovis omnia plena.

They care no more for the ministers I have mentioned,
than they do for those sturdy royalists who for £60 per
annum stand behind his Majesty's carriage, arrayed in
scarlet and in gold. If the present ministers opposed the
Court instead of flattering it, they would not command
twenty votes.

Do not imagine by these observations that I am not
loyal: without joining in the common cant of the best of
kings, I respect the King most sincerely as a good man.
His religion is better than the religion of Mr. Perceval,

[1] See p. 295.

his old morality very superior to the old morality of Mr.
Canning, and I am quite certain he has a safer understanding than both of them put together. Loyalty within
the bounds of reason and moderation, is one of the great
instruments of English happiness; but the love of the King
may easily become more strong than the love of the kingdom, and we may lose sight of the public welfare in our
exaggerated admiration of him who is appointed to reign
only for its promotion and support. I detest Jacobinism;
and if I am doomed to be a slave at all, I would rather be
the slave of a king than a cobbler. God save the King,
you say, warms your heart like the sound of a trumpet.
I cannot make use of so violent a metaphor; but I am
delighted to hear it, when it is the cry of genuine affection;
I am delighted to hear it, when they hail not only the individual man, but the outward and living sign of all English
blessings. These are noble feelings, and the heart of
every good man must go with them; but God save the
King, in these times, too often means God save my pension
and my place, God give my sisters an allowance out of the
privy purse,—make me clerk of the irons, let me survey
the meltings, let me live upon the fruits of other men's
industry, and fatten upon the plunder of the public.

What is it possible to say to such a man as the Gentleman
of Hampstead, who really believes it feasible to convert
the four million Irish Catholics to the Protestant religion,
and considers this as the best remedy for the disturbed
state of Ireland? It is not possible to answer such a man
with arguments; we must come out against him with
beads, and a cowl, and push him into an hermitage. It is
really such trash—that it is an abuse of the privilege of
reasoning to reply to it. Such a project is well worthy
the statesman who would bring the French to reason by
keeping them without rhubarb, and exhibit to mankind
the awful spectacle of a nation deprived of neutral salts.
This is not the dream of a wild apothecary indulging in his
own opium; this is not the distempered fancy of a pounder
of drugs, delirious from smallness of profits: but it is the
sober, deliberate, and systematic scheme of a man to
whom the public safety is entrusted, and whose appointment is considered by many as a masterpiece of political
sagacity. What a sublime thought, that no purge can

now be taken between the Weser and the Garonne; that the bustling pestle is still, the canorous mortar mute, and the bowels of mankind locked up for fourteen degrees of latitude! When, I should be curious to know, were all the powers of crudity and flatulence fully explained to his Majesty's ministers? At what period was this great plan of conquest and constipation fully developed? In whose mind was the idea of destroying the pride and the plasters of France first engendered? Without castor oil they might, for some months, to be sure, have carried on a lingering war; but can they do without bark? Will the people live under a government where antimonial powders cannot be procured? Will they bear the loss of mercury? "There's the rub." Depend upon it, the absence of the materia medica will soon bring them to their senses, and the cry of *Bourbon and bolus* burst forth from the Baltic to the Mediterranean.

You ask me for any precedent in our history where the oath of supremacy has been dispensed with. It was dispensed with to the Catholics of Canada in 1774. They are only required to take a simple oath of allegiance. The same, I believe, was the case in Corsica. The reason of such exemption was obvious; you could not possibly have retained either of these countries without it. And what did it signify, whether you retained them or not? In cases where you might have been foolish without peril, you were wise; when nonsense and bigotry threaten you with destruction, it is impossible to bring you back to the alphabet of justice and common sense. If men are to be fools, I would rather they were fools in little matters than in great; dulness turned up with temerity, is a livery all the worse for the facings; and the most tremendous of all things is the magnanimity of a dunce.

It is not by any means necessary, as you contend, to repeal the Test Act if you give relief to the Catholic; what the Catholics ask for is to be put on a footing with the Protestant Dissenters, which would be done by repealing that part of the law which compels them to take the oath of supremacy and to make the declaration against transubstantiation: they would then come into parliament as all other Dissenters are allowed to do, and the penal laws to which they were exposed for taking office would be

suspended every year, as they have been for this half
century past towards Protestant Dissenters. Perhaps,
after all, this is the best method,—to continue the persecuting law, and to suspend it every year,—a method which
while, it effectually destroys the persecution itself, leaves
to the great mass of mankind the exquisite gratification
of supposing that they are enjoying some advantage from
which a particular class of their fellow-creatures are excluded. We manage the Corporation and Test Acts at
present much in the same manner as if we were to persuade
parish boys who had been in the habit of beating an ass
to spare the animal, and beat the skin of an ass stuffed
with straw; this would preserve the semblance of tormenting without the reality, and keep boy and beast in
good humour.

How can you imagine that a provision for the Catholic
clergy affects the 5th article of the Union? Surely I am
preserving the Protestant Church in Ireland, if I put it
in a better condition than that in which it now is. A
tithe proctor in Ireland collects his tithes with a blunder-
buss, and carries his tenth hay-cock by storm, sword in
hand: to give him equal value in a more pacific shape
cannot, I should imagine, be considered as injurious to
the Church of Ireland; and what right has that Church
to complain, if parliament chooses to fix upon the empire
the burthen of supporting a double ecclesiastical establishment? Are the revenues of the Irish Protestant clergy
in the slightest degree injured by such provision? On the
contrary, is it possible to confer a more serious benefit
upon that Church, than by quieting and contenting those
who are at work for its destruction?

It is impossible to think of the affairs of Ireland without
being forcibly struck with the parallel of Hungary. Of
her seven millions of inhabitants, one half were Protestants,
Calvinists, and Lutherans, many of the Greek Church, and
many Jews; such was the state of their religious dissensions,
that Mahomet had often been called in to the aid of Calvin,
and the crescent often glittered on the walls of Buda and
of Presburg. At last, in 1791, during the most violent
crisis of disturbance, a diet was called, and by a great
majority of voices a decree was passed, which secured to
all the contending sects the fullest and freest exercise of

religious worship and education; ordained (let it be heard
in Hampstead) that churches and chapels should be
erected for all on the most perfectly equal terms; that
the Protestants of both confessions should depend upon
their spiritual superiors alone; liberated them from swearing by the usual oath, "the holy Virgin Mary, the saints,
and chosen of God"; and then the decree adds "*that
public offices and honours, high or low, great or small, shall
be given to natural-born Hungarians who deserve well of
their country, and possess the other qualifications, let their
religion be what it may.*" Such was the line of policy
pursued in a diet consisting of four hundred members, in
a state whose form of government approaches nearer to
our own than any other, having a Roman Catholic establishment of great wealth and power, and under the influence
of one of the most bigoted Catholic Courts in Europe.
This measure has now the experience of eighteen years
in its favour; it has undergone a trial of fourteen years of
revolution such as the world never witnessed, and more
than equal to a century less convulsed: What have been
its effects? When the French advanced like a torrent
within a few days' march of Vienna, the Hungarians rose
in a mass; they formed what they called the sacred insurrection, to defend their sovereign, their rights and liberties,
now common to all; and the apprehension of their approach
dictated to the reluctant Bonaparte the immediate signature of the treaty of *Leoben*. The Romish hierarchy of
Hungary exists in all its former splendour and opulence;
never has the slightest attempt been made to diminish it;
and those revolutionary principles, to which so large a
portion of civilised Europe has been sacrificed, have here
failed in making the smallest successful inroad.

The whole history of this proceeding of the Hungarian
Diet is so extraordinary, and such an admirable comment
upon the Protestantism of Mr. Spencer Perceval, that I
must compel you to read a few short extracts from the
law itself:—"The Protestants of both confessions shall,
in religious matters, depend upon their own spiritual
superiors alone. The Protestants may likewise retain their
trivial [1] and grammar schools. The Church dues which
the Protestants have hitherto paid to the Catholic parish

[1] See p. 295.

priests, schoolmasters, or other such officers, either in money, productions, or labour, shall in future entirely cease, and after three months from the publishing of this law, be no more any where demanded. In the building or repairing of churches, parsonage-houses, and schools, the Protestants are not obliged to assist the Catholics with labour, nor the Catholics the Protestants. The pious foundations and donations of the Protestants which already exist, or which in future may be made for their churches, ministers, schools and students, hospitals, orphan-houses and poor, cannot be taken from them under any pretext, nor yet the care of them; but rather the unimpeded administration shall be entrusted to those from among them to whom it legally belongs, and those foundations which may have been taken from them under the last government, shall be returned to them without delay. All affairs of marriage of the Protestants are left to their own consistories; all landlords and masters of families, under the penalty of public persecution, are ordered not to prevent their subjects and servants, whether they be Catholic or Protestant, from the observance of the festivals and ceremonies of their religion," etc. etc. etc.—By what strange chances are mankind influenced! A little Catholic barrister of Vienna might have raised the cry of *No Protestantism*, and Hungary would have panted for the arrival of a French army as much as Ireland does at this moment; arms would have been searched for; Lutheran and Calvinist houses entered in the dead of the night; and the strength of Austria exhausted in guarding a country from which under the present liberal system, she may expect, in a moment of danger, the most powerful aid: and let it be remembered, that this memorable example of political wisdom took place at a period when many great monarchies were yet unconquered in Europe; in a country where the two religious parties were equal in number; and where it is impossible to suppose indifference in the party which relinquished its exclusive privileges. Under all these circumstances, the measure was carried in the Hungarian Diet by a majority of 280 to 120. In a few weeks, we shall see every concession denied to the Catholics by a much larger majority of Protestants, at a moment when every other power is subjugated but ourselves, and in a country where the oppressed are four times as numerous as their oppressors. So much for the wisdom of our ancestors—so much for the nineteenth century—so much for the superiority of the English over all the nations of the Continent.

Are you not sensible, let me ask you, of the absurdity of trusting the lowest Catholics with offices correspondent to their situation in life, and of denying such privilege to the higher? A Catholic may serve in the militia, but a Catholic cannot come into Parliament; in the latter case you suspect combination, and in the former case you suspect no combination; you deliberately arm ten or twenty thousand of the lowest of the Catholic people;—and the moment you come to a class of men whose education, honour, and talents, seem to render all mischief less probable, then you see the danger of employing a Catholic, and cling to your investigating tests and disabling laws. If you tell me you have enough of members of Parliament, and not enough of militia, without the Catholics—I beg leave to remind you, that, by employing the physical force of any sect, at the same time when you leave them in a state of utter disaffection, you are not adding strength to your armies, but weakness and ruin.—If you want the vigour of their common people, you must not disgrace their nobility, and insult their priesthood.

I thought that the terror of the Pope had been confined to the limits of the nursery, and merely employed as a means to induce young master to enter into his small-clothes with greater speed, and to eat his breakfast with greater attention to decorum. For these purposes, the name of the Pope is admirable; but why push it beyond? Why not leave to Lord Hawkesbury all further enumeration of the Pope's powers? For a whole century, you have been exposed to the enmity of France, and your succession was disputed in two rebellions; what could the Pope do at the period when there was a serious struggle, whether England should be Protestant or Catholic, and when the issue was completely doubtful? Could the Pope induce the Irish to rise in 1715? Could he induce them to rise in 1745? You had no Catholic enemy when half this island was in arms; and what did the Pope attempt in the last rebellion in Ireland? But if he had as much power over the minds

of the Irish as Mr. Wilberforce has over the mind of a
young Methodist converted the preceding quarter, is this
a reason why we are to disgust men, who may be acted
upon in such a manner by a foreign power? or is it not an
additional reason why we should raise up every barrier of
affection and kindness against the mischief of foreign
influence? But the true answer is, the mischief does not
exist. Gog and Magog have produced as much influence
upon human affairs as the Pope has done for this half
century past; and by spoiling him of his possessions, and
degrading him in the eyes of all Europe, Bonaparte has
not taken quite the proper method of increasing his influence.

But why not a Catholic king, as well as a Catholic member
of Parliament, or of the Cabinet?—Because it is probable
that the one would be mischievous, and the other not.
A Catholic king might struggle against the Protestantism
of the country, and if the struggle were not successful, it
would at least be dangerous; but the efforts of any other
Catholic would be quite insignificant, and his hope of success
so small, that it is quite improbable the effort would ever
be made: my argument is, that in so Protestant a country
as Great Britain, the character of her parliaments and
her cabinet could not be changed by the few Catholics
who would ever find their way to the one or the other.
But the power of the Crown is immeasurably greater than
the power which the Catholics could obtain from any other
species of authority in the state; and it does not follow,
because the lesser degree of power is innocent, that the
greater should be so too. As for the stress you lay upon
the danger of a Catholic chancellor, I have not the least
hesitation in saying, that his appointment would not do a
ten-thousandth part of the mischief to the English Church
that might be done by a Methodistical chancellor of the
true Clapham breed; and I request to know, if it is really
so very necessary that a chancellor should be of the religion
of the Church of England, how many chancellors you have
had within the last century who have been bred up in the
Presbyterian religion?—And again, how many you have
had who notoriously have been without any religion at all?

Why are you to suppose that eligibility and election are
the same thing, and that all the cabinet *will* be Catholics
whenever all the cabinet *may* be Catholics? You have a

right, you say, to suppose an extreme case, and to argue upon it—so have I: and I will suppose that the hundred Irish members will one day come down in a body, and pass a law compelling the King to reside in Dublin. I will suppose that the Scotch members, by a similar stratagem, will lay England under a large contribution of meal and sulphur: no measure is without objection, if you sweep the whole horizon for danger; it is not sufficient to tell me of what may happen, but you must show me a rational probability that it will happen: after all, I might, contrary to my real opinion, admit all your dangers to exist; it is enough for me to contend, that all other dangers taken together are not equal to the danger of losing Ireland from disaffection and invasion.

I am astonished to see you, and many good and well-meaning clergymen beside you, painting the Catholics in such detestable colours; two-thirds, at least, of Europe are Catholics,—they are Christians, though mistaken Christians; how can I possibly admit that any sect of Christians, and above all, that the oldest and the most numerous sect of Christians, are incapable of fulfilling the common duties and relations of life: though I do differ from them in many particulars—God forbid I should give such a handle to infidelity, and subscribe to such blasphemy against our common religion!

Do you think mankind never change their opinions without formally expressing and confessing that change? When you quote the decisions of ancient Catholic councils, are you prepared to defend all the decrees of English convocations and universities since the reign of Queen Elizabeth? I could soon make you sick of your uncandid industry against the Catholics, and bring you to allow that it is better to forget times past, and to judge and be judged by present opinions and present practice.

I must beg to be excused from explaining and refuting all the mistakes about the Catholics made by my Lord Redesdale; and I must do that nobleman the justice to say, that he has been treated with great disrespect. Could any thing be more indecent than to make it a morning lounge in Dublin to call upon his Lordship, and to cram him with Arabian-night stories about the Catholics? Is this proper behaviour to the representative of Majesty, the

H

child of Themis, and the keeper of the conscience in West Britain? Whoever reads the Letters of the Catholic Bishops, in the Appendix to Sir John Hippesly's [1] very sensible book, will see to what an excess this practice must have been carried with the pleasing and Protestant nobleman whose name I have mentioned, and from thence I wish you to receive your answer about excommunication, and all the trash which is talked against the Catholics.

A sort of notion has, by some means or another, crept into the world, that difference of religion would render men unfit to perform together the offices of common and civil life: that Brother Wood and Brother Grose could not travel together the same circuit if they differed in creed, nor Cockell and Mingay be engaged in the same cause if Cockell was a Catholic and Mingay a Muggletonian. It is supposed that Huskisson and Sir Harry Englefield [2] would squabble behind the Speaker's chair about the Council of Lateran, and many a turnpike bill miscarry by the sarcastical controversies of Mr. Hawkins Brown and Sir John Throckmorton upon the real presence. I wish I could see some of these symptoms of earnestness upon the subject of religion; but it really seems to me that, in the present state of society, men no more think about inquiring concerning each other's faith than they do concerning the colour of each other's skins. There may have been times in England when the quarter sessions would have been disturbed by theological polemics: but now, after a Catholic justice had once been seen on the bench and it had been clearly ascertained that he spoke English, had no tail, only a single row of teeth, and that he loved port wine,—after all the scandalous and infamous reports of his physical conformation had been clearly proved to be false,—he would be reckoned a jolly fellow, and very superior in flavour to a sly Presbyterian. Nothing, in fact, can be more uncandid and unphilosophical * than to say that a man has a tail, because you cannot agree with him upon religious subjects; it appears to be ludicrous: but I am convinced it has done infinite mischief to the Catholics, and made a very serious impression upon the minds of many gentlemen of large landed property.

[1] See p. 295.   [2] See p. 295.
* *Vide* Lord Bacon, Locke and Descartes.

In talking of the impossibility of Catholic and Protestant living together with equal privilege under the same government, do you forget the Cantons of Switzerland? You might have seen there a Protestant congregation going into a church which had just been quitted by a Catholic congregation; and I will venture to say that the Swiss Catholics were more bigoted to their religion than any people in the whole world. Did the kings of Prussia ever refuse to employ a Catholic? Would Frederick the Great have rejected an able man on this account? We have seen Prince Czartorinski, a Catholic secretary of state in Russia; in former times, a Greek patriarch and an apostolic vicar acted together in the most perfect harmony in Venice; and we have seen the Emperor of Germany in modern times entrusting the care of his person and the command of his guard to a Protestant Prince, Ferdinand of Wirtemberg. But what are all these things to Mr. Perceval? He has looked at human nature from the top of Hampstead Hill, and has not a thought beyond the little sphere of his own vision. "The snail," say the Hindoos, "sees nothing but his own shell, and thinks it the grandest palace in the universe."

I now take a final leave of this subject of Ireland; the only difficulty in discussing it is a want of resistance, a want of something difficult to unravel, and something dark to illumine. To agitate such a question is to beat the air with a club, and cut down gnats with a scimitar; it is a prostitution of industry, and a waste of strength. If a man say, I have a good place, and I do not choose to lose it, this mode of arguing upon the Catholic question I can well understand; but that any human being with an understanding two degrees elevated above that of an Anabaptist preacher, should conscientiously contend for the expediency and propriety of leaving the Irish Catholics in their present state, and of subjecting us to such tremendous peril in the present condition of the world, it is utterly out of my power to conceive. Such a measure as the Catholic question is entirely beyond the common game of politics; it is a measure in which all parties ought to acquiesce, in order to preserve the place where and the stake for which they play. If Ireland is gone, where are jobs? where are reversions? where is my brother, Lord

Arden[1]? where are my dear and near relations? The
game is up, and the Speaker of the House of Commons
will be sent as a present to the menagerie at Paris. We
talk of waiting from particular considerations, as if centuries of joy and prosperity were before us: in the next
ten years our fate must be decided; we shall know, long
before that period, whether we can bear up against the
miseries by which we are threatened, or not: and yet,
in the very midst of our crisis, we are enjoined to abstain
from the most certain means of increasing our strength,
and advised to wait for the remedy till the disease is removed
by death or health. And now, instead of the plain and
manly policy of increasing unanimity at home, by equalising
rights and privileges, what is the ignorant, arrogant, and
wicked system which has been pursued? Such a career
of madness and of folly was, I believe, never run in so short
a period. The vigour of the ministry is like the vigour
of a grave-digger,—the tomb becomes more ready and
more wide for every effort which they make. There is
nothing which it is worth while either to take or to retain,
and a constant train of ruinous expeditions have been
kept up. Every Englishman felt proud of the integrity
of his country; the character of the country is lost for ever.
It is of the utmost consequence to a commercial people at
war with the greatest part of Europe, that there should
be a free entry of neutrals into the enemy's ports; the
neutrals who carried our manufactures we have not only
excluded, but we have compelled them to declare war
against us. It was our interest to make a good peace, or
convince our own people that it could not be obtained;
we have not made a peace, and we have convinced the
people of nothing but of the arrogance of the Foreign
Secretary: and all this has taken place in the short space
of a year, because a King's Bench barrister and a writer
of epigrams, turned into Ministers of State, were determined to show country gentlemen that the late administration had no vigour. In the mean time commerce
stands still, manufactures perish, Ireland is more and
more irritated, India is threatened, fresh taxes are accumulated upon the wretched people, the war is carried on
without it being possible to conceive any one single object

[1] See p. 295.

which a rational being can propose to himself by its continuation; and in the midst of this unparalleled insanity we are told that the Continent is to be reconquered by the want of rhubarb and plums.* A better spirit than exists in the English people never existed in any people in the world; it has been misdirected, and squandered upon party purposes in the most degrading and scandalous manner; they have been led to believe that they were benefiting the commerce of England by destroying the commerce of America, that they were defending their Sovereign by perpetuating the bigoted oppression of their fellow-subjects; their rulers and their guides have told them that they would equal the vigour of France by equalling her atrocity; and they have gone on wasting that opulence, patience, and courage, which, if husbanded by prudent and moderate counsels, might have proved the salvation of mankind. The same policy of turning the good qualities of Englishmen to their own destruction, which made Mr. Pitt omnipotent, continues his power to those who resemble him only in his vices; advantage is taken of the loyalty of Englishmen to make them meanly submissive; their piety is turned into persecution, their courage into useless and obstinate contention; they are plundered because they are ready to pay, and soothed into asinine stupidity because they are full of virtuous patience. If England must perish at last, so let it be; that event is in the hands of God; we must dry up our tears and submit. But that England should perish swindling and stealing; that it should perish waging war against lazar houses, and hospitals; that it should perish persecuting with monastic bigotry; that it should calmly give itself up to be ruined by the flashy arrogance of one man, and the narrow fanaticism of another; these events are within the power of human beings, and I did not think that the magnanimity of Englishmen would ever stoop to such degradations.

Longum vale!

PETER PLYMLEY.

* Even Allen Park (accustomed as he has always been to be delighted by all administrations) says it is too bad; and Hall and Morris are said to have actually blushed in one of the divisions.

SELECTED WRITINGS

BENTHAM'S BOOK OF FALLACIES [1]

THERE are a vast number of absurd and mischievous fallacies, which pass readily in the world for sense and virtue, while in truth they tend only to fortify error and encourage crime. Mr. Bentham has enumerated the most conspicuous of these in the book before us.

Whether it be necessary there should be a middleman between the cultivator and the possessor, learned economists have doubted; but neither gods, men, nor booksellers can doubt the necessity of a middleman between Mr. Bentham and the public. Mr. Bentham is long; Mr. Bentham is occasionally involved and obscure; Mr. Bentham invents new and alarming expressions; Mr. Bentham loves division and sub-division—and he loves method itself, more than its consequences. Those only, therefore, who know his originality, his knowledge, his vigour, and his boldness, will recur to the works themselves. The great mass of readers will not purchase improvement at so dear a rate; but will choose rather to become acquainted with Mr. Bentham through the medium of Reviews —after that eminent philosopher has been washed, trimmed, shaved, and forced into clean linen. One great use of a Review, indeed, is to make men wise in ten pages, who have no appetite for a hundred pages; to condense nourishment, to work with pulp and essence, and to guard the stomach from idle burden and unmeaning bulk. For half a page, sometimes for a whole page, Mr. Bentham writes with a power which few can equal; and by selecting and omitting, an admirable style may be formed from the text. Using this liberty, we shall endeavour to give an account of Mr. Bentham's doctrines, for the most part in his own words. Wherever any expression is particularly happy, let it be considered to be Mr. Bentham's:—the dulness we take to ourselves.

Our Wise Ancestors—the Wisdom of our Ancestors— the Wisdom of Ages—venerable Antiquity—Wisdom of Old

[1] See p. 295.

89

Times.—This mischievous and absurd fallacy springs from
the grossest perversion of the meaning of words. Experience is certainly the mother of wisdom, and the old have,
of course, a greater experience than the young; but the
question is, who are the old? and who are the young? Of
individuals living at the same period, the oldest has, of
course, the greatest experience; but among *generations* of
men the reverse of this is true. Those who come first
(our ancestors), are the young people, and have the least
experience. We have added to their experience the
experience of many centuries; and, therefore, as far as
experience goes, are wiser, and more capable of forming
an opinion than they were. The real feeling should be,
not, can we be so presumptuous as to put our opinions in
opposition to those of our ancestors? but can such young,
ignorant, and inexperienced persons as our ancestors necessarily were, be expected to have understood a subject
as well as those who have seen so much more, lived so much
longer, and enjoyed the experience of so many centuries?
All this cant, then, about our ancestors is merely an abuse
of words, by transferring phrases true of contemporary
men to succeeding ages. Whereas (as we have before
observed) of living men the oldest has, *cæteris paribus*,
the most experience; of generations, the oldest has, *cæteris
paribus*, the least experience. Our ancestors, up to the
Conquest, were children in arms; chubby boys in the time
of Edward the First; striplings under Elizabeth; men in
the reign of Queen Anne; and *we* only are the white-
bearded, silver-headed ancients, who have treasured up,
and are prepared to profit by, all the experience which
human life can supply. We are not disputing with our
ancestors the palm of talent, in which they may or may not
be our superiors, but the palm of experience, in which it is
utterly impossible they can be our superiors. And yet,
whenever the Chancellor comes forward to protect some
abuse, or to oppose some plan which has the increase of
human happiness for its object, his first appeal is always
to the wisdom of our ancestors; and he himself, and many
noble lords who vote with him, are, to this hour, persuaded
that all alterations and amendments on their devices are
an unblushing controversy between youthful temerity and
mature experience!—and so, in truth, they are,—only

that much-loved magistrate mistakes the young for the old, and the old for the young—and is guilty of that very sin against experience which he attributes to the lovers of innovation.

We cannot of course be supposed to maintain that our ancestors wanted wisdom, or that they were necessarily mistaken in their institutions, because their means of information were more limited than ours. But we do confidently maintain that when we find it expedient to change any thing which our ancestors have enacted, we are the experienced persons, and not they. The quantity of talent is always varying in any great nation. To say that we are more or less able than our ancestors, is an assertion that requires to be explained. All the able men of all ages, who have ever lived in England, probably possessed, if taken all together, more intellect than all the able men now in England can boast of. But if authority must be resorted to rather than reason, the question is, What was the wisdom of that single age which enacted the law, compared with the wisdom of the age which proposes to alter it? What are the eminent men of one and the other period? If you say that our ancestors were wiser than us, mention your date and year. If the splendour of names is equal, are the circumstances the same? If the circumstances are the same, we have a superiority of experience, of which the difference between the two periods is the measure. It is necessary to insist upon this; for upon sacks of wool, and on benches forensic, sit grave men, and agricolous persons in the Commons, crying out "Ancestors, Ancestors! *hodie non*! Saxons, Danes, save us! Fiddlefrig, help us! Howel, Ethelwolf, protect us!"—Any cover for nonsense —any veil for trash—any pretext for repelling the in-novations of conscience and of duty!

So long as they keep to vague generalities—so long as the two objects of comparison are each of them taken in the lump —wise ancestors in one lump, ignorant and foolish mob of modern times in the other—the weakness of the fallacy may escape detection. But let them assign for the period of superior wisdom any determinate period whatsoever, not only will the groundlessness of the notion be apparent (class being compared with class in that period and the present one), but, unless the antecedent period be comparatively speaking a very modern one, so wide will be the disparity, and to such an amount in favour of modern times, that, in comparison of the lowest class of the people in modern times, (always supposing them proficients in the art of reading, and their proficiency employed in the reading of newspapers,) the very highest and best informed class of these wise ancestors will turn out to be grossly ignorant.

Take, for example, any year in the reign of Henry the Eighth, from 1509 to 1546. At that time the House of Lords would probably have been in possession of by far the larger proportion of what little instruction the age afforded: in the House of Lords, among the laity, it might even then be a question whether, without exception, their lordships were all of them able so much as to read. But even supposing them all in the fullest possession of that useful art, political science being the science in question, what instruction on the subject could they meet with at that time of day?

On no one branch of legislation was any book extant from which, with regard to the circumstances of the then present times, any useful instruction could be derived: distributive law, penal law, international law, political economy, so far from existing as sciences, had scarcely obtained a name: in all those departments, under the head of *quid faciendum*, a mere blank: the whole literature of the age consisted of a meagre chronicle or two, containing short memorandums of the usual occurrences of war and peace, battles, sieges, executions, revels, deaths, births, processions, ceremonies, and other external events; but with scarce a speech or an incident that could enter into the composition of any such work as a history of the human mind—with scarce an attempt at investigation into causes, characters, or the state of the people at large. Even when at last, little by little, a scrap or two of political instruction came to be obtainable, the proportion of error and mischievous doctrine mixed up with it was so great, that whether a blank unfilled might not have been less prejudicial than a blank thus filled, may reasonably be matter of doubt.

If we come down to the reign of James the First, we shall find that Solomon of his time eminently eloquent as well as learned not only among crowned but among uncrowned heads, marking out for prohibition and punishment the practices of devils and witches, and without any the slightest objection on the part of the great characters of that day in their high situations, consigning men to death and torment for the misfortune of not being so well acquainted as he was with the composition of the Godhead.

Under the name of Exorcism the Catholic liturgy contains a form of procedure for driving out devils;—even with the help of this instrument, the operation cannot be performed with the desired success, but by an operator qualified by holy orders for the working of this as well as so many other wonders.   In our days and in our country the same object is attained, and beyond comparison more effectually, by so cheap an instrument as a common newspaper: before this talisman, not only devils but ghosts, vampires, witches, and all their kindred tribes, are driven out of the land, never to return again! The touch of holy water is not so intolerable to them as the bare smell of printers' ink.—(pp. 74–7.)

Fallacy of irrevocable Laws.—A law, says Mr. Bentham (no matter to what effect), is proposed to a legislative assembly, who are called upon to reject it, upon the single ground, that by those who in some former period exercised the same power, a regulation was made, having for its object to preclude for ever, or to the end of an unexpired period, all succeeding legislators from enacting a law to any such effect as that now proposed.

Now it appears quite evident that, at every period of time, every Legislature must be endowed with all those powers which the exigency of the times may require: and any attempt to infringe on this power is inadmissible and absurd.   The sovereign power, at any one period, can only form a blind guess at the measures which may be necessary for any future period: but by this principle of immutable laws, the government is transferred from those who are necessarily the best judges of what they want, to others who can know little or nothing about the matter.   The thirteenth century decides for the fourteenth.   The fourteenth makes laws for the fifteenth.   The fifteenth hermetically seals up the sixteenth, which tyrannises over the seventeenth, which again tells the eighteenth how it is to act, under circumstances which cannot be foreseen, and how it is to conduct itself in exigencies which no human wit can anticipate.

Men who have a century more of experience to ground their judgments on, surrender their intellect to men who had a century less experience, and who, unless that deficiency constitutes a claim, have no claim to preference.   If the prior generation were, in respect of intellectual qualification, ever so much superior to the subsequent generation—if it understood so much better than the subsequent generation itself the interest of that subsequent generation—could it have been in an equal degree anxious to promote that interest, and consequently equally attentive to those facts with which, though in order to form a judgment it ought to have been, it is impossible that it should have been acquainted? In a word, will its love for that subsequent generation be quite so great as that same generation's love for itself?

Not even here, after a moment's deliberate reflection, will the assertion be in the affirmative. And yet it is their prodigious anxiety for the welfare of their posterity that produces the propensity of these sages to tie up the hands of this same posterity for evermore—to act as guardians to its perpetual and incurable weakness, and take its conduct for ever out of its own hands.

If it be right that the conduct of the nineteenth century should be determined not by its own judgment, but by that of the eighteenth, it will be equally right that the conduct of the twentieth century should be determined, not by its own judgment, but by that of the nineteenth. And if the same principle were still pursued, what at length would be the consequence?—that in process of time the practice of legislation would be at an end. The conduct and fate of all men would be determined by those who neither knew nor cared anything about the matter; and the aggregate body of the Living would remain for ever in subjection to an inexorable tyranny, exercised as it were by the aggregate body of the Dead.—(pp. 84–6.)

The despotism, as Mr. Bentham well observes, of Nero or Caligula, would be more tolerable than an *irrevocable law*. The despot, through fear or favour, or in a lucid interval, might relent; but how are the Parliament, who made the Scotch Union, for example, to be awakened from that dust in which they repose—the jobber and the patriot, the speaker and the doorkeeper, the silent voters and the men of rich allusions—Cannings and cultivators, Barings and beggars—making irrevocable laws for men who toss their remains about with spades, and use the relics of these legislators, to give breadth to broccoli, and to aid the vernal eruption of asparagus?

If the law be good, it will support itself; if bad, it should not be supported by the *irrevocable theory*, which is never resorted to but as the veil of abuses. All living men must possess the supreme power over their own happiness at every particular period. To suppose that there is any thing which a whole nation cannot do, which they deem to be essential to their happiness, and that they cannot do it, because *another* generation, long ago dead and gone, said it must not be done, is mere nonsense. While you are captain of the vessel, do what you please; but the moment you quit the ship, I become as omnipotent as you. You may leave me as much *advice* as you please, but you cannot leave me *commands*; though, in fact, this is the only meaning which can be applied to what are called irrevocable laws. It appeared to the Legislature for the time being to be of immense importance to make such and such a law. Great good was gained, or great evil avoided by enacting it. Pause before you alter an institution which has been deemed to be of so much importance. This is prudence and common sense; the rest is the exaggeration of fools, or the artifice of knaves who eat up fools. What endless nonsense has been talked of our navigation laws! What wealth has been sacrificed to either before they were repealed! How impossible it appeared to Noodledom to repeal them! They were considered of the irrevocable class—a kind of law over which the dead only were omnipotent, and the living had no power. Frost, it is true, cannot be put off by act of Parliament, nor can Spring be accelerated by any majority of both Houses. It is, however, quite a mistake to suppose that any alteration of any of the Articles of Union is as much out of the jurisdiction of Parliament as these meteorological changes. In every year, and every day of that year, living men have a right to make their own laws, and manage their own affairs; to break through the tyranny of the ante-spirants —the people who breathed before them, and to do what they please for themselves. Such supreme power cannot indeed be well exercised by the people at large; it must be exercised therefore by the delegates, or Parliament, whom the people choose; and such Parliament, disregarding the superstitious reverence for *irrevocable laws*, can have no other criterion of wrong and right than that of public utility.

When a law is considered as immutable, and the immutable law happens at the same time to be too foolish and mischievous to be endured, instead of being repealed, it is clandestinely evaded, or openly violated; and thus the authority of all law is weakened.

Where a nation has been ancestorially bound by foolish and improvident treaties, ample notice must be given of their termination. Where the state has made ill-advised

grants, or rash bargains with individuals, it is necessary
to grant proper compensation. The most difficult case,
certainly, is that of the union of nations, where a smaller
number of the weaker nation is admitted into the larger
senate of the greater nation, and will be overpowered if
the question come to a vote; but the lesser nation must
run this risk: it is not probable that any violation of articles
will take place, till they are absolutely called for by extreme
necessity. But let the danger be what it may, no danger
is so great, no supposition so foolish, as to consider any
human law as irrevocable. The shifting attitude of
human affairs would often render such a condition an
intolerable evil to all parties. The absurd jealousy of our
countrymen at the Union secured heritable jurisdiction
to the owners; nine and thirty years afterwards they were
abolished, in the very teeth of the Act of Union, and to the
evident promotion of the public good.

Continuity of a Law by Oath.—The Sovereign of England
at his Coronation takes an oath to maintain the laws of
God, the true profession of the Gospel, and the Protestant
religion as established by law, and to preserve to the
Bishops and Clergy of this realm the rights and privileges
which by law appertain to them, and to preserve inviolate
the doctrine, discipline, worship, and government of the
Church. It has been suggested that by this oath the
King stands precluded from granting those indulgencies
to the Irish Catholics, which are included in the bill for
their emancipation. The true meaning of these provisions is of course to be decided, if doubtful, by the same
legislative authority which enacted them. But a different
notion it seems is now afloat. The King for the time
being (we are putting an imaginary case) thinks as an
individual, that he is not maintaining the doctrine, discipline, and rights of the Church of England, if he grant
any extension of civil rights to those who are not members
of that Church, that he is violating his oath by so doing.
This oath, then, according to this reasoning, is the great
palladium of the Church. As long as it remains inviolate
the Church is safe. How then can any monarch who has
taken it ever consent to repeal it? How can he, consistently with his oath for the preservation of the privileges
of the Church, contribute his part to throw down so strong

a bulwark as he deems this oath to be! The oath, then, cannot be altered. It must remain under all circumstances of society the same. The King, who has taken it, is bound to continue it, and to refuse his sanction to any bill for its future alteration; because it prevents him, and, he must needs think, will prevent others, from granting dangerous immunities to the enemies of the Church.

Here, then, is an irrevocable law—a piece of absurd tyranny exercised by the rulers of Queen Anne's time upon the government of 1825—a certain art of potting and preserving a kingdom, in one shape, attitude, and flavour—and in this way it is that an institution appears like old Ladies' Sweet-meats and made Wines—Apricot Jam, 1822—Currant Wine, 1819—Court of Chancery, 1427—Penal Laws against Catholics, 1676. The difference is, that the Ancient Woman is a better judge of mouldy commodities than the liberal part of his Majesty's Ministers. The potting lady goes sniffing about and admitting light and air to prevent the progress of decay; while to him of the Woolsack, all seems doubly dear in proportion as it is antiquated, worthless, and unusable. It ought not to be in the power of the Sovereign to tie up his own hands, much less the hands of his successors. If the Sovereign be to oppose his own opinion to that of the two other branches of the legislature, and himself to decide what he considers to be for the benefit of the Protestant Church, and what not, a king who has spent his whole life in the frivolous occupation of a court, may, by perversion of understanding, conceive measures most salutary to the Church to be most pernicious; and persevering obstinately in his own error, may frustrate the wisdom of his Parliament, and perpetuate the most inconceivable folly! If Henry VIII. had argued in this manner, we should have had no Reformation. If George III. had always argued in this manner, the Catholic Code would never have been relaxed. And thus, a king, however incapable of forming an opinion upon serious subjects, has nothing to do but to pronounce the word *Conscience*, and the whole power of the country is at his feet.

Can there be greater absurdity than to say that a man is acting contrary to his conscience who surrenders his opinion upon any subject to those who must understand

I

the subject better than himself? I think my ward has a claim to the estate; but the best lawyers tell me he has none. I think my son capable of undergoing the fatigues of a military life; but the best physicians say he is much too weak. My Parliament say this measure will do the Church no harm; but I think it very pernicious to the Church. Am I acting contrary to my conscience because I apply much higher intellectual powers than my own to the investigation and protection of these high interests?

According to the form in which it is conceived, any such engagement is in effect either a check or a licence:—a licence under the appearance of a check, and for that very reason but the more efficiently operative.

Chains to the man in power? Yes:—but only such as he figures with on the stage: to the spectators as imposing, to himself as light as possible. Modelled by the wearer to suit his own purposes, they serve to rattle, but not to restrain.

Suppose a King of Great Britain and Ireland to have expressed his fixed determination, in the event of any proposed law being tendered to him for his assent, to refuse such assent, and this not on the persuasion that the law would not be "for the utility of the subjects," but that by his coronation oath he stands precluded from so doing:—the course proper to be taken by parliament, the course pointed out by principle and precedent, would be, a vote of abdication:—a vote declaring the king to have abdicated his royal authority, and that, as in case of death or incurable mental derangement, now is the time for the person next in succession to take his place.

In the celebrated case in which a vote to this effect was actually passed, the declaration of abdication was in lawyers' language a fiction—in plain truth a falsehood—and that falsehood a mockery; not a particle of his power was it the wish of James to abdicate, to part with; but to increase it to a maximum was the manifest object of all his efforts. But in the case here supposed, with respect to a part, and that a principal part, of the royal authority, the will and purpose to abdicate is actually declared: and this, being such a part, without which the remainder cannot, "to the utility of the subjects," be exercised, the remainder must of necessity be, on their part, and for their sake, added.—(pp. 110, 111.)

Self-trumpeter's Fallacy.—Mr. Bentham explains the self-trumpeter's fallacy as follows:—

There are certain men in office who, in discharge of their functions, arrogate to themselves a degree of probity, which is to exclude all imputations and all inquiry. Their assertions

are to be deemed equivalent to proof; their virtues are guar-
antees for the faithful discharge of their duties; and the most
implicit confidence is to be reposed in them on all occasions.
If you expose any abuse, propose any reform, call for securities,
inquiry, or measures to promote publicity, they set up a cry
of surprise, amounting almost to indignation, as if their
integrity were questioned, or their honour wounded. With
all this, they dexterously mix up intimations, that the most
exalted patriotism, honour, and perhaps religion, are the only
sources of all their actions.—(p. 120.)

Of course every man will try what he can effect by these
means; but (as Mr. Bentham observes) if there be any one
maxim in politics more certain than another, it is that no
possible degree of virtue in the governor can render it
expedient for the governed to dispense with good laws and
good institutions. Madame de Staël (to her disgrace) said
to the Emperor of Russia, "Sire, your character is a
constitution for your country, and your conscience its
guarantee." His reply was, "Quand cela serait, je ne
serais jamais qu'un accident heureux"; and this we think
one of the truest and most brilliant replies ever made by
monarch.

Laudatory Personalities.—The object of laudatory personalities is to effect the rejection of a measure on account of the
alleged good character of those who oppose it: and the argument advanced is, "The measure is rendered unnecessary by
the virtues of those who are in power—their opposition is a
sufficient authority for the rejection of the measure. The
measure proposed implies a distrust of the members of His
Majesty's Government; but so great is their integrity, so
complete their disinterestedness, so uniformly do they prefer
the public advantage to their own, that such a measure is
altogether unnecessary. Their disapproval is sufficient to
warrant an opposition; precautions can only be requisite where
danger is apprehended: here, the high character of the individuals in question is a sufficient guarantee against any ground
of alarm."—(pp. 123, 124.)

The panegyric goes on increasing with the dignity of
the lauded person. All are honourable and delightful
men. The person who opens the door of the office is a
person of approved fidelity; the junior clerk is a model of
assiduity; all the clerks are models—seven years' models,
eight years' models, nine years' models and upwards.

The first clerk is a paragon — and ministers the very perfection of probity and intelligence; and as for the highest magistrate of the state, no adulation is equal to describe the extent of his various merits! It is too condescending perhaps to refute such folly as this. But we would just observe, that if the propriety of the measure in question be established by direct arguments, these must be at least as conclusive against the character of those who oppose it, as their character can be against the measure.

The effect of such an argument is, to give men of good, or reputed good character, the power of putting a negative on any question—not agreeable to their inclinations.

In every public trust, the legislator should, for the purpose of prevention, suppose the trustee disposed to break the trust in every imaginable way in which it would be possible for him to reap, from the breach of it, any personal advantage. This is the principle on which public institutions ought to be formed; and when it is applied to all men indiscriminately, it is injurious to none. The practical inference is, to oppose to such possible (and what will always be probable) breaches of trust, every bar that can be opposed, consistently with the power requisite for the efficient and due discharge of the trust. Indeed, these arguments, drawn from the supposed virtues of men in power, are opposed to the first principles on which all laws proceed.

Such allegations of individual virtue are never supported by specific proof, are scarce ever susceptible of specific disproof; and specific disproof, if offered, could not be admitted in either House of Parliament. If attempted elsewhere, the punishment would fall, not on the unworthy trustee, but on him by whom the unworthiness had been proved.—(pp. 125, 126.)

Fallacies of pretended Danger.—Imputation of bad design —of bad character—of bad motives—of inconsistency— of suspicious connections.

The object of this class of fallacies is to draw aside attention from the measure to the man, and this in such a manner, that, for some real or supposed defect in the author of the measure, a corresponding defect shall be imputed to the measure itself. Thus, "the author of the measure entertains a bad design; therefore the measure is bad. His character is bad, therefore the measure is bad; his motive is bad, I will vote against the measure. On former occasions, this same person who proposed the measure was its enemy, therefore the measure is bad. He is on a footing of intimacy with this or that dangerous man, or has been seen in his company, or is suspected of entertaining some of his opinions, therefore the measure is bad. He bears a name that at a former period was borne by a set of men now no more, by whom bad principles were entertained—therefore the measure is bad!"

Now, if the measure be really inexpedient, why not at once show it to be so? If the measure be good, is it bad because a bad man is its author? If bad, is it good because a good man has produced it? What are these arguments, but to say to the assembly who are to be the judges of any measure, that their imbecility is too great to allow them to judge of the measure by its own merits, and that they must have recourse to distant and feebler probabilities for that purpose?

In proportion to the degree of efficiency with which a man suffers these instruments of deception to operate upon his mind he enables bad men to exercise over him a sort of power, the thought of which ought to cover him with shame. Allow this argument the effect of a conclusive one, you put it into the power of any man to draw you at pleasure from the support of every measure which in your own eyes is good, to force you to give your support to any and every measure which in your own eyes is bad. Is it good?—the bad man embraces it, and, by the supposition, you reject it. Is it bad?—he vituperates it, and that suffices for driving you into its embrace. You split upon the rocks, because he has avoided them; you miss the harbour, because he has steered into it! Give yourself up to any such blind antipathy, you are no less in the power of your adversaries, than if, by a correspondently irrational sympathy and obsequiousness, you put yourself into the power of your friends.—(pp. 132, 133.)

Besides, nothing but laborious application, and a clear and comprehensive intellect, can enable a man, on any given subject, to employ successfully relevant arguments drawn from the subject itself. To employ personalities, neither labour nor intellect is required. In this sort of contest, the most idle and the most ignorant are quite on a par with, if not superior to, the most industrious and the most highly-gifted individuals. Nothing can be more convenient for those who would speak without the trouble of thinking. The same ideas are brought forward over and over again, and all that is required is to vary the turn of expression. Close and relevant arguments have very little hold on the passions, and serve rather to quell than to inflame them; while in personalities there is always something stimulant, whether on the part of him who praises or him who blames. Praise forms a kind of connection between the party praising and the party praised, and vituperation gives an air of courage and independence to the party who blames.

Ignorance and indolence, friendship and enmity, concurring and conflicting interest, servility and independence, all conspire to give personalities the ascendency they so unhappily maintain. The more we lie under the influence of our own passions, the more we rely on others being affected in a similar degree. A man who can repel these injuries with dignity, may often convert them into triumph: "Strike me, but hear," says he, and the fury of his antagonist redounds to his own discomfiture.—(pp. 141, 142.)

No Innovation !—To say that all new things are bad, is to say that all old things were bad in their commencement: for of all the old things ever seen or heard of, there is not one that was not once new. Whatever is now establishment was once innovation. The first inventor of pews and parish clerks, was no doubt considered as a Jacobin in his day. Judges, juries, criers of the court, are all the inventions of ardent spirits, who filled the world with alarm, and were considered as the great precursors of ruin and dissolution. No inoculation, no turnpikes, no reading, no writing, no popery! The fool sayeth in his heart, and crieth with his mouth, "I will have nothing new!"

Fallacy of Distrust !—"*What's at the Bottom ?*"—This fallacy begins with a virtual admission of the propriety of the measure considered in itself, and thus demonstrates its own futility, and cuts up from under itself the ground which it endeavours to make. A measure is to be rejected for something that, by bare possibility, may be found amiss in some other measure! This is vicarious reprobation; upon this principle Herod instituted his massacre. It is the argument of a driveller to other drivellers, who says, We are not able to decide upon the evil when it arises —our only safe way is to act upon the general apprehension of evil.

Official Malefactor's Screen.—"*Attack us—you attack Government.*"

If this notion is acceded to, every one who derives at present any advantage from misrule has it in fee-simple; and all abuses, present and future, are without remedy.

So long as there is any thing amiss in conducting the business of government, so long as it can be made better, there can be no other mode of bringing it nearer to perfection, than the indication of such imperfections as at the time being exist.

But so far is it from being true that a man's aversion or contempt for the hands by which the powers of Government, or even for the system under which they are exercised, is a proof of his aversion or contempt towards Government itself, that, even in proportion to the strength of that aversion or contempt, it is a proof of the opposite affection. What, in consequence of such contempt or aversion, he wishes for, is, not that there be no hands at all to exercise these powers, but that the hands may be better regulated;—not that those powers should not be exercised at all, but that they should be better exercised;—not that in the exercise of them, no rules at all should be pursued, but that the rules by which they are exercised should be a better set of rules.

All government is a trust; every branch of government is a trust; and immemorially acknowledged so to be: it is only by the magnitude of the scale that public differ from private trusts. I complain of the conduct of a person in the character of guardian, as domestic guardian, having the care of a minor or insane person. In so doing, do I say that guardianship is a bad institution? Does it enter into the head of any one to suspect me of so doing? I complain of an individual in the character of a commercial agent, or assignee of the effects of an insolvent. In so doing, do I say that commercial agency is a bad thing? that the practice of vesting in the hands of trustees or assignees the effects of an insolvent, for the purpose of their being divided among his creditors, is a bad practice? Does any such conceit ever enter into the head of man, as that of suspecting me of so doing?—(pp. 162, 163.)

There are no complaints against government in Turkey —no motions in Parliament, no *Morning Chronicles*, and no *Edinburgh Reviews*: yet of all countries in the world, it is that in which revolts and revolutions are the most frequent.

It is so far from true, that no good government can exist consistently with such disclosure, that no good government can exist without it. It is quite obvious, to all who are capable of reflection, that by no other means than by lowering the governors in the estimation of the people, can there be hope or chance of beneficial change. To infer from this wise endeavour to lessen the existing rulers in the estimation of the people, a wish of dissolving the government, is either artifice or error. The physician who intentionally weakens the patient by bleeding him has no intention he should perish.

The greater the quantity of respect a man receives, independently of good conduct, the less good is his behaviour likely to be. It is the interest, therefore, of the public, in the case of each, to see that the respect paid to him should, as completely as possible, depend upon the goodness of his behaviour in the execution of his trust. But it is, on the contrary, the interest of the trustee, that the respect, the money, or any other advantage he receives in virtue of his office, should be as great, as secure, and as independent of conduct as possible. Soldiers expect to be shot at; public men must expect to be attacked, and sometimes unjustly. It keeps up the habit of considering their conduct as exposed to scrutiny; on the part of the people at large, it keeps alive the expectation of witnessing such attacks, and the habit of looking out for them. The friends and supporters of government have always greater facility in keeping and raising it up, than its adversaries have for lowering it.

Accusation-scarer's Device.—"*Infamy must attach somewhere.*"

This fallacy consists in representing the character of a calumniator as necessarily and justly attaching upon him who, having made a charge of misconduct against any persons possessed of political power or influence, fails of producing evidence sufficient for their conviction.

If taken as a general proposition, applying to all public accusations, nothing can be more mischievous as well as fallacious. Supposing the charge unfounded, the delivery of it may have been accompanied with *mala fides* (consciousness of its injustice), with *temerity* only, or it may have been perfectly blameless. It is in the first case alone that infamy can with propriety attach upon him who brings it forward. A charge really groundless may have been honestly *believed* to be well founded, i.e. believed with a sort of provisional credence, sufficient for the purpose of engaging a man to do his part towards the bringing about an investigation, but without sufficient reasons. But a charge may be perfectly groundless without attaching the smallest particle of blame upon him who brings it forward. Suppose him to have heard from one or more, presenting themselves to him in the character of percipient witnesses, a story, which, either *in toto*, or perhaps only in *circumstances*, though in circumstances of the most material importance, should prove false and mendacious—how is the person who hears this, and acts accordingly, to blame?   What sagacity can enable a man previously to legal investigation, a man who has no power that can enable him to insure correctness or completeness on the part of this extrajudicial testimony, to guard against deception in such a case?—(pp. 185, 186.)

Fallacy of False Consolation.—"What is the matter with you?—What would you have? Look at the people there, and there; think how much better off you are than they are. Your prosperity and liberty are objects of their envy; your institutions models of their imitation."

It is not the desire to look to the bright side that is blamed: but when a particular suffering, produced by an assigned cause, has been pointed out, the object of many apologists is to turn the eyes of inquirers and judges into any other quarter in preference.   If a man's tenants were to come with a general encomium on the prosperity of the country, instead of a specified sum, would it be accepted? In a court of justice, in an action for damages, did ever any such device occur as that of pleading assets in the hands of a third person?   There is, in fact, no country so poor and so wretched in every element of prosperity, in which matter for this argument might not be found.   Were the prosperity of the country tenfold as great as at present, the absurdity of the argument would not in the least degree be lessened. Why should the smallest evil be endured, which can be cured, because others suffer patiently under greater evils? Should the smallest improvement attainable be neglected, because others remain contented in a state of still greater inferiority?

Seriously and pointedly in the character of a bar to any measure of relief, no, nor to the most trivial improvement, can it ever be employed.   Suppose a bill brought in for converting an impassable road anywhere into a passable one, would any man stand up to oppose it who could find nothing better to urge against it than the multitude and goodness of the roads we have already?   No: when in the character of a serious bar to the measure in hand, be that measure what it may, an argument so palpably inapplicable is employed, it can only be for the purpose of creating a diversion;—of turning aside the minds of men from the subject really in hand, to a picture, which by its beauty, it is hoped, may engross the attention of the assembly, and make them forget for the moment for what purpose they came there.—(pp. 196, 197.)

The Quietist, or no Complaint.—A new law or measure being proposed in the character of a remedy for some incontestable abuse or evil, an objection is frequently started to the following effect:—"The measure is unnecessary. Nobody complains of disorder in that shape, in which it is the aim of your measure to propose a remedy to it. But even when *no* cause of complaint has been found to exist, especially under governments which admit of complaints, men have in general not been slow to complain; much less where any just cause of complaint has existed." The argument amounts to this:—Nobody complains, therefore nobody suffers. It amounts to a *veto* on all measures of precaution or prevention, and goes to establish a maxim in legislation directly opposed to the most ordinary prudence of common life;—it enjoins us to build no parapets to a bridge till the number of accidents has raised an universal clamour.—(pp. 190, 191.)

Procrastinator's Argument.—"*Wait a little, this is not the time.*"

This is the common argument of men, who, being in reality hostile to a measure, are ashamed or afraid of appearing to be so. *To-day* is the plea—*eternal exclusion* commonly the object. It is the same sort of quirk as a plea of abatement in law—which is never employed but on the side of a dishonest defendant, whose hope it is to obtain an ultimate triumph by overwhelming his adversary with despair, impoverishment, and lassitude. Which is the properest day to do good? which is the properest day to remove a nuisance? we answer, the very first day a man can be found to propose the removal of it; and whoever opposes the removal of it on that day will (if he dare) oppose it on every other. There is in the minds of many feeble friends to virtue and improvement, an imaginary period for the removal of evils, which it would certainly be worth while to wait for, if there was the smallest chance of its ever arriving—a period of unexampled peace and prosperity, when a patriotic king and an enlightened mob united their ardent efforts for the amelioration of human affairs; when the oppressor is as delighted to give up the oppression, as the oppressed is to be liberated from it; when the difficulty and the unpopularity would be to con-

tinue the evil, not to abolish it!   These are the periods when
fair-weather philosophers are willing to venture out, and
hazard a little for the general good.   But the history of
human nature is so contrary to all this, that almost all
improvements are made after the bitterest resistance, and
in the midst of tumults and civil violence—the worst
period at which they can be made, compared to which any
period is eligible, and should be seized hold of by the
friends of salutary reform.

*Snail's Pace argument.—One thing at a time !   Not too fast !
Slow and sure !*—Importance of the business—extreme difficulty of the business—danger of innovation—need of caution
and circumspection — impossibility of foreseeing all consequences—danger of precipitation—every thing should be
gradual—one thing at a time—this is not the time—great
occupation at present—wait for more leisure—people well
satisfied—no petitions presented—no complaints heard—no
such mischief has yet taken place—stay till it has taken
place!—Such is the prattle which the magpie in office, who,
understanding nothing, yet understands that he must have
something to say on every subject, shouts out among his
auditors as a succedaneum to thought.—(pp. 203, 204.)

Vague Generalities.—Vague generalities comprehend a
numerous class of fallacies resorted to by those who, in
preference to the determinate expressions which they might
use, adopt others more vague and indeterminate.

Take, for instance, the terms, government, laws, morals,
religion.   Everybody will admit that there are in the world
bad governments, bad laws, bad morals, and bad religions.
The bare circumstance, therefore, of being engaged in
exposing the defects of government, law, morals, and
religion, does not of itself afford the slightest presumption
that a writer is engaged in any thing blameable.   If his
attack be only directed against that which is bad in each,
his efforts may be productive of good to any extent.   This
essential distinction, however, the defender of abuses
uniformly takes care to keep out of sight; and boldly
imputes to his antagonists an intention to subvert all
government, law, morals, and religion.   Propose any thing
with a view to the improvement of the existing practice,
in relation to law, government, and religion, he will treat
you with an oration upon the necessity and utility of law,

government, and religion. Among the several cloudy appellatives which have been commonly employed as cloaks for misgovernment, there is none more conspicuous in this atmosphere of illusion than the word order. As often as any measure is brought forward which has for its object to lessen the sacrifice made by the many to the few, *social order* is the phrase commonly opposed to its progress.

> By a defalcation made from any part of the mass of factitious delay, vexation, and expense, out of which, and in proportion to which, lawyers' profit is made to flow—by any defalcation made from the mass of needless and worse than useless emolument to office, with or without service or pretence of service—by any addition endeavoured to be made to the quantity, or improvement in the quality of service rendered, or time bestowed in service rendered in return for such emolument—by every endeavour that has for its object the persuading the people to place their fate at the disposal of any other agents than those in whose hands breach of trust is certain, due fulfilment of it morally and physically impossible —*social order* is said to be endangered, and threatened to be destroyed.—(p. 234.)

In the same way *Establishment* is a word in use to protect the bad parts of establishments, by charging those who wish to remove or alter them, with a wish to subvert all good establishments.

Mischievous fallacies also circulate from the convertible use of what Mr. B. is pleased to call dyslogistic and eulogistic terms. Thus a vast concern is expressed for the *liberty of the press*, and the utmost abhorrence for its *licentiousness*: but then, by the licentiousness of the press is meant every disclosure by which any abuse is brought to light and exposed to shame—by the *liberty of the press* is meant only publications from which no such inconvenience is to be apprehended; and the fallacy consists in employing the sham approbation of liberty as a mask for the real opposition to all free discussion. To write a pamphlet so ill that nobody will read it; to animadvert in terms so weak and insipid upon great evils, that no disgust is excited at the vice, and no apprehension in the evil-doer, is a fair use of the liberty of the press, and is not only pardoned by the friends of government, but draws from them the most fervent eulogium. The licentiousness of the press consists in doing the thing boldly and well, in striking terror into the guilty, and in rousing the attention of the public to the defence of their highest interests. This is the licentiousness of the press held in the greatest horror by timid and corrupt men, and punished by semianimous, semicadaverous judges, with a captivity of many years. In the same manner the dyslogistic and eulogistic fallacies are used in the case of reform.

Between all abuses whatsoever, there exists that connexion —between all persons who see each of them, any one abuse in which an advantage results to himself, there exists, in point of interest, that close and sufficiently understood connexion, of which intimation has been given already. To no one abuse can correction be administered without endangering the existence of every other.

If, then, with this inward determination not to suffer, so far as depends upon himself, the adoption of any reform which he is able to prevent, it should seem to him necessary or advisable to put on for a cover, the profession or appearance of a desire to contribute to such reform—in pursuance of the device or fallacy here in question, he will represent that which goes by the name of reform as distinguishable into two species; one of them a fit subject for approbation, the other for disapprobation. That which he thus professes to have marked for approbation, he will accordingly, for the expression of such approbation, characterise by some adjunct of the *eulogistic* cast, such as moderate, for example, or temperate, or practical, or practicable.

To the other of these nominally distinct species, he will, at the same time, attach some adjunct of the *dyslogistic* cast, such as violent, intemperate, extravagant, outrageous, theoretical, speculative, and so forth.

Thus, then, in profession and to appearance, there are in his conception of the matter two distinct and opposite species of reform, to one of which his approbation, to the other his disapprobation, is attached. But the species to which his approbation is attached is an *empty* species—a species in which no individual is, or is intended to be, contained.

The species to which his disapprobation is attached is, on the contrary, a crowded species, a receptacle in which the whole contents of the *genus*—of the genus *Reform*, are intended to be included.—(pp. 277, 278.)

Anti-rational Fallacies.—When reason is in opposition to a man's interests, his study will naturally be to render the faculty itself, and whatever issues from it, an object of hatred and contempt. The sarcasm and other figures of speech employed on the occasion are directed not merely against reason, but against thought, as if there were something in the faculty of thought that rendered the exercise of it incompatible with useful and successful practice. Sometimes a plan, which would not suit the official person's interest, is without more ado pronounced a *speculative* one; and, by this observation, all need of rational and deliberate discussion is considered to be superseded. The first effort of the corruptionist is to fix the epithet *Speculative* upon any scheme which he thinks may cherish the spirit of reform. The expression is hailed with the greatest delight by bad and feeble men, and repeated with the most unwearied energy; and to the word Speculative, by way of reinforcement, are added, *theoretical, visionary, chimerical, romantic, Utopian.*

Sometimes a distinction is taken, and thereupon a concession made. The plan is *good in theory*, but it would be *bad in practice*, i.e. its being good in theory does not hinder its being bad in practice.

Sometimes, as if in consequence of a farther progress made in the art of irrationality, the plan is pronounced to be *too good to be practicable*; and its being so good as it is, is thus represented as the very cause of its being bad in practice.

In short, such is the perfection at which this art is at length arrived, that the very circumstance of a plan's being susceptible of the appellation of a *plan*, has been gravely stated as a circumstance sufficient to warrant its being rejected: rejected, if not with hatred, at any rate with a sort of accompaniment, which, to the million, is commonly felt still more galling—with contempt.—(p. 296.)

There is a propensity to push theory too far; but what is the just inference? not that theoretical propositions (i.e. all propositions of any considerable comprehension or extent) should, from such their extent, be considered to be false *in toto*, but only that, in the particular case, inquiry should be made whether, supposing the proposition to be in the character of a rule generally true, an exception ought to be taken out of it. It might almost be imagined that there was something wicked or unwise in the exercise of thought; for everybody feels a necessity for disclaiming it. "I am not given to speculation, I am no friend to theories." Can a man disclaim theory, can he disclaim speculation, without disclaiming thought?

The description of persons by whom this fallacy is chiefly employed are those who, regarding a plan as adverse to their interests, and not finding it on the ground of general utility exposed to any preponderant objection, have recourse to this objection in the character of an instrument of contempt, in the view of preventing those from looking into it who might have been otherwise disposed. It is by the fear of seeing it practised that they are drawn to speak of it as impracticable. "Upon the face of it (exclaims some feeble or pensioned gentleman), it carries that air of plausibility, that, if you were not upon your guard, might engage you to bestow more or less of attention upon it; but were you to take the trouble, you would find that (as it is with all these plans which promise so much) practicability would at last be wanting to it. To save yourself from this trouble, the wisest course you can take is to put the plan aside, and to think no more about the matter." This is always accompanied with a peculiar grin of triumph.

The whole of these fallacies may be gathered together in a little oration, which we will denominate the

Noodle's Oration

"What would our ancestors say to this, Sir? How does this measure tally with their institutions? How does it agree with their experience? Are we to put the wisdom of yesterday in competition with the wisdom of centuries? (*Hear, hear!*) Is beardless youth to show no respect for the decisions of mature age? (*Loud cries of hear! hear!*) If this measure be right, would it have escaped the wisdom of those Saxon progenitors to whom we are indebted for so many of our best political institutions? Would the Dane have passed it over? Would the Norman have rejected it? Would such a notable discovery have been reserved for these modern and degenerate times? Besides, Sir, if the measure itself is good, I ask the honourable gentleman if this is the time for carrying it into execution —whether, in fact, a more unfortunate period could have been selected than that which he has chosen? If this were an ordinary measure, I should not oppose it with so much vehemence; but, Sir, it calls in question the wisdom of an irrevocable law—of a law passed at the memorable period of the Revolution. What right have we, Sir, to break down this firm column, on which the great men of that day stamped a character of eternity? Are not all authorities against this measure—Pitt, Fox, Cicero, and the Attorney and Solicitor General? The proposition is new, Sir; it is the first time it was ever heard in this House. I am not prepared, Sir—this House is not prepared, to receive it. The measure implies a distrust of his Majesty's government; their disapproval is sufficient to warrant opposition. Precaution only is requisite where danger is apprehended. Here the high character of the individuals in question is a sufficient guarantee against any ground of alarm. Give not, then, your sanction to this measure; for, whatever be its character, if you do give your sanction to it, the same man by whom this is proposed, will propose to you others to which it will be impossible to give your consent. I care very little, Sir, for the ostensible measure; but what is there behind? What are the honourable gentleman's future schemes? If we pass this bill, what fresh concessions may he not require? What further degradation is he planning for his country? Talk of evil and inconvenience, Sir! look to other countries—study other aggregations and societies of men, and then see whether the laws of this country demand a remedy or deserve a panegyric. Was the honourable gentleman (let me ask him) always of this way of thinking? Do I not remember when he was the advocate in this House of very opposite opinions? I not only quarrel with his present sentiments, Sir, but I declare very frankly, I do not like the party with which he acts. If his own motives were as pure as possible, they cannot but suffer contamination from those with whom he is politically associated. This measure may be a boon to the constitution; but I will accept no favour to the constitution from such hands. (*Loud cries of hear! hear!*) I profess myself, Sir, an honest and upright member of the British Parliament, and I am not afraid to profess myself an enemy to all change and all innovation. I am satisfied with things as they are; and it will be my pride and pleasure to hand down this country to my children as I received it from those who preceded me. The honourable gentleman pretends to justify the severity with which he has attacked the noble Lord who presides in the Court of Chancery; but I say such attacks are pregnant with mischief to Government itself. Oppose Ministers, you oppose Government: disgrace Ministers, you disgrace Government: bring Ministers into contempt, you bring Government into contempt; and anarchy and civil war are the consequences. Besides, Sir, the measure is unnecessary. Nobody complains of disorder in that shape in which it is the aim of your measure to propose a remedy to it. The business is one of the greatest importance; there is need of the greatest caution and circumspection. Do not let us be precipitate, Sir. It is impossible to foresee all consequences. Everything should be gradual: the example of a neighbouring nation should fill us with alarm! The honourable gentleman has taxed me with illiberality, Sir. I deny the charge. I hate innovation; but I love improvement. I am an enemy to the corruption of Government; but I defend its influence. I dread reform; but I dread it only when it is intemperate. I consider the liberty of the Press as the great Palladium of the Constitution; but, at the same time, I hold the licentiousness of the Press in the greatest abhorrence. Nobody is more conscious than I am of the splendid abilities of the honourable mover; but I tell him at once, his scheme is too good to be practicable. It savours of Utopia. It looks well in theory; but it won't do in practice. It will not do, I repeat, Sir, in practice; and so the advocates of the measure will find, if, unfortunately, it should find its way through Parliament. (*Cheers.*) The source of that corruption to which the honourable member alludes, is in the minds of the people: so rank and extensive is that corruption, that no political reform can have any effect in removing it. Instead of reforming others—instead of reforming the State, the Constitution, and every thing that is most excellent, let each man reform himself! let him look at home; he will find there enough to do, without looking abroad, and aiming at what is out of his power. (*Loud cheers.*) And now, Sir, as it is frequently the custom in this House to end with a quotation, and as the gentleman who preceded me in the debate has anticipated me in my favourite quotation of 'The strong pull and the long pull,'—I shall end with the memorable words of the assembled Barons— '*Nolumus leges Angliæ mutari.*'"

K

Upon the whole, the following are the characters which appertain in common to all the several arguments here distinguished by the name of fallacies:—

1. Whatsoever be the measure in hand, they are, with relation to it, irrelevant.

2. They are all of them such, that the application of these irrelevant arguments affords a presumption either of the weakness or total absence of relevant arguments on the side on which they are employed.

3. To any good purpose they are all of them unnecessary.

4. They are all of them not only capable of being applied, but actually in the habit of being applied, and with advantage, to bad purposes; viz. to the obstruction and defeat of all such measures as have for their object the removal of the abuses or other imperfections still discernible in the frame and practice of the government.

5. By means of their irrelevancy, they all of them consume and misapply time, thereby obstructing the course and retarding the progress of all necessary and useful business.

6. By that irritative quality which, in virtue of their irrelevancy, with the improbity or weakness of which it is indicative, they possess, all of them, in a degree more or less considerable, but in a more particular degree such of them as consist in personalities, they are productive of ill-humour, which in some instances has been productive of bloodshed, and is continually productive, as above, of waste of time and hindrance of business.

7. On the part of those who, whether in spoken or written discourses, give utterance to them, they are indicative either of improbity or intellectual weakness, or of a contempt for the understanding of those on whose minds they are destined to operate.

8. On the part of those on whom they operate, they are indicative of intellectual weakness; and on the part of those in and by whom they are pretended to operate, they are indicative of improbity, viz. in the shape of insincerity.

The practical conclusion is, that in proportion as the acceptance, and thence the utterance, of them can be prevented, the understanding of the public will be strengthened, the morals of the public will be purified, and the practice of government improved.

PERSECUTING BISHOPS [1]

It is a great point in any question to clear away encumbrances, and to make a naked circle about the object in dispute, so that there may be a clear view of it on every side. In pursuance of this disencumbering process, we shall first acquit the Bishop [2] of all wrong intentions. He has a very bad opinion of the practical effects of high Calvinistic doctrines upon the common people; and he thinks it his duty to exclude those clergymen who profess them from his diocese. There is no moral wrong in this. He has accordingly devised no fewer than *eighty-seven* interrogatories, by which he thinks he can detect the smallest taint of Calvinism that may lurk in the creed of the candidate; and in this also, whatever we may think of his reasoning, we suppose his purpose to be blameless. He believes, finally, that he has legally the power so to interrogate and exclude; and in this, perhaps, he is not mistaken. His intentions, then, are good, and his conduct, perhaps, not amenable to the law. All this we admit in his favour: but against him we must maintain, that his conduct upon the points in dispute has been singularly injudicious, extremely harsh, and, in its effects (though not in its intentions), very oppressive and vexatious to the Clergy.

We have no sort of intention to avail ourselves of an anonymous publication to say unkind, uncivil, or disrespectful things to a man of rank, learning, and character —we hope to be guilty of no such impropriety; but we cannot believe we are doing wrong in ranging ourselves on the weaker side, in the cause of propriety and justice. The Mitre protects its wearer from indignity; but it does not secure impunity.

It is a strong presumption that a man is wrong, when

[1] See p. 295.
[2] Dr. Herbert Marsh, Bishop of Peterborough.

115

all his friends, whose habits naturally lead them to coincide with him, think him wrong. If a man were to indulge in taking medicine till the apothecary, the druggist, and the physician, all called upon him to abandon his philo-cathartic propensities—if he were to gratify his convivial habits till the landlord demurred, and the waiter shook his head—we should naturally imagine that advice so wholly disinterested was not given before it was wanted, and that it merited some little attention and respect. Now, though the Bench of Bishops certainly love power, and love the Church, as well as the Bishop of Peterborough, yet not one defended him—not one rose to say, "I have done, or I would do, the same thing." It was impossible to be present at the last debate on this question, without perceiving that his Lordship stood alone—and this in a very gregarious profession, that habitually combines and butts against an opponent with a very extended front. If a lawyer is wounded, the rest of the profession pursue him, and put him to death. If a churchman is hurt, the others gather round for his protection, stamp with their feet, push with their horns, and demolish the dissenter who did the mischief.

The Bishop has at least done a very unusual thing in his Eighty-seven Questions. The two Archbishops, and we believe every other Bishop, and all the Irish hierarchy, admit curates into their dioceses without any such pre-cautions. The necessity of such severe and scrupulous inquisition, in short, has been apparent to nobody but the Bishop of Peterborough; and the authorities by which he seeks to justify it are anything but satisfactory. His Lord-ship states, that forty years ago he was himself examined by written interrogatories, and that he is not the only Bishop who has done it; but he mentions no names; and it was hardly worth while to state such extremely slight precedents for so strong a deviation from the common practice of the Church.

The Bishop who rejects a curate upon the Eighty-seven Questions is necessarily and inevitably opposed to the Bishop who ordained him. The Bishop of Gloucester ordains a young man of twenty-three years of age, not thinking it necessary to put to him these interrogatories, or putting them, perhaps, and approving of answers diametrically opposite to those that are required by the Bishop of Peterborough. The young clergyman then comes to the last-mentioned Bishop; and the Bishop, after *putting him to the Question*, says, "You are unfit for a clergyman,"—though, ten days before, the Bishop of Gloucester has made him one! It is bad enough for ladies to pull caps, but still worse for Bishops to pull mitres. Nothing can be more mischievous or indecent than such scenes; and no man of common prudence, or knowledge of the world, but must see that they ought immediately to be put a stop to. If a man is a captain in the army in one part of England, he is a captain in all. The general who commands north of the Tweed does not say, You shall never appear in my district, or exercise the functions of an officer, if you do not answer eighty-seven questions on the art of war, according to my notions. The same officer who commands a ship of the line in the Mediterranean, is considered as equal to the same office in the North Seas. The sixth commandment is suspended, by one medical diploma, from the north of England to the south. But, by this new system of interrogation, a man may be admitted into orders at Barnet, rejected at Stevenage, readmitted at Brogden, kicked out as a Calvinist at Witham Common, and hailed as an ardent Arminian on his arrival at York.

It matters nothing to say that sacred things must not be compared with profane. In their importance, we allow, they cannot; but in their order and discipline they may be so far compared as to say, that the discrepancy and contention which would be disgraceful and pernicious in worldly affairs, should, in common prudence, be avoided in the affairs of religion. Mr. Greenough has made a map of England, according to its geological varieties;—blue for the chalk, green for the clay, red for the sand, and so forth. Under this system of Bishop Marsh, we must petition for the assistance of the geologist in the fabrication of an ecclesiastical map. All the Arminian districts must be purple. Green for one theological extremity—sky-blue for another—as many colours as there are Bishops—as many shades of these colours as there are Archdeacons— a tailor's pattern card—the picture of vanity, fashion, and caprice.

The Bishop seems surprised at the resistance he meets with; and yet, to what purpose has he read ecclesiastical history, if he expect to meet with anything but the most determined opposition? Does he think that every sturdy supralapsarian bullock whom he tries to sacrifice to the Genius of Orthodoxy, will not kick, and push, and toss; that he will not, if he *can*, shake the axe from his neck, and hurl his mitred butcher into the air? His Lordship has undertaken a task of which he little knows the labour or the end. We know these men fully as well as the Bishop; he has not a chance of success against them. If one motion in Parliament will not do, they will have twenty. They will ravage, roar, and rush, till the very chaplains, and the Masters and Misses Peterborough request his Lordship to desist. He is raising up a storm in the English Church of which he has not the slightest conception; and which will end, as it ought to end, in his Lordship's disgrace and defeat.

The longer we live, the more we are convinced of the justice of the old saying, that an *ounce of mother wit is worth a pound of clergy*; that discretion, gentle manners, common sense, and good nature, are, in men of high ecclesiastical station, of far greater importance than the greatest skill in discriminating between sublapsarian and supralapsarian doctrines. Bishop Marsh should remember, that all men wearing the mitre work by character, as well as doctrine; that a tender regard to men's rights and feelings, a desire to avoid sacred squabbles, a fondness for quiet, and an ardent wish to make everybody happy, would be of far more value to the Church of England than all his learning and vigilance of inquisition. The Irish Tithes will probably fall next session of Parliament; the common people are regularly receding from the Church of England—baptising, burying, and confirming for themselves. Under such circumstances, what would the worst enemy of the English Church require?—a bitter, bustling, theological Bishop, accused by his clergy of tyranny and oppression—the cause of daily petitions and daily debates in the House of Commons—the idoneous vehicle of abuse against the Establishment—a stalking-horse to bad men for the introduction of revolutionary opinions, mischievous ridicule, and irreligious feelings. Such will be the advantages which Bishop Marsh will secure for the English Establishment in the ensuing session. It is inconceivable how such a prelate shakes all the upper works of the Church, and ripens it for dissolution and decay. Six such Bishops, multiplied by eighty-seven, and working with five hundred and twenty-two questions, would fetch everything to the ground in less than six months. But what if it pleased Divine Providence to afflict every prelate with the spirit of putting eighty-seven queries, and the two Archbishops with the spirit of putting twice as many, and the Bishop of Sodor and Man with the spirit of putting only forty-three queries?—there would then be a grand total of two thousand three hundred and thirty-five interrogations flying about the English Church; and sorely vexed would the land be with Question and Answer.

We will suppose this learned Prelate, without meanness or undue regard to his worldly interests, to feel that fair desire of rising in his profession, which any man, in any profession, may feel without disgrace. Does he forget that his character in the ministerial circles will soon become that of a violent impracticable man—whom it is impossible to place in the highest situations—who has been trusted with too much already, and must be trusted with no more? Ministers have something else to do with their time, and with the time of Parliament, than to waste them in debating squabbles between Bishops and their Clergy. They naturally wish, and, on the whole, reasonably expect, that every thing should go on silently and quietly in the Church. They have no objection to a learned Bishop; but they deprecate one atom more of learning than is compatible with moderation, good sense, and the soundest discretion. It must be the grossest ignorance of the world to suppose that the Cabinet has any pleasure in watching Calvinists.

The Bishop not only puts the questions, but he actually assigns the limits within which they are to be answered. Spaces are left in the paper of interrogations, to which limits the answer is to be confined;—two inches to original sin: an inch and a half to justification; three-quarters to predestination; and to free will only a quarter of an inch. But if his Lordship gives them an inch, they will take an ell. His Lordship is himself a theological writer, and by no means remarkable for his conciseness. To deny space to his brother theologians, who are writing on the most difficult subjects, not from choice, but necessity; not for fame, but for bread; and to award rejection as the penalty of prolixity, does appear to us no slight deviation from Christian gentleness. The tyranny of calling for such short answers is very strikingly pointed out in a letter from Mr. Thurtell to the Bishop of Peterborough; the style of which pleads, we think, very powerfully in favour of the writer.

BECCLES, SUFFOLK, *August 28th*, 1821.

MY LORD,

I ought, in the first place, to apologise for delaying so long to answer your Lordship's letter: but the difficulty in which I was involved, by receiving another copy of your Lordship's Questions, with positive directions to give short answers, may be sufficient to account for that delay.

It is my sincere desire to meet your Lordship's wishes, and to obey your Lordship's directions in every particular; and I would therefore immediately have returned answers, without any "restrictions or modifications," to the Questions which your Lordship has thought fit to send me, if, in so doing, I could have discharged the obligations of my conscience, by showing what my opinions really are. But it appears to me, that the Questions proposed to me by your Lordship are so constructed as to elicit only two sets of opinions; and that, by answering them in so concise a manner, I should be representing myself to your Lordship as one who believes in either of two particular creeds, to neither of which I do *really* subscribe. For instance, to answer Question I. chap. ii. in the manner your Lordship desires, I am reduced to the alternative of declaring, either that "mankind are a mass of *mere* corruption," which expresses more than I intend, or of leaving room for the inference, that they are only *partially* corrupt, which is opposed to the plainest declarations of the Homilies; such as these, "Man is *altogether* spotted and defiled" (Hom. on Nat.), "without a *spark* of goodness in him" (Serm. on Mis. of Man, etc.).

Again, by answering the Questions comprised in the chapter on "Free Will," according to your Lordship's directions, I am compelled to acknowledge, either that man has such a share in the work of his own salvation as to exclude the *sole* agency of God, or that he has no share whatever; when the Homilies for Rogation Week and Whitsunday positively declare, that God is the "only Worker," or, in other words, *sole* Agent; and at the same time assign to man a certain share in the work of his own salvation. In short, I could, with your Lordship's permission, point out twenty Questions, involving doctrines

of the utmost importance, which I am unable to answer, so
as to convey my real sentiments, without more room for
explanation than the printed sheet affords.

In this view of the subject, therefore, and in the most deliberate exercise of my judgment, I deem it indispensable to my
acting with that candour and truth with which it is my wish
and duty to act, and with which I cannot but believe your
Lordship desires I should act, to state my opinions in that
language which expresses them most fully, plainly, and un-
reservedly. This I have endeavoured to do in the answers
now in the possession of your Lordship. If any further
explanation be required, I am most willing to give it, even to a
minuteness of opinion beyond what the Articles require. At
the same time, I would humbly and respectfully appeal to
your Lordship's candour, *whether it is not hard to demand my
decided opinion upon points which have been the themes of
volumes ; upon which the most pious and learned men of the
Church have conscientiously differed ; and upon which the
Articles, in the judgment of Bishop Burnet, have pronounced
no definite sentence.* To those Articles, my Lord, I have
already subscribed; and I am willing again to subscribe to
every one of them, "in its literal and grammatical sense,"
according to His Majesty's declaration prefixed to them.

I hope, therefore, in consideration of the above statement,
that your Lordship will not compel me, by the conciseness
of my answers, to assent to doctrines which I do not believe,
or to expose myself to inferences which do not fairly and
legitimately follow from my opinions.

I am, my Lord, etc. etc.

We are not much acquainted with the practices of courts of
justice; but, if we remember right, when a man is going
to be hanged, the judge lets him make his defence in his
own way, without complaining of its length. We should
think a Christian Bishop might be equally indulgent to a
man who is going to be ruined. The answers are required
to be clear, concise, and correct—short, plain, and positive. In other words, a poor curate, extremely agitated
at the idea of losing his livelihood, is required to write
with brevity and perspicuity on the following subjects:—
Redemption by Jesus Christ—Original Sin—Free Will—
Justification—Justification in reference to its causes—
Justification in reference to the time when it takes place
—Everlasting Salvation—Predestination—Regeneration or
the New Birth—Renovation, and the Holy Trinity. As a
specimen of these questions, the answer to which is required

to be so brief and clear, we shall insert the following quotation:—

Section II.—Of Justification, in reference to its cause

1. Does not the eleventh Article declare, that we are "justified by Faith *only*"?
2. Does not the expression "Faith only" derive additional strength from the negative expression in the same Article "and *not* for our own works"?
3. Does not therefore the eleventh Article *exclude* good works from all share in the office of Justifying? Or can we so construe the term "Faith" in that Article as to make it *include* good works?
4. Do not the twelfth and thirteenth Articles *further* exclude them, the one by asserting that good works *follow after* Justification, the other by maintaining that they *cannot precede* it?
5. Can that which never precedes an effect be reckoned among the *causes* of that effect?
6. Can we then, consistently with our Articles, reckon the performance of good works among the *causes* of Justification, whatever qualifying epithet be used with the term *cause*?

We entirely deny that the Calvinistical Clergy are bad members of their profession. We maintain that as many instances of good, serious, and pious men—of persons zealously interesting themselves in the temporal and spiritual welfare of their parishioners, are to be found among them, as among the clergy who put an opposite interpretation on the Articles. The Articles of Religion are older than Arminianism, *eo nomine*. The early reformers leant to Calvinism; and would, to a man, have answered the Bishop's questions in a way which would have induced him to refuse them ordination and curacies; and those who drew up the Thirty-nine Articles, if they had not prudently avoided all precise interpretation of their Creed on free will, necessity, absolute decrees, original sin, reprobation and election, would have, in all probability, given an interpretation of them like that which the Bishop considers as a disqualification for Holy Orders. Laud's Lambeth Articles were illegal, mischievous, and are generally condemned. The Irish Clergy in 1641 drew up one hundred and four articles as the creed of their Church; and these are

Calvinistic and not Arminian. They were approved and signed by Usher, and never abjured by him; though dropt as a test or qualification. Usher was promoted (even in the days of Arminianism) to bishoprics and archbishoprics—so little did a Calvinistic interpretation of the Articles in a man's own breast, or even an avowal of Calvinism beyond what was required by the Articles, operate even then as a disqualification for the cure of souls, or any other office in the Church. Throughout Charles II. and William III.'s time, the best men and greatest names of the Church not only allowed latitude in interpreting the Articles, but thought it would be wise to diminish their number, and render them more lax than they are; and be it observed, that these latitudinarians leant to Arminianism rather than to high Calvinism; and thought, consequently, that the Articles, if objectionable at all, were exposed to the censure of being "too Calvinistic," rather than too Arminian. How preposterous, therefore, to twist them, and the subscription to them required by law, by the machinery of a long string of explanatory questions, into a barrier against Calvinists, and to give the Arminians a monopoly in the Church!

Archbishop Wake, in 1716, after consulting all the Bishops then attending Parliament, thought it incumbent on him *"to employ the authority which the ecclesiastical laws then in force, and the custom and laws of the realm vested in him,"* in taking care that *"no unworthy person might hereafter be admitted into the sacred Ministry of the Church"*; and he drew up twelve recommendations to the Bishops of England, in which he earnestly exhorts them not to ordain persons of bad conduct or character, or incompetent learning; but he does not require from the candidates for Holy Orders or preferment any explanation whatever of the Articles which they had signed.

The Correspondence of the same eminent Prelate with Professor Turretin in 1718, and with Mr. Le Clerc and the Pastors and Professors of Geneva in 1719, printed in London, 1782, recommends union among Protestants, and the omission of controverted points in Confessions of Faith, as a means of obtaining that union; and a constant reference to the practice of the Church of England is made, in elucidation of the charity and wisdom of such policy.

Speaking of men who act upon a contrary principle he says,
O quantum potuit insana φιλαντια!

These passages, we think, are conclusive evidence of the practice of the Church till 1719. For Wake was not only at the time Archbishop of Canterbury, but both in his circular recommendations to the Bishops of England, and in his correspondence with foreign Churches, was acting in the capacity of metropolitan of the Anglican Church. He, a man of prudence and learning, publicly boasts to Protestant Europe, that his Church does *not* exact, and that he *de facto* has never avowed, and never will, his opinions on those very points upon which Bishop Marsh obliges every poor curate to be explicit, upon pain of expulsion from the Church.

It is clear, then, the practice was, to extract subscription, and nothing else, as the test of orthodoxy—to that Wake is an evidence. As far as he is authority on a point of opinion, it is his conviction that this practice was wholesome, wise, and intended to preserve peace in the Church; that it would be wrong at least, if not illegal, to do otherwise; and that the observance of this forbearance is the only method of preventing schism. The Bishop of Peterborough, however, is of a different opinion; he is so thoroughly convinced of the pernicious effects of Calvinistic doctrines, that he does what no other Bishop does, or ever did do, for their exclusion. This may be either wise or injudicious, but it is at least zealous and bold; it is to encounter rebuke, and opposition, from a sense of duty. It is impossible to deny this merit to his Lordship. And we have no doubt, that, in pursuance of the same theological gallantry, he is preparing a set of interrogatories for those clergymen who are presented to benefices in his diocese. The patron will have his action of *Quare impedit*, it is true; and the judge and jury will decide whether the Bishop has the right of interrogation at all; and whether Calvinistical answers to his interrogatories disqualify any man from holding preferment in the Church of England. If either of these points are given against the Bishop of Peterborough, he is in honour and conscience bound to give up his examination of curates. If Calvinistic ministers are, in the estimation of the Bishops, so dangerous as curates, they are of course much more dangerous as rectors and vicars. He has as much right to examine one as the other. Why then does he pass over the greater danger, and guard against the less? Why does he not show his zeal when he would run some risk, and where the excluded person (if excluded unjustly) could appeal to the laws of his country? If his conduct be just and right, has he any thing to fear from that appeal? What should we say of a police officer who acted in all cases of petty larceny, where no opposition was made, and let off all persons guilty of felony who threatened to knock him down? If the Bishop value his own character, he is bound to do less, —or to do more. God send his choice may be right! The law, as it stands at present, certainly affords very unequal protection to rector and to curate; but if the Bishop will not act so as to improve the law, the law must be so changed as to improve the Bishop; an action of *Quare impedit* must be given to the curate also—and then the fury of interrogation will be calmed.

We are aware that the Bishop of Peterborough, in his speech, disclaims the object of excluding the Calvinists by this system of interrogation. We shall take no other notice of his disavowal, than expressing our sincere regret that he ever made it; but the question is not at all altered by the intention of the interrogator. Whether he aim at the Calvinists only, or includes them with other heterodox respondents—the fact is, they *are* included in the proscription, and excluded from the Church, the practical effect of the practice being, that men are driven out of the Church who have as much right to exercise the duties of clergymen as the Bishop himself. If heterodox opinions are the great objects of the Bishop's apprehensions, he has his Ecclesiastical Courts, where regular process may bring the offender to punishment, and from whence there is an appeal to higher courts. This would be the fair thing to do. The Curate and the Bishop would be brought into the light of day, and subjected to the wholesome restraint of public opinion.

His Lordship boasts, that he has excluded only two curates. So the Emperor of Hayti boasted that he had only cut off two persons' heads for disagreeable behaviour at his table. In spite of the paucity of the visitors executed, the example operated as a considerable impediment to conversation; and the intensity of the punishment was found to be a full compensation for its rarity. How many persons have been deprived of curacies which they might have enjoyed, but for the tenor of these interrogatories? How many respectable clergymen have been deprived of the assistance of curates connected with them by blood, friendship, or doctrine, and compelled to choose persons for no other qualification than that they could pass through the eye of the Bishop's needle? Violent measures are not to be judged of merely by the number of times they have been resorted to, but by the terror, misery, and restraint which the severity is likely to have produced.

We never met with any style so entirely clear of all redundant and vicious ornament, as that which the ecclesiastical Lord of Peterborough has adopted towards his clergy. It, in fact, may be all reduced to these few words— "Reverend Sir, I shall do what I please. Peterborough." —Even in the House of Lords, he speaks what we must call very plain language. Among other things, he says, that the allegations of the petitions are *false*. Now, as every Bishop is, besides his other qualities, a gentleman; and as the word *false* is used only by laymen who mean to hazard their lives by the expression; and as it cannot be supposed that foul language is ever used because it can be used with personal impunity, his Lordship must therefore be intended to mean not *false*, but *mistaken*— not a wilful deviation from truth, but an accidental and unintended departure from it.

His Lordship talks of the drudgery of wading through ten pages of answers to his eighty-seven questions. Who has occasioned this drudgery, but the person who means to be so much more active, useful, and important, than all other Bishops, by proposing questions which nobody has thought to be necessary but himself? But to be intolerably strict and harsh to a poor curate, who is trying to earn a morsel of hard bread, and then to complain of the drudgery of reading his answers, is much like knocking a man down with a bludgeon, and then abusing him for splashing you with his blood, and pestering you with his groans. It is quite monstrous, that a man who inflicts eighty-seven new questions in Theology upon his fellow-creatures, should talk of the drudgery of reading their answers.

A Curate—there is something which excites compassion in the very name of a Curate!!! How any man of Purple, Palaces, and Preferment, can let himself loose against this poor working man of God, we are at a loss to conceive,— a learned man in an hovel, with sermons and saucepans, lexicons and bacon, Hebrew books and ragged children— good and patient—a comforter and a preacher—the first and purest pauper in the hamlet, and yet showing, that, in the midst of his worldly misery, he has the heart of a gentleman, and the spirit of a Christian, and the kindness of a pastor; and this man, though he has exercised the duties of a clergyman for twenty years—though he has most ample testimonies of conduct from clergymen as respectable as any Bishop—though an Archbishop add his name to the list of witnesses, is not good enough for Bishop Marsh; but is pushed out in the street, with his wife and children, and his little furniture, to surrender his honour, his faith, his conscience, and his learning—or to starve!

An obvious objection to these innovations is, that there can be no end to them. If eighty-three questions are assumed to be necessary by one Bishop, eight hundred may be considered as the minimum of interrogation by another. When once the ancient faith marks of the Church are lost sight of and despised, any misled theologian may launch out on the boundless sea of polemical vexation.

The Bishop of Peterborough is positive, that the Arminian interpretation of the Articles is the right interpretation, and that Calvinists should be excluded from it; but the country gentlemen who are to hear these matters debated in the Lower House, are to remember, that other Bishops have written upon these points before the Bishop of Peterborough, and have arrived at conclusions diametrically opposite. When curates are excluded because their answers are Calvinistical, a careless layman might imagine that this interpretation of the Articles had never been heard of before in the Church—that it was a gross and palpable perversion of their sense, which had been scouted by all writers on Church matters, from the day the Articles were promulgated, to this hour—that such an unheard-of monster as a Calvinistical Curate had never leapt over the pale before, and been detected browsing in the sacred pastures.

The following is the testimony of Bishop Sherlock:—

"The Church has left a latitude of sense to prevent schisms and breaches upon every different opinion. It is evident the Church of England has so done in some Articles, which are most liable to the hottest disputes; which yet are penned with that temper as to be willingly subscribed by men of different apprehensions in those matters."—(Sherlock's *Defence of Stillingfleet's Unreasonableness of Separation*.)

Bishop Cleaver, describing the difficulties attending so great an undertaking as the formation of a national creed, observes:—

"These difficulties, however, do not seem to have discouraged the great leaders in this work from forming a design as wise as it was liberal, that of framing a confession, which, in the enumeration and method of its several articles, should meet the approbation, and engage the consent, of the whole reformed world.

"If upon trial it was found that a comprehension so extensive could not be reduced to practice, still as large a comprehension as could be contrived, within the narrower limits of the kingdom, became, for the same reasons which first suggested the idea, at once an object of prudence and duty, in the formation and government of the English Church."

After dwelling on the means necessary to accomplish this object, the Bishop proceeds to remark:—"Such evidently appears to have been the origin, and such the actual complexion of the confession comprised in the Articles of our Church; *the true scope and design of which will not, I conceive, be correctly apprehended in any other view than that of one drawn up and adjusted with an intention to comprehend the assent of all, rather than to exclude that of any who concurred in the necessity of a reformation.*

"The means of comprehension intended were, not any general ambiguity or equivocation of terms, *but a prudent forbearance in all parties not to insist on the full extent of their opinions in matters not essential or fundamental ; and in all cases to waive, as much as possible, tenets which might divide, where they wish to unite.*" (*Remarks on the Design and Formation of the Articles of the Church of England*, by William, Lord Bishop of Bangor, 1802.—pp. 23-5.)

We will finish with Bishop Horsley.

It has been the fashion of late to talk about Arminianism as the system of the Church of England, and of Calvinism as something opposite to it, to which the Church is hostile. That I may not be misunderstood in what I have stated, or may have occasion further to say upon this subject, I must here declare, that I use the words Arminianism and Calvinism in that restricted sense in which they are now generally taken, to denote the doctrinal part of each system, as unconnected with the principles either of Arminians or Calvinists upon Church discipline and Church government. This being premised, I assert, what I often have before asserted, and by God's grace I will persist in the assertion to my dying day, that so far is it from the truth that the Church of England is decidedly Arminian, and hostile to Calvinism, that the truth is this, *that upon the principal points in dispute between the Arminians and the Calvinists—upon all the points of doctrine characteristic of the two sects, the Church of England maintains an absolute neutrality ; her Articles explicitly assert nothing but what is believed both by Arminians and by Calvinists.* The Calvinists indeed hold some opinions relative to the same points, which the Church of England has not gone the length of asserting in her Articles; but neither has she gone the length of explicitly contradicting those opinions; insomuch, that *there is nothing to hinder the Arminian and the highest supralapsarian Calvinist from walking together in the Church of England and Ireland as friends and brothers, if they both approve the discipline of the Church, and both are willing to submit to it.* Her discipline has been approved; it has been submitted to; it has been in former times most ably and zealously defended by the highest supralapsarian Calvinists. Such was the great Usher; such was Whitgift; such were many more, burning and shining lights of our Church in her early days (when first she shook off the Papal tyranny), long since gone to the resting-place of the spirits of the just.—(*Bishop* HORSLEY'S *Charges*, p. 216.—pp. 25, 26.)

So that these unhappy Curates are turned out of their bread for an exposition of the Articles which such men as Sherlock, Cleaver, and Horsley think may be fairly given of their meaning. We do not quote their authority, to show that the right interpretation is decided, but that it is doubtful—that there is a balance of authorities—that the opinion which Bishop Marsh has punished with poverty and degradation, has been considered to be legitimate, by men at least as wise and learned as himself. In fact, it is to us perfectly clear, that the Articles were originally framed to prevent the very practices which Bishop Marsh has used for their protection—they were purposely so worded, that Arminians and Calvinists could sign them without blame. They were intended to combine both these descriptions of Protestants, and were meant principally for a bulwark against the Catholics.

L

Thus [says Bishop Burnet] was the doctrine of the Church cast into a short and plain form; in which they took care both to establish the positive articles of religion, and to cut off the errors formerly introduced in the time of Popery, or of late broached by the Anabaptists and enthusiasts of Germany; *avoiding the niceties of schoolmen, or the peremptoriness of the writers of controversy; leaving, in matters that are more justly controvertible, a liberty to divines to follow their private opinions without thereby disturbing the peace of the Church.*—(*History of the Reformation,* Book I. part ii. p. 168, folio edition.)

The next authority is that of Fuller.

In the Convocation now sitting, wherein Alexander Nowel, Dean of St. Paul's, was Prolocutor, the nine-and-thirty Articles were composed. For the main they agree with those set forth in the reign of King Edward the Sixth, though in some particulars allowing more liberty to dissenting judgments. For instance, in this King's Articles it is said, that it is to be believed that Christ went down to hell (to preach to the spirits there); which last clause is left out in these Articles, and men left to a latitude concerning the cause, time, and manner of his descent.

Hence some have unjustly taxed the composers for too much favour extended in their large expressions, clean through the contexture of these Articles, which should have tied men's consciences up closer, in more strict and particularising propositions, *which indeed proceeded from their commendable moderation.* Children's clothes ought to be made of the biggest, because afterwards their bodies will grow up to their garments. Thus the Articles of this English Protestant Church, in the infancy thereof, they thought good to draw up in general terms, foreseeing that posterity would grow up to fill the same: I mean these holy men did prudently prediscover, that differences in judgments would unavoidably happen in the Church, *and were loath to unchurch any, and drive them off from an ecclesiastical communion, for such petty differences, which made them pen the Articles in comprehensive words, to take in all who, differing in the branches, meet in the root of the same religion.*

Indeed most of them had formerly been sufferers themselves, and cannot be said, in compiling these Articles, (an acceptable service, no doubt,) to offer to God what cost them nothing, some having paid imprisonment, others exile, all losses in their estates, for this their experimental knowledge in religion, *which made them the more merciful and tender in stating those points,* seeing such who themselves have been most patient in bearing, will be most pitiful in burdening the consciences of others.—(See FULLER's *Church History,* book ix. p. 72, folio edit.)

But this generous and pacific spirit gives no room for the display of zeal and theological learning. The gate of admission has been left too widely open. I may as well be without power at all, if I cannot force my opinions upon other people. What was purposely left indefinite, I must make finite and exclusive. Questions of contention and difference must be laid before the servants of the Church, and nothing like neutrality in theological metaphysics allowed to the ministers of the Gospel. *I come not to bring peace*, etc.

The Bishop, however, seems to be quite satisfied with himself, when he states, that he has a *right to do* what he has done—just as if a man's character with his fellow-creatures depended upon legal rights alone, and not upon a discreet exercise of those rights. A man may persevere in doing what he has a right to do, till the Chancellor shuts him up in Bedlam, or till the mob pelt him as he passes. It must be presumed, that all men whom the law has invested with rights, Nature has invested with common sense to use those rights. For these reasons, children have no rights till they have gained some common sense, and old men have no rights after they lose their common sense. All men are at all times accountable to their fellow-creatures for the discreet exercise of every right they possess.

Prelates are fond of talking of *my* see, *my* clergy, *my* diocese, as if these things belonged to them, as their pigs and dogs belonged to them. They forget that the clergy, the diocese, and the Bishops themselves, all exist only for the public good; that the public are a third, and principal party in the whole concern. It is not simply the tormenting Bishop *versus* the tormented Curate, but the public against the system of tormenting; as tending to bring scandal upon religion and religious men. By the late alteration in the laws, the labourers in the vineyard are given up to the power of the inspectors of the vineyard. If he have the meanness and malice to do so, an inspector may worry and plague to death any labourer against whom he may have conceived an antipathy. As often as such cases are detected, we believe they will meet, in either House of Parliament, with the severest reprehension. The noblemen and gentlemen of England will never allow their parish clergy to be treated with cruelty, injustice, and caprice, by men who were parish clergymen themselves yesterday, and who were trusted with power for very different purposes.

The Bishop of Peterborough complains of the insolence of the answers made to him. This is certainly not true of Mr. Grimshawe, Mr. Neville, or of the author of the Appeal. They have answered his Lordship with great force, great manliness, but with perfect respect. Does the Bishop expect that humble men, as learned as himself, are to be driven from their houses and homes by his new theology, and then to send him letters of thanks for the kicks and cuffs he has bestowed upon them? Men of very small incomes, be it known to his Lordship, have very often very acute feelings; and a Curate trod on feels a pang as great as when a Bishop is refuted.

We shall now give a specimen of some answers, which, we believe, would exclude a curate from the diocese of Peterborough, and contrast these answers with the Articles of the Church to which they refer. The 9th Article of the Church of England is upon Original Sin. Upon this point his Lordship puts the following question:—

Did the fall of Adam produce such an effect on his posterity, that mankind became thereby a mass of mere corruption, or of absolute and entire depravity? Or is the effect only such, that we are very *far gone* from original righteousness, and of our own nature *inclined* to evil?

Excluding Answer

The fall of Adam produced such an effect on his posterity, that mankind became thereby a mass of mere corruption, or of absolute and entire depravity.

The Ninth Article

Original sin standeth not in the following of Adam (as the Pelagians do vainly talk); but it is the fault or corruption of the nature of every man, that naturally is engendered of the offspring of Adam, whereby man is very far gone from original righteousness, and is of his own nature inclined to evil, so that the flesh lusteth always contrary to the spirit; and therefore, in every person born into the world, it deserveth God's wrath and damnation.

The 9th Question, Cap. 3d, on Free Will, is as follows:— Is it not contrary to Scripture to say, that man has no share in the work of his salvation?

Excluding Answer

It is quite agreeable to Scripture to say, that man has no share in the work of his own salvation.

Tenth Article

The condition of man after the fall of Adam is such, that he cannot turn and prepare himself, by his own natural strength and good works, to faith, and calling upon God. Wherefore, we have no power to do good works pleasant and acceptable to God, without the grace of God by Christ preventing us, that we may have a good will, and working with us when we have that good will.

On Redemption, his Lordship has the following question, Cap. 1st, Question 1st:—Did Christ die for all men, or did he die only for a chosen few?

Excluding Answer

Christ did not die for all men, but only for a chosen few.

Part of Article Seventh

Predestination to life is the everlasting purpose of God, whereby (before the foundations of the world were laid) he hath constantly decreed by his counsel, secret to us, to deliver from curse and damnation those whom he hath chosen in Christ out of mankind, and to bring them by Christ unto everlasting salvation, as vessels made to honour.

Now, whether these answers are right or wrong, we do not presume to decide; but we cannot help saying, there appears to be some little colour in the language of the Articles for the errors of the respondent. It does not appear at first sight to be such a deviation from the plain, literal, and grammatical sense of the Articles, as to merit rapid and ignominious ejectment from the bosom of the Church.

Now we have done with the Bishop. We give him all he asks as to his legal right; and only contend, that he is acting a very indiscreet and injudicious part—fatal to his quiet—fatal to his reputation as a man of sense—blamed by Ministers—blamed by all the Bench of Bishops— vexatious to the Clergy, and highly injurious to the Church. We mean no personal disrespect to the Bishop; we are as ignorant of him as of his victims. We should have been heartily glad if the debate in Parliament had put an end to these blameable excesses; and our only object, in meddling with the question, is to restrain the arm of Power within the limits of moderation and justice—one of the great objects which first led to the establishment of this Journal, and which, we hope, will always continue to characterise its efforts.

POOR-LAWS [1]

OUR readers, we fear, will require some apology for being asked to look at anything upon the Poor-Laws. No subject, we admit, can be more disagreeable, or more trite. But, unfortunately, it is the most important of all the important subjects which the distressed state of the country is now crowding upon our notice.

A pamphlet on the Poor-Laws generally contains some little piece of favourite nonsense, by which we are gravely told this enormous evil may be perfectly cured. The first gentleman recommends little gardens; the second cows; the third a village shop; the fourth a spade; the fifth Dr. Bell, and so forth. Every man rushes to the press with his small morsel of imbecility; and is not easy till he sees his impertinence stitched in blue covers. In this list of absurdities, we must not forget the project of supporting the poor from national funds, or, in other words, of immediately doubling the expenditure, and introducing every possible abuse into the administration of it. Then there are worthy men, who call upon gentlemen of fortune and education to become overseers—meaning, we suppose, that the present overseers are to perform the higher duties of men of fortune. Then Merit is set up as the test of relief; and their worships are to enter into a long examination of the life and character of each applicant, assisted, as they doubtless would be, by candid overseers, and neighbours divested of every feeling of malice and partiality. The children are next to be taken from their parents, and lodged in immense pedagogueries of several acres each, where they are to be carefully secluded from those fathers and mothers they are commanded to obey and honour, and are to be brought up in virtue by the churchwardens. —And this is gravely intended as a corrective of the Poor-Laws; as if (to pass over the many other objections which might be made to it) it would not set mankind populating faster than carpenters and bricklayers could cover in their

[1] See p. 295.

children, or separate twigs to be bound into rods for their flagellation. An extension of the Poor-Laws to personal property is also talked of. We should be very glad to see any species of property exempted from these laws, but have no wish that any which is now exempted should be subjected to their influence. The case would infallibly be like that of the Income-tax,—the more easily the tax was raised, the more profligate would be the expenditure. It is proposed also that alehouses should be diminished, and that the children of the poor should be catechised publicly in the church,—both very respectable and proper suggestions, but of themselves hardly strong enough for the evil. We have every wish that the poor should accustom themselves to habits of sobriety; but we cannot help reflecting, sometimes, that an alehouse is the only place where a poor tired creature, haunted with every species of wretchedness, can purchase three or four times a year three pennyworth of ale, a liquor upon which wine-drinking moralists are always extremely severe. We must not forget, among other nostrums, the eulogy of small farms—in other words, of small capital, and profound ignorance in the arts of agriculture;—and the evil is also thought to be curable by periodical contributions from men who have nothing, and can earn nothing without charity. To one of these plans, and perhaps the most plausible, Mr. Nicol has stated, in the following passage, objections that are applicable to almost all the rest.

The district school would no doubt be well superintended and well regulated; magistrates and country gentlemen would be its visitors. The more excellent the establishment, the greater the mischief; because the greater the expense. We may talk what we will of economy, but where the care of the poor is taken exclusively into the hands of the rich, comparative extravagance is the necessary consequence: to say that the gentleman, or even the overseer, would never permit the poor to live at the district school as they live at home, is saying far too little. English humanity will never see the poor in anything like want, when that want is palpably and visibly brought before it; first, it will give necessaries, next comforts; until its fostering care rather pampers, than merely relieves. The humanity itself is highly laudable; but if practised on an extensive scale, its consequences must entail an almost unlimited expenditure.

Mr. Locke computes that the labour of a child from three to

fourteen, being set against its nourishment and teaching, the result will be exoneration of the parish from expense. Nothing could prove more decisively the incompetency of the Board of Trade to advise on this question. Of the productive labour of the workhouse, I shall have to speak hereafter; I will only observe in this place, that after the greatest care and attention bestowed on the subject, after expensive looms purchased, etc., the fifty boys of the Blue Coat School [1] earned in the year 1816, £59 10s. 3d.; the forty girls earned, in the same time, £40 7s. 9d. The ages of these children are from eight to sixteen. They earn about one pound in the year and cost about twenty.

The greater the call for labour in public institutions, be they prisons, workhouses, or schools, the more difficult to be procured that labour must be. There will thence be both much less of it for the comparative numbers, and it will afford a much less price; to get any labour at all, one school must underbid another.

It has just been observed, that "the child of a poor cottager, half clothed, half fed, with the enjoyment of home and liberty, is not only happier but better than the little automaton of a parish workhouse"; and this I believe is accurately true. I scarcely know a more cheering sight, though certainly many more elegant ones, than the youthful gambols of a village green. They call to mind the description given by Paley of the shoals of the fry of fish: "They are so happy that they know not what to do with themselves; their attitude, their vivacity, their leaps out of the water, their frolics in it, all conduce to show their excess of spirits, and are simply the effects of that excess."

Though politeness may be banished from the cottage, and though the anxious mother may sometimes chide a little too sharply, yet here both maternal endearments and social affection exist in perhaps their greatest vigour; the attachments of lower life, where independent of attachment there is so little to enjoy, far outstrip the divided if not exhausted sensibility of the rich and great; and in depriving the poor of these attachments, we may be said to rob them of their little all.

But it is not to happiness only I here refer: it is to morals. I listen with great reserve to that system of moral instruction, which has not social affection for its basis, or the feelings of the heart for its ally. It is not to be concealed, that everything may be taught, yet nothing learned, that systems planned with care and executed with attention, may evaporate into unmeaning forms, where the imagination is not roused, or the sensibility impressed.

Let us suppose the children of the "district school," nurtured with that superabundant care which such institutions, when

[1] See p. 295.

supposed to be well conducted, are wont to exhibit; they rise with the dawn; after attending to the calls of cleanliness, prayers follow; then a lesson; then breakfast; then work, till noon liberates them, for perhaps an hour, from the walls of their prison to the walls of their prison court. Dinner follows; and then, in course, work, lessons, supper, prayers; at length, after a day dreary and dull, the counterpart of every day which has preceded, and of all that are to follow, the children are dismissed to bed.—This system may construct a machine, but it will not form a man. Of what does it consist? of prayers parroted without one sentiment in accord with the words uttered: of moral lectures which the understanding does not comprehend, or the heart feel; of endless bodily constraint, intolerable to youthful vivacity, and injurious to the perfection of the human frame.—The cottage day may not present so imposing a scene; no decent uniform; no well-trimmed locks; no glossy skin; no united response of hundreds of conjoined voices; no lengthened procession, misnamed exercise; but if it has less to strike the eye, it has far more to engage the heart. A trifle in the way of cleanliness must suffice; the prayer is not forgot; it is perhaps imperfectly repeated, and confusedly understood; but it is not muttered as a vain sound; it is an earthly parent that tells of an heavenly one; duty, love, obedience, are not words without meaning, when repeated by a mother to her child: to God—the great unknown Being that made all things, all thanks, all praise, all adoration is due. The young religionist may be in some measure bewildered by all this; his notions may be obscure, but his feelings will be roused, and the foundation at least of true piety will be laid.

Of moral instruction, the child may be taught less at home than at school, but he will be taught better; that is, whatever he is taught he will feel; he will not have abstract propositions of duty coldly presented to his mind; but precept and practice will be conjoined; what he is told it is right to do will be instantly done. Sometimes the operative principle on the child's mind will be love, sometimes fear, sometimes habitual sense of obedience; it is always something that will impress, always something that will be remembered.

There are two points which we consider as now admitted by all men of sense,—1st, That the Poor-Laws must be abolished; 2dly, That they must be *very gradually* abolished.[1]

[1] I am not quite so wrong in this as I seem to be, nor after all our experience am I satisfied that there has not been a good deal of rashness and precipitation in the conduct of this admirable measure. You have not been able to carry the law into manufacturing counties. Parliament will compel you to soften some of the more severe clauses.

We hardly think it worth while to throw away pen and ink upon any one who is still inclined to dispute either of these propositions.

With respect to the gradual abolition, it must be observed, that the present redundant population of the country has been entirely produced by the Poor-Laws: and nothing could be so grossly unjust, as to encourage people to such a vicious multiplication, and then, when you happen to discover your folly, immediately to starve them into annihilation. You have been calling upon your population for two hundred years to beget more children—furnished them with clothes, food, and houses—taught them to lay up nothing for matrimony, nothing for children, nothing for age—but to depend upon Justices of the Peace for every human want. The folly is now detected; but the people, who are the fruit of it, remain. It was madness to call them in this manner into existence; but it would be the height of cold-blooded cruelty to get rid of them by any other than the most gentle and gradual means; and not only would it be cruel, but extremely dangerous, to make the attempt. Insurrections of the most sanguinary and ferocious nature would be the immediate consequence of any very sudden change in the system of the Poor-Laws; not partial, like those which proceed from an impeded or decaying state of manufactures, but as universal as the Poor-Laws themselves, and as ferocious as insurrections always are which are led on by hunger and despair.

These observations may serve as an answer to those angry and impatient gentlemen, who are always crying out, What has the Committee of the House of Commons done?—What have they to show for their labours?—Are the rates lessened?—Are the evils removed? The Committee of the House of Commons would have shown themselves to be a set of the most contemptible charlatans, if they had proceeded with any such indecent and perilous haste, or paid the slightest regard to the ignorant folly which required it at their hands. They have very properly begun, by collecting all possible information upon the subject; by consulting speculative and practical men;

It has been the nucleus of general insurrection and chartism. The Duke of Wellington wisely recommended that the experiment should be first tried in a few counties round the metropolis.

by leaving time for the press to contribute whatever it
could of thought or knowledge to the subject; and by introducing measures, the effects of which will be, and are
intended to be, gradual. The Lords seemed at first to
have been surprised that the Poor-Laws were not abolished
before the end of the first session of Parliament; and accordingly set up a little rival Committee of their own, which
did little or nothing, and will not, we believe, be renewed.
We are so much less sanguine than those noble legislators,
that we shall think the improvement immense, and a
subject of very general congratulation, if the Poor-rates
are perceptibly diminished, and if the system of pauperism
is clearly going down in twenty or thirty years hence.

We think, upon the whole, that Government have been
fortunate in the selection of the gentleman who is placed
at the head of the Committee for the revision of the Poor-
Laws; or rather, we should say (for he is a gentleman of
very independent fortune), who has consented that he
should be placed there. Mr. Sturges Bourne is undoubtedly a man of business, and of very good sense: he has
made some mistakes; but, upon the whole, sees the subject
as a philosopher and a statesman ought to do. Above all,
we are pleased with his good nature and good sense in
adhering to his undertaking, after the Parliament has
flung out two or three of his favourite bills. Many men
would have surrendered so unthankful and laborious an
undertaking in disgust; but Mr. Bourne knows better
what appertains to his honour and character, and, above
all, what he owes to his country. It is a great subject;
and such as will secure to him the gratitude and favour
of posterity, if he bring it to a successful issue.

We have stated our opinion, that all remedies, without gradual abolition, are of little importance. With a
foundation laid for such gradual abolition, every auxiliary
improvement of the Poor-Laws (while they do remain)
is worthy the attention of Parliament: and, in suggesting
a few alterations as fit to be immediately adopted, we wish
it to be understood, that we have in view the gradual
destruction of the system, as well as its amendment while
it continues to operate.

It seems to us, then, that one of the first and greatest
improvements of this unhappy system would be a complete

revision of the Law of Settlement. Since Mr. East's act
for preventing the removal of the poor till they are actually
chargeable, any man may live where he pleases, till he
becomes a beggar, and ask alms of the place where he
resides. To gain a settlement, then, is nothing more than
to gain a right of begging: it is not, as it used to be before
Mr. East's act, a power of residing where, in the judgment
of the resident, his industry and exertion will be best re-
warded; but a power of taxing the industry and exertions
of other persons in the place where his settlement falls.
This privilege produces all the evil complained of in the
Poor-Laws; and instead therefore of being conferred with
the liberality and profusion which it is at present, it should
be made of very difficult attainment, and liable to the
fewest possible changes. The constant policy of our
Courts of Justice has been, to make settlements easily
obtained. Since the period we have before alluded to,
this has certainly been a very mistaken policy. It would
be a far wiser course to abolish all other means of settlement than those of Birth, Parentage, and Marriage,—not
for the limited reason stated in the Committee, that it
would diminish the law expenses, (though that, too, is of
importance,) but because it would invest fewer residents
with the fatal privilege of turning beggars, exempt a
greater number of labourers from the moral corruption of
the Poor-Laws, and stimulate them to exertion and
economy, by the fear of removal if they are extravagant
and idle. Of ten men who leave the place of their birth,
four, probably, get a settlement by yearly hiring, and
four others by renting a small tenement; while two or three
may return to the place of their nativity, and settle there.
Now, under the present system, here are eight men settled
where they have a right to beg without being removed.
The probability is, that they will all beg; and that their
virtue will give way to the incessant temptation of the
Poor-Laws: but if these men had felt from the very beginning, that removal from the place where they wished most
to live would be the sure consequence of their idleness
and extravagance, the probability is, that they would
have escaped the contagion of pauperism, and been much
more useful members of society than they now are. The
best labourers in a village are commonly those who are

living where they are legally settled, and have therefore
no right to ask charity—for the plain reason, that they
have nothing to depend upon but their own exertions: in
short, for them the Poor-Laws hardly exist; and they are
such as the great mass of English peasantry would be, if
we had escaped the curse of these laws altogether.

It is incorrect to say, that no labourer would settle
out of the place of his birth, if the means of acquiring a
settlement were so limited. Many men begin the world
with strong hope and much confidence in their own fortune,
and without any intention of subsisting by charity; but
they see others subsisting in greater ease, without their
toil—and their spirit gradually sinks to the meanness
of mendicity.

An affecting picture is sometimes drawn of a man falling
into want in the decline of life, and compelled to remove
from the place where he has spent the greatest part of his
days. These things are certainly painful enough to him
who has the misfortune to witness them. But they must
be taken upon a large scale; and the whole good and evil
which they produce diligently weighed and considered.
The question then will be, whether any thing can be more
really humane, than to restrain a system which relaxes
the sinews of industry, and places the dependence of
laborious men upon anything but themselves. We must
not think only of the wretched sufferer who is removed, and,
at the sight of his misfortunes, call out for fresh facilities
to beg. We must remember the industry, the vigour, and
the care which the dread of removal has excited, and the
number of persons who owe their happiness and their
wealth to that salutary feeling. The very person who,
in the decline of life, is removed from the spot where he has
spent so great a part of his time, would perhaps have been
a pauper half a century before, if he had been afflicted
with the right of asking alms in the place where he lived.

It has been objected that this plan of abolishing all
settlements but those of birth, would send a man, the
labour of whose youth had benefited some other parish,
to pass the useless part of his life in a place for which he
existed only as a burthen. Supposing that this were the
case, it would be quite sufficient to answer, that any given
parish would probably send away as many useless old men

as it received; and after all, little inequalities must be borne for the general good. But, in truth, it is rather ridiculous to talk of a parish not having benefited by the labour of the man who is returned upon their hands in his old age. If such parish resemble most of those in England, the absence of a man for thirty or forty years has been a great good instead of an evil; they have had many more labourers than they could employ; and the very man whom they are complaining of supporting for his few last years, would, in all probability, have been a beggar forty years before, if he had remained among them; or, by pushing him out of work, would have made some other man a beggar. Are the benefits derived from prosperous manufactures limited to the parishes which contain them? The industry of Halifax, Huddersfield, or Leeds is felt across the kingdom as far as the Eastern Sea. The prices of meat and corn at the markets of York and Malton are instantly affected by any increase of demand and rise of wages in the manufacturing districts to the west. They have benefited these distant places, and found labour for their superfluous hands by the prosperity of their manufactures. Where then would be the injustice, if the manufacturers, in the time of stagnation and poverty, were returned to their birth settlements? But as the law now stands, *population tumors*, of the most dangerous nature, may spring up in any parish:— a manufacturer, concealing his intention, may settle there, take two hundred or three hundred apprentices, fail, and half ruin the parish which has been the scene of his operations. For these reasons, we strongly recommend to Mr. Bourne to narrow as much as possible, in all his future bills, the means of acquiring settlements,[1] and to reduce them ultimately to parentage, birth, and marriage— convinced that, by so doing, he will, in furtherance of the great object of abolishing the Poor-Laws, be only *limiting the right of begging*, and preventing the resident and almsman from being (as they now commonly are) one and the same person. But, before we dismiss this part of the subject, we must say a few words upon the methods by which settlements are now gained.

In the settlement by hiring it is held, that a man has a

---

[1] This has been done.

claim upon the parish for support where he has laboured for a year; and yet another, who has laboured there for twenty years by short hirings, gains no settlement at all. When a man was not allowed to live where he was not settled, it was wise to lay hold of any plan for extending settlements. But the whole question is now completely changed; and the only point which remains is, to find out what mode of conferring settlements produces the least possible mischief. We are convinced it is by throwing every possible difficulty in the way of acquiring them. If a settlement hereafter should not be obtained in that parish in which labourers have worked for many years, it will be because it contributes materially to their happiness that they should not gain a settlement there; and this is a full answer to the apparent injustice.

Then, upon what plea of common sense should a man gain a power of taxing a parish to keep him, because he has rented a tenement of ten pounds a year there? or, because he has served the office of clerk, or sexton, or hog-ringer, or bought an estate of thirty pounds value? However good these various pleas might be for conferring settlements, if it were desirable to increase the facility of obtaining them, they are totally inefficacious if it can be shown, that the means of gaining new settlements should be confined to the limits of the strictest necessity.

These observations (if they have the honour of attracting his attention) will show Mr. Bourne our opinion of his bill, for giving the privilege of settlement only to a certain length of residence. In the first place, such a bill, would be the cause of endless vexation to the poor, from the certainty of their being turned out of their cottages, before they pushed their legal taproot into the parish; and, secondly, it would rapidly extend all the evils of the Poor-Laws, by identifying, much more than they are at present identified, the resident and the settled man—the very opposite of the policy which ought to be pursued.

Let us suppose, then, that we have got rid of all the means of gaining a settlement, or right to become a beggar, except by birth, parentage, and marriage; for the wife, of course, must fall into the settlement of the husband; and the children, till emancipated, must be removed, if their parents are removed. This point gained, the task of regulating the law expenses of the Poor-Laws would be nearly accomplished: for the most fertile causes of dispute would be removed. Every first settlement is an inexhaustible source of litigation and expense to the miserable rustics. Upon the simple fact, for example, of a farmer hiring a ploughman for a year, arise the following afflicting questions:—Was it an expressed contract? Was it an implied contract? Was it an implied hiring of the ploughman, rebutted by circumstances? Was the ploughman's contract for a year's prospective service? Was it a customary hiring of the ploughman? Was it a retrospective hiring of the ploughman? Was it a conditional hiring? Was it a general hiring? Was it a special, or a special yearly hiring, or a special hiring with wages reserved weekly? Did the farmer make it a special conditional hiring with warning, or an exceptive hiring? Was the service of the ploughman actual or constructive? Was there any dispensation expressed or implied?—or was there a dissolution implied?—by new agreement?—or mutual consent?—or by Justices?—or by any other of the ten thousand means which the ingenuity of lawyers has created? Can any one be surprised, after this, to learn, that the amount of appeals for removals, in the four Quarter Sessions ending Midsummer, 1817, were *four thousand seven hundred* ? [1] Can any man doubt that it is necessary to reduce the hydra to as few heads as possible? or can any other objection be stated to such reduction, than the number of attorneys and provincial counsel, whom it will bring into the poor-house?—Mr. Nicol says, that the greater number of modes of settlement do not increase litigation. He may just as well say, that the number of the streets in the Seven Dials does not increase the difficulty of finding the way. The modes of settlement we have, are by far the simplest, and the evidence is assisted by registers.

Under the head of Law Expenses, we are convinced a great deal may be done, by making some slight alteration in the law of removals. At present, removals are made without any warning to the parties to whom the pauper is removed; and the first intimation which the defendant parish receives of the projected increase of their population

[1] Commons' Report, 1817.

M

is, by the arrival of the father, mother, and eight or nine children at the overseer's door—where they are tumbled out, with the Justice's order about their necks, and left as a spectacle to the assembled and indignant parishioners. No sooner have the poor wretches become a little familiarised to their new parish, than the order is appealed against, and they are recarted with the same precipitate indecency—*Quo fata trahunt, retrahuntque.*

No removal should ever take place without due notice to the parish to which the pauper is to be removed, nor till the time in which it may be appealed against is past by. Notice to be according to the distance—either by letter or personally; and the decision should be made by the Justices at their petty sessions, with as much care and attention as if there were no appeal from their decision. An absurd notion prevails among Magistrates, that they need not take much trouble in the investigation of removals, because their errors may be corrected by a superior court; whereas it is an object of great importance, by a fair and diligent investigation in the nearest and cheapest court, to convince the country people which party is right and which is wrong; and in this manner to prevent them from becoming the prey of Law Vermin. We are convinced that this subject of the removal of poor is well worthy a short and separate bill. Mr. Bourne thinks it would be very difficult to draw up such a bill. We are quite satisfied we could draw up one in ten minutes that would completely answer the end proposed, and cure the evil complained of.

We proceed to a number of small details, which are well worth the attention of the Legislature.—Overseers' accounts should be given in quarterly, and passed by the Justices, as they now are, annually. The office of Overseers should be triennial. The accounts which have nothing to do with the poor, such as the Constable's account, should be kept and passed separately from them; and the vestry should have the power of ordering a certain portion of the superfluous poor upon the roads. But we beseech all speculators in Poor-Laws to remember, that the machinery they must work with is of a very coarse description. An overseer must always be a limited, uneducated person, but little interested in what he is about, and with much business of his own on his hands. The extensive interference of gentlemen with those matters is quite visionary and impossible. If gentlemen were tide-waiters, the Custom-house would be better served; if gentlemen would become petty constables, the police would be improved; if bridges were made of gold, instead of iron, they would not rust. —But there are not enough of these articles for such purposes.

A great part of the evils of the Poor-Laws has been occasioned by the large powers intrusted to individual Justices. Everybody is full of humanity and good-nature when he can relieve misfortune by putting his hand—in his neighbour's pocket. Who can bear to see a fellow-creature suffering pain and poverty, when he can order other fellow-creatures to relieve them? Is it in human nature, that A should see B in tears and misery, and not order C to assist him? Such a power must, of course, be liable to every degree of abuse; and the sooner the power of ordering relief can be taken out of the hands of Magistrates, the sooner shall we begin to experience some mitigation of the evils of the Poor-Laws. The Special-Vestry Bill is good for this purpose, as far as it goes; but it goes a very little way; and we much doubt if it will operate as any sort of abridgment to the power of Magistrates in granting relief. A single Magistrate must not act under this bill, but in cases of special emergency. But every case of distress is a case of special emergency: and the double Magistrates, holding their petty sessions at some little alehouse, and overwhelmed with all the monthly business of the hundred, cannot possibly give to the pleadings of the overseer and pauper half the attention they would be able to afford them at their own houses.

The common people have been so much accustomed to resort to Magistrates for relief, that it is certainly a delicate business to wean them from this bad habit; but it is essential to the great objects which the Poor-Committee have in view, that the power of Magistrates of ordering relief should be gradually taken away. When this is once done, half the difficulties of the abolition are accomplished. We will suggest a few hints as to the means by which this desirable end may be promoted.

A poor man now comes to a Magistrate any day in the week, and any hour in any day, to complain of the

Overseers, or of the Select Committee. Suppose he were to be made to wait a little, and to feel for a short time the bitterness of that poverty which, by idleness, extravagance, and hasty marriage, he has probably brought upon himself. To effect this object, we would prohibit all orders for relief, by Justices, between the 1st and 10th day of the month; and leave the poor entirely in the hands of the Overseers, or of the Select Vestry, for that period. Here is a beginning—a gradual abolition of one of the first features of the Poor-Laws. And it is without risk of tumult; for no one will run the risk of breaking the laws for an evil to which he anticipates so speedy a termination. This Decameron of overseers' despotism, and paupers' suffering, is the very thing wanted. It will teach the parishes to administer their own charity responsibly, and to depend upon their own judgment. It will teach the poor the miseries of pauperism and dependence; and will be a warning to unmarried young men not hastily and rashly to place themselves, their wives and children, in the same miserable situation; and it will effect all these objects gradually, and without danger. It would of course be the same thing on principle, if relief were confined to three days between the 1st and the 10th of each month; three between the 10th and the 20th; three between the 20th and the end of the month;—or in any other manner that would gradually [1] crumble away the power, and check the gratuitous munificence, of Justices,—give authority over their own affairs to the heads of the parish, and teach the poor, by little and little, that they must suffer if they are imprudent. It is understood in all these observations, that the Overseers are bound to support their poor without any order of Justices; and that death arising from absolute want should expose those officers to very severe punishments, if it could be traced to their inhumanity and neglect. The time must come when we must do without this; but we are not got so far yet—and are at present only getting rid of Justices, not of Overseers.

Mr. Davison seems to think that the plea of old age stands upon a different footing, with respect to the Poor-Laws, from all other pleas. But why should this plea be

---

[1] All gradation and caution have been banished since the Reform Bill—rapid high pressure wisdom is the only agent in public affairs.

more favoured than that of sickness? why more than losses
in trade, incurred by no imprudence? In reality, this
plea is less entitled to indulgence. Every man knows he is
exposed to the helplessness of age; but sickness and sudden
ruin are very often escaped—comparatively seldom happen.
Why is a man exclusively to be protected against that evil
which he must have foreseen longer than any other, and
has had the longest time to guard against? Mr. Davison's
objections to a limited expenditure are much more satisfactory. These we shall lay before our readers; and we
recommend them to the attention of the Committee.

I shall advert next to the plan of a limitation upon the
amount of rates to be assessed in future. This limitation, as it
is a pledge of some protection to the property now subjected
to the maintenance of the poor against the indefinite encroach-
ment which otherwise threatens it, is, in that light, certainly
a benefit; and supposing it were rigorously adhered to, the
very knowledge, among the parish expectants, that there was
some limit to their range of expectation, some barrier which
they could not pass, might incline them to turn their thoughts
homeward again to the care of themselves. But it is an
expedient, at the best, far from being satisfactory. In the
first place, there is much reason to fear that such a limitation
would not eventually be maintained, after the example of a
similar one having failed before, and considering that the
urgency of the applicants, as long as they retain the principle
of dependence upon the parish unqualified in any one of its
main articles, would probably overbear a mere barrier of
figures in the parish account. Then there would be much
real difficulty in the proceedings, to be governed by such a
limiting rule. For the use of the limitation would be chiefly,
or solely, in cases where there is some struggle between the
ordinary supplies of the parish rates and the exigencies of
the poor, or a kind of run and pressure upon the parish by a
mass of indigence: and in circumstances of this kind it would
be hard to know how to distribute the supplies under a fair
proportion to the applicants, known or expected; hard to
know how much might be granted for the present, and how
much should be kept in reserve for the remainder of the year's
service. The real intricacy in such a distribution of account
would show itself in disproportions and inequalities of allowance, impossible to be avoided; and the applicants would
have one pretext more for discontent.

The limitation itself in many places would be only in words
and figures. It would be set, I presume, by an average of
certain preceding years. But the average taken upon the
preceding years might be a sum exceeding in its real value the

highest amount of the assessments of any of the averaged years, under the great change which has taken place in the value of money itself. A given rate, or assessment nominally the same, or lower, might in this way be a greater real money value than it was some time before. In many of the most distressed districts, where the parochial rates have nearly equalled the rents, a nominal average would therefore be no effectual benefit; and yet it is in those districts that the alleviation of the burthen is the most wanted.

It is manifest, also, that a peremptory restriction of the whole amount of money applicable to the parochial service, though abundantly justified in many districts by their particular condition being so impoverished as to make the measure, for them, almost a measure of necessity, if nothing can be substituted for it; and where the same extreme necessity does not exist, still justified by the prudence of preventing in some way the interminable increase of the parochial burthens; still, that such a restriction is an ill-adjusted measure in itself, and would in many instances operate very inequitably. It would fall unfairly in some parishes, where the relative state of the poor and the parish might render an increase of the relief as just and reasonable as it is possible for anything to be under the Poor-Laws at all. It would deny to many possible fair claimants the whole, or a part, of that degree of relief commonly granted elsewhere to persons in their condition, on this or that account of claim. Leaving the reason of the present demands wholly unimpeached, and unexplained; directing no distinct warning or remonstrance to the parties in the line of their affairs, by putting a check to their expectations upon positive matters implicated in their conduct; which would be speaking to them in a definite sense, and a sense applicable to all: this plan of limitation would nurture the whole mass of the claim in its origin, and deny the allowance of it to thousands, on account of reasons properly affecting a distant quarter, of which they know nothing. The want of a clear method, and of a good principle at the bottom of it, in this direct compulsory restriction, renders it, I think, wholly unacceptable, unless it be the only possible plan that can be devised for accomplishing the same end. If a parish had to keep its account with a single dependant, the plan would be much more useful in that case. For the ascertained fact of the total amount of his expectations might set his mind at rest, and put him on a decided course of providing for himself. But, in the limitation proposed to be made, the ascertained fact is of a general amount only, not of each man's share in it. Consequently, each man has his indefinite expectations left to him, and every separate specific ground of expectation remaining as before.

Mr. Davison talks of the propriety of refusing to find

labour for able labourers after the lapse of ten years; as
if it was some ordinary bill he was proposing, unaccom-
panied by the slightest risk. It is very easy to make such
laws, and to propose them; but it would be of immense
difficulty to carry them into execution. Done it must be,
everybody knows that; but the real merit will consist in
discovering the gradual and gentle means by which the
difficulties of getting parish labour may be increased, and
the life of a parish pauper be rendered a life of salutary
and deterring hardship. A law that rendered such request
for labour perfectly lawful for ten years longer, and then
suddenly abolished it, would merely bespeak a certain,
general, and violent insurrection for the year 1830. The
legislator, thank God, is in his nature a more cunning and
gradual animal.

Before we drop Mr. Davison, who writes like a very
sensible man, we wish to say a few words about his style.
If he would think less about it, he would write much better.
It is always as plethoric and full-dressed as if he were
writing a treatise *de finibus bonorum et malorum.* He is
sometimes obscure; and is occasionally apt to dress up
common-sized thoughts in big clothes, and to dwell a little
too long in proving what every man of sense knows and
admits. We hope we shall not offend Mr. Davison by these
remarks; and we have really no intention of doing so.
His views upon the Poor-Laws are, generally speaking,
very correct and philosophical; he writes like a gentleman,
a scholar, and a man capable of eloquence; and we hope
he will be a bishop. If his mitred productions are as
enlightened and liberal as this, we are sure he will confer
as much honour on the Bench as he receives from it. There
is a good deal, however, in Mr. Davison's book about the
"virtuous marriages of the poor." To have really the
charge of a family as a husband and a father, we are told,
—to have the privilege of laying out his life in their service.
is the poor man's boast,—his home is the school of his
sentiments," etc. etc. This is viewing human life through
a Claude Lorraine glass, and decorating it with colours
which do not belong to it. A ploughman marries a plough-
woman because she is plump; generally uses her ill; thinks
his children an incumbrance; very often flogs them; and,
for sentiment, has nothing more nearly approaching to it

than the ideas of broiled bacon and mashed potatoes. This is the state of the lower orders of mankind—deplorable, but true—and yet rendered much worse by the Poor-Laws.

The system of roundsmen is much complained of; as well as that by which the labour of paupers is paid, partly by the rate, partly by the master — and a long string of Sussex Justices send up a petition on the subject. But the evil we are suffering under is an excess of population. There are ten men applying for work, when five only are wanted; of course, such a redundance of labouring persons must depress the rate of their labour far beyond what is sufficient for the support of their families. And how is that deficiency to be made up but from the parish rates, unless it is meant suddenly and immediately to abolish the whole system of the Poor-Laws? To state that the rate of labour is lower than a man can live by, is merely to state that we *have had*, and *have* Poor-Laws—of which this practice is at length the inevitable consequence; and nothing could be more absurd than to attempt to prevent, by Acts of Parliament, the natural depreciation of an article which exists in much greater abundance than it is wanted. Nor can any thing be more unjust than the complaint, that roundsmen are paid by their employers at an inferior rate, and that the difference is made up by the parish funds. A roundsman is commonly an inferior description of labourer who cannot get regularly hired;—he comes upon his parish for labour commonly at those seasons when there is the least to do;—he is not a servant of the farmer's choice, and probably does not suit him;—he goes off to any other labour at a moment's warning, when he finds it more profitable;—and the farmer is forced to keep nearly the same number of labourers as if there were no roundsmen at all. Is it just, then, that a labourer, combining every species of imperfection, should receive the same wages as a chosen, regular, stationary person, who is always ready at hand, and whom the farmer has selected for his dexterity and character?

Those persons who do not, and cannot employ labourers, have no kind of right to complain of the third or fourth part of the wages being paid by the rates; for if the farmers did not agree among themselves to take such occasional

labourers, the whole of their support must be paid by the
rates, instead of one-third. The order is, that the pauper
shall be paid such a sum as will support himself and family;
and if this agreement to take roundsmen was not entered
into by the farmers, they must be paid, by the rates, the
whole of the amount of the order, for doing nothing. If
a circulating labourer, therefore, with three children, to
whom the Justices would order 12s. per week, receives 8s.
from his employer, and 4s. from the rates, the parish is
not burthened by this system to the amount of 4s., but
relieved to the amount of 8s. A parish manufacture,
conducted by overseers, is infinitely more burthensome to
the rates than any system of roundsmen. There are
undoubtedly a few instances to the contrary. Zeal and
talents will cure the original defects of any system; but to
suppose that average men can do what extraordinary men
have done, is the cause of many silly projects and extravagant blunders. Mr. Owen may give his whole heart
and soul to the improvement of one of his parochial parallel-
ograms; but who is to succeed to Mr. Owen's enthusiasm?
Before we have quite done with the subject of roundsmen,
we cannot help noticing a strange assertion of Mr. Nicol,
that the low rate of wages paid by the master is an injustice
to the pauper—that he is cheated, forsooth, out of 8s. or
10s. per week by this arrangement. Nothing, however,
can possibly be more absurd than such an allegation.
The whole country is open to him. Can he gain more anywhere else? If not, this is the market price of his labour;
and what right has he to complain? or how can he say he is
defrauded? A combination among farmers to lower the
price of labour would be impossible, if labour did not exist
in much greater quantities than was wanted. All such
things, whether labour, or worsted stockings, or broad
cloth, are, of course, always regulated by the proportion
between the supply and demand. Mr. Nicol cites an instance
of a parish in Suffolk, where the labourer receives sixpence
from the farmers, and the rest is made up by the rates;
and for this he reprobates the conduct of the farmers. But
why are they not to take labour as cheap as they can get it?
Why are they not to avail themselves of the market price
of this, as of any other commodity? The rates are a
separate consideration: let them supply what is wanting;

but the farmer is right to get his iron, his wood, and his labour, as cheap as he can. It would, we admit, come nearly to the same thing, if £100 were paid in wages rather than £25 in wages, and £75 by rate; but then, if the farmers were to agree to give wages above the market price, and sufficient for the support of the labourers without any rate, such an agreement could never be adhered to. The base and the crafty would make their labourers take less, and fling heavier rates upon those who adhered to the contract; whereas the agreement, founded upon giving as little as can be given, is pretty sure of being adhered to; and he who breaks it, lessens the rate to his neighbour, and does not increase it. The problem to be solved is this: If you have ten or twenty labourers who say they can get no work, and you cannot dispute this, and the Poor-Laws remain, what better scheme can be devised, than that the farmers of the parish should employ them in their turns? —and what more absurd than to suppose that farmers so employing them should give one farthing more than the market price for their labour?

It is contended, that the statute of Elizabeth, rightly interpreted, only compels the overseer to assist the sick and old, and not to find labour for strong and healthy men. This is true enough; and it would have been eminently useful to have attended to it a century past: but to find employment for all who apply, is now, by long use, become a practical part of the Poor-Laws, and will require the same care and dexterity for its abolition as any other part of that pernicious system. It would not be altogether prudent suddenly to tell a million of stout men, with spades and hoes in their hands, that the 43rd of Elizabeth had been misconstrued, and that no more employment would be found for them. It requires twenty or thirty years to state such truths to such numbers.

We think, then, that the diminution of the claims of settlement, and of the authority of Justices, coupled with the other subordinate improvements we have stated, will be the best steps for beginning the abolition of the Poor-Laws. When these have been taken, the description of persons entitled to relief may be narrowed by degrees. But let no man hope to get rid of these laws, even in the gentlest and wisest method, without a great deal of misery,

and some risk of tumult. If Mr. Bourne thinks only of
avoiding risk, he will do nothing. Some risk must be
incurred; but the secret is gradation; and the true reason
for abolishing these laws is, not that they make the rich
poor, but that they make the poor poorer.[1]

[1] The boldness of modern legislation has thrown all my caution
into the background. Was it wise to encounter such a risk? Is
the danger over? Can the vital parts of the Bill be maintained?

GAME LAWS [1]

ABOUT the time of the publication of this little pamphlet of Mr. Herbert, a Committee of the House of Commons published a Report on the Game Laws, containing a great deal of very curious information respecting the sale of game, an epitome of which we shall now lay before our readers. The country higglers who collect poultry, gather up the game from the depôts of the poachers, and transmit it in the same manner as poultry, and in the same packages, to the London poulterers, by whom it is distributed to the public; and this traffic is carried on (as far as game is concerned) even from the distance of Scotland. The same business is carried on by the porters of stage coaches; and a great deal of game is sold clandestinely by lords of manors, or by gamekeepers, without the knowledge of lords of manors; and principally, as the evidence states, from Norfolk and Suffolk, the great schools of steel traps and spring guns.[2] The supply of game, too, is proved to be quite as regular as the supply of poultry; the number of hares and partridges supplied rather exceeds that of pheasants; but any description of game may be had to any amount. Here is a part of the evidence.

Can you at any time procure any quantity of game? I have no doubt of it.—If you were to receive almost an unlimited order, could you execute it? Yes; I would supply the whole city of London, any fixed day once a week, all the year through, so that every individual inhabitant should have game for his table. Do you think you could procure a thousand pheasants? Yes; I would be bound to produce *ten thousand* a week.—You would be bound to provide every family in London with a dish of game? Yes; a partridge, or a pheasant, or a hare, or a grouse, or something or other.—How would you set about doing it? I should, of course, request the persons with whom I am in the habit of dealing, to use their influence to bring me what they could by a certain day; I should speak to the dealers and the mail-guards, and coachmen, to produce a quantity; and I should send to my own connections in one or

[1] See p. 295.   [2] See p. 295.

two manors where I have the privilege of selling for those gentlemen; and should send to Scotland to say, that every week the largest quantity they could produce was to be sent. Being but a petty salesman, I sell a very small quantity; but I have had about four thousand head direct from one man.— Can you state the quantity of game which has been sent to you during the year? No: I may say, perhaps, ten thousand head; mine is a limited trade; I speak comparatively to that of others; I only supply private families.—(*Report*, p. 20.)

Poachers who go out at night cannot, of course, like regular tradesmen, proportion the supply to the demand, but having once made a contract, they kill all they can; and hence it happens that the game market is sometimes very much overstocked, and great quantities of game either thrown away, or disposed of by Irish hawkers to the common people at very inferior prices.

Does it ever happen to you to be obliged to dispose of poultry at the same low prices you are obliged to dispose of game? It depends upon the weather; often when there is a considerable quantity on hand, and, owing to the weather, it will not keep till the following day, I am obliged to take any price that is offered; but we can always turn either poultry or game into some price or other; and if it was not for the Irish hawkers, hundreds and hundreds of heads of game would be spoiled and thrown away. It is out of the power of any person to conceive for one moment the quantity of game that is hawked in the streets. I have had opportunity more than other persons of knowing this; for I have sold, I may say, more game than any other person in the city; and we serve hawkers indiscriminately, persons who come and purchase probably six fowls or turkeys and geese, and they will buy heads of game with them.—(*Report*, p. 22.)

Live birds are sent up as well as dead; eggs as well as birds. The price of pheasants' eggs last year was 8s. per dozen; of partridges' eggs, 2s. The price of hares was from 3s. to 5s. 6d.; of partridges, from 1s. 6d. to 2s. 6d.; of pheasants, from 5s. to 5s. 6d. each, and sometimes as low as 1s. 6d.

What have you given for game this year? It is very low indeed; I am sick of it; I do not think I shall ever deal again. We have got game this season as low as half-a-crown a brace (birds), and pheasants as low as 7s. a brace. It is so plentiful, there has been no end to spoiling it this season. It is so plentiful, it is of no use. In war time it was worth having; then they fetched 7s. and 8s. a brace.—(*Report*, p. 33.)

All the poulterers, too, even the most respectable, state,
that it is absolutely necessary they should carry on this
illegal traffic in the present state of the game laws; because
their regular customers for poultry would infallibly leave
any poulterer's shop from whence they could not be supplied
with game.

I have no doubt that it is the general wish at present of the
trade not to deal in the article; but they are all, of course,
compelled from their connections. If they cannot get game
from one person they can from another.
Do you believe that poulterers are not to be found who
would take out licences, and would deal with those very persons
for the purposes of obtaining a greater profit than they would
have dealing as you would do? I think the poulterers in
general are a respectable set of men, and would not countenance
such a thing; they feel now that they are driven into a corner;
that there may be men who would countenance irregular
proceedings, I have no doubt.—Would it be their interest to
do so, considering the penalty? No, I think not. The
poulterers are perfectly well aware that they are committing
a breach of the law at present. Do you suppose that those
persons, respectable as they are, who are now committing
a breach of the law, would not equally commit that breach
if the law were altered? No, certainly not; at present it is so
connected with their business that they cannot help it.—You
said just now, that they were driven into a corner; what did
you mean by that? We are obliged to aid and abet those
men who commit those depredations, because of the constant
demand for game, from different customers whom we supply
with poultry.—Could you carry on your business as a poulterer,
if you refused to supply game? By no means; because some
of the first people in the land require it of me.—(*Report*, p. 15.)

When that worthy Errorist, Mr. Bankes, brought in his
bill of additional severities against poachers, there was no
man of sense and reflection who did not anticipate the
following consequences of the measure:—

Do you find that less game has been sold in consequence of
the bill rendering it penal to sell game? Upon my word, it
did not make the slightest difference in the world.—Not
immediately after it was made? No; I do not think it made
the slightest difference.—It did not make the slightest sensation? No; I never sold a bird less.—Was not there a
resolution of the poulterers not to sell game? I was secretary
to that committee.—What was the consequence of that
resolution? A great deal of ill blood in the trade. One

gentleman who just left the room did not come in to my ideas.
I never had a head of game in my house; all my neighbours
sold it; and as we had people on the watch who were ready
to watch it into the houses, it came to this, we were prepared
to bring our actions against certain individuals, after sitting,
perhaps, from three to four months, every week which we
did at the Crown and Anchor in the Strand; but we did not
proceed with our actions, to prevent ill blood in the trade.
We regularly met, and, as we conceived at the time, formed a
committee of the most respectable of the trade. I was secretary of that committee. The game was sold in the city, in
the vicinity of the Royal Exchange, cheaper than ever was
known, because the people at our end of the town were afraid.
I, as a point of honour, never had it in my house. I never
had a head of game in my house that season.—What was the
consequence? I lost my trade, and gave offence to gentlemen:
a nobleman's steward, or butler, or cook, treated it as con-
tumely; "Good God! what is the use of your running your
head against the wall?"—You were obliged to begin the
trade again? Yes, and sold more than ever.—(*Report*, p. 18.)

These consequences are confirmed by the evidence of
every person before the Committee.

All the evidence is very strong as to the fact, that dealing
in game is not discreditable; that there are a great number
of respectable persons, and, among the rest, the first
poulterers in London, who buy game knowing it to have
been illegally procured, but who would never dream of
purchasing any other article procured by dishonesty.

Are there not, to your knowledge, a great many people in
this town who deal in game, by buying or selling it, that would
not on any account buy or sell stolen property? Certainly;
there are many capital tradesmen, poulterers, who deal in
game, that would have nothing to do with stolen property;
and yet I do not think there is a poulterer's shop in London,
where they could not get game, if they wanted it.—Do you
think any discredit attaches to any man in this town for buying
or selling game? I think none at all; and I do not think that
the men to whom I have just referred would have any thing
to do with stolen goods.—Would it not, in the opinion of the
inhabitants of London, be considered a very different thing
dealing in stolen game or stolen poultry? Certainly.—The
one would be considered disgraceful, and the other not?
Certainly; they think nothing of dealing in game; and the
farmers in the country will not give information; they will
have a hare or two of the very men who work for them; and
they are afraid to give us information.—(*Report*, p. 31.)

The evidence of Daniel Bishop, one of the Bow Street officers, who has been a good deal employed in the apprehension of poachers, is curious and important, as it shows the enormous extent of the evil, and the ferocious spirit which the game laws engender in the common people. "The poachers," he says, "came sixteen miles. The whole of the village from which they were taken were poachers; the constable of the village, and the shoemaker, and other inhabitants of the village. I fetched one man twenty-two miles. There was the son of a respectable gardener; one of these was a sawyer, and another a baker, who kept a good shop there. If the village had been alarmed, we should have had some mischief; but we were all prepared with fire-arms. If poachers have a spite with the gamekeeper, that would induce them to go out in numbers to resist him. This party I speak of had something in their hats to distinguish them. They take a delight in setting-to with the gamekeepers; and talk it over afterwards how they served so and so. They fought with the butt-ends of their guns at Lord Howe's; they beat the gamekeepers shockingly."—Does it occur to you (Bishop is asked) to have had more applications, and to have detected more persons this season than in any former one? Yes; I think within four months there have been twenty-one transported that I have been at the taking of, and through one man turning evidence in each case, and without that they could not have been identified; the gamekeepers could not, or would not, identify them. The poachers go to the public-house and spend their money; if they have a good night's work, they will go and get drunk with the money. The gangs are connected together at different public-houses, just like a club at a public-house; they are all sworn together. If the keeper took one of them, they would go and attack him for so doing."

Mr. Stafford, chief clerk of Bow Street, says, "All the offences against the game laws which are of an atrocious description I think are generally reported to the public office in Bow Street, more especially in cases where the keepers have either been killed, or dangerously wounded, and the assistance of an officer from Bow Street is required. The applications have been much more numerous of late

years [1] than they were formerly. Some of them have
been cases of murder; but I do not think many have
amounted to murder. There are many instances in which
keepers have been very ill-treated—they have been
wounded, skulls have been fractured, and bones broken;
and they have been shot at. A man takes a hare, or a
pheasant, with a very different feeling from that with
which he would take a pigeon or a fowl out of a farmyard.
The number of persons that assemble together is more for
the purpose of protecting themselves against those that
may apprehend them, than from any idea that they are
actually committing depredation upon the property of
another person; they do not consider it as property. I
think there is a sense of morality and a distinction of crime
existing in the men's minds, although they are mistaken
about it. Men feel that if they go in a great body together,
to break into a house, or to rob a person, or to steal his
poultry, or his sheep, they are committing a crime against
that man's property; but I think with respect to the game,
they do not feel that they are doing any thing which is
wrong: but think they have committed no crime when
they have done the thing, and their only anxiety is to
escape detection." In addition, Mr. Stafford states that
he remembers not *one single conviction under Mr. Bankes's
Act against buying game*; and not one conviction for buying
or selling game within the last year has been made at
Bow Street.

The inferences from these facts are exactly as we predicted, and as every man of common sense must have
predicted—that to prevent the sale of game is absolutely
impossible. If game be plentiful, and cannot be obtained
at any lawful market, an illicit trade will be established,
which it is utterly impossible to prevent by any increased
severity of the laws. There never was a more striking
illustration of the necessity of attending to public opinion
in all penal enactments. Mr. Bankes (a perfect repre-

---

[1] It is only of late years that men have been transported for
shooting at night. There are instances of men who have been
transported at the Sessions for night poaching, who made no resistance at all when taken; but then their characters as old poachers
weighed against them—characters estimated probably by the very
lords of manors who had lost their game. This disgraceful law is
the occasion of all the murders committed for game.

N

sentative of all the ordinary notions about forcing mankind by pains and penalties) took the floor. To buy a
partridge (though still considered as inferior to murder)
was visited with the very heaviest infliction of the law;
and yet, though game is sold as openly in London as apples
and oranges, though three years have elapsed since this
legislative mistake, the officers of the police can hardly
recollect a single instance where the information has been
laid, or the penalty levied; and why? because every man's
feelings and every man's understanding tell him, that it is
a most absurd and ridiculous tyranny to prevent one man,
who has more game than he wants, from exchanging it
with another man, who has more money than he wants—
because magistrates will not (if they can avoid it) inflict
such absurd penalties—because even common informers
know enough of the honest indignation of mankind, and
are too well aware of the coldness of pump and pond, to
act under the bill of the Lycurgus of Corfe Castle.

The plan now proposed is, to undersell the poacher,
which may be successful or unsuccessful; but the threat
is, if you attempt this plan there will be no game—and if
there is no game, there will be no country gentlemen.
We deny every part of this enthymeme—the last proposition as well as the first. We really cannot believe that
all our rural mansions would be deserted, although no
game was to be found in their neighbourhood. Some
come into the country for health, some for quiet, for
agriculture, for economy, from attachment to family
estates, from love of retirement, from the necessity of
keeping up provincial interests, and from a vast variety
of causes. Partridges and pheasants, though they form
nine-tenths of human motives, still leave a small residue,
which may be classed under some other head. Neither are
a great proportion of those whom the love of shooting
brings into the country of the smallest value or importance
to the country. A Colonel of the Guards, the second son
just entered at Oxford, three diners-out from Piccadilly
—Major Rock, Lord John, Lord Charles, the Colonel of
the regiment quartered at the neighbouring town, two
Irish Peers, and a German Baron;—if all this honourable
company proceed with fustian jackets, dog-whistles, and
chemical inventions, to a solemn destruction of pheasants,

how is the country benefited, by their presence? or how would earth, air, or sea, be injured by their annihilation? There are certainly many valuable men brought into the country by a love of shooting, who, coming there for that purpose, are useful for many better purposes; but a vast multitude of shooters are of no more service to the country than the ramrod which condenses the charge, or the barrel which contains it. We do not deny that the annihilation of the game laws would thin the aristocratical population of the country; but it would not thin that population so much as is contended; and the loss of many of the persons so banished would be a good rather than a misfortune. At all events, we cannot at all comprehend the policy of alluring the better classes of society into the country, by the temptation of petty tyranny and injustice, or of monopoly in sports. How absurd it would be to offer to the higher orders the exclusive use of peaches, nectarines, and apricots, as the premium of rustication—to put vast quantities of men into prison as apricot eaters, apricot buyers, and apricot sellers—to appoint a regular day for beginning to eat, and another for leaving off—to have a lord of the manor for greengages — and to rage with a penalty of five pounds against the unqualified eater of the gage! And yet the privilege of shooting a set of wild poultry is stated to be the bonus for the residence of country gentlemen. As far as this immense advantage can be obtained without the sacrifice of justice and reason, well and good—but we would not oppress any order of society, or violate right and wrong, to obtain any population of squires, however dense. It is the grossest of all absurdities to say the present state of the law is absurd and unjust, but it must not be altered, because the alteration would drive gentlemen out of the country! If gentlemen cannot breathe fresh air without injustice, let them putrefy in Cranborne Alley. Make just laws, and let squires live and die where they please.

The evidence collected in the House of Commons respecting the Game Laws is so striking and so decisive against the gentlemen of the trigger, that their only resource is to represent it as not worthy of belief. But why not worthy of belief? It is not stated what part of it is incredible. Is it the plenty of game in London for sale? the infrequency of convictions? the occasional but frequent excess of supply above demand in an article supplied by stealing; or its destruction when the sale is not without risk, and the price extremely low? or the readiness of grandees to turn the excess of their game into fish or poultry? All these circumstances appear to us so natural and so likely, that we should, without any evidence, have had little doubt of their existence. There are a few absurdities in the evidence of one of the poulterers; but, with this exception, we see no reason whatever for impugning the credibility and exactness of the mass of testimony prepared by the Committee.

It is utterly impossible to teach the common people to respect property in animals bred the possessor knows not where—which he cannot recognise by any mark, which may leave him the next moment, which are kept, not for his profit, but for his amusement. Opinion never will be in favour of such property: if the *animus furandi* exists, the propensity will be gratified by poaching. It is in vain to increase the severity of the protecting laws. They make the case weaker instead of stronger; and are more resisted and worse executed, exactly in proportion as they are contrary to public opinion:—the case of the game laws is a memorable lesson upon the philosophy of legislation. If a certain degree of punishment does not cure the offence, it is supposed by the Bankes School, that there is nothing to be done but to multiply this punishment by two, and then again and again, till the object is accomplished. The efficient maximum of punishment, however, is not what the Legislature chooses to enact, *but what the great mass of mankind think the maximum ought to be.* The moment the punishment passes this Rubicon, it becomes less and less, instead of greater and greater. Juries and Magistrates will not commit—informers [1] are afraid of public indig-

---

[1] There is a remarkable instance of this in the new Turnpike Act. The penalty for taking more than the legal number of outside passengers is ten pounds per head, if the coachman is in part or wholly the owner. This will rarely be levied; because it is too much. A penalty of £100 would produce perfect impunity. The maximum of practical severity would have been about five pounds. Any magistrate would cheerfully levy this sum; while doubling it will produce reluctance in the Judge, resistance in the culprit, and unwillingness in the informer.

nation—poachers will not submit to be sent to Botany Bay without a battle—blood is shed for pheasants—the public attention is called to this preposterous state of the law—and even ministers (whom nothing pesters so much as the interests of humanity) are at last compelled to come forward and do what is right. Apply this to the game laws. It was before penal to sell game: within these few years it has been made penal to buy it. From the scandalous cruelty of the law, night poachers are transported for seven years. And yet, never was so much game sold, or such a spirit of ferocious resistance excited to the laws. One-fourth of all the commitments in Great Britain are for offences against the game laws. There is a general feeling that some alteration *must* take place—a feeling not only among Reviewers, who never see nor eat game, but among the double-barrelled, shot-belted members of the House of Commons, who are either alarmed or disgusted by the vice and misery which their cruel laws and childish passion for amusement are spreading among the lower orders of mankind.

It is said, "In spite of all the game sold, there is game enough left; let the laws therefore remain as they are"; and so it was said formerly, "There is sugar enough; let the slave trade remain as it is." But at what expense of human happiness is this quantity of game or of sugar, and this state of poacher law and slave law, to remain! The first object of a good government is not that rich men should have their pleasures in perfection, but that all orders of men should be good and happy; and if crowded covies and chuckling cock-pheasants are only to be procured by encouraging the common people in vice, and leading them into cruel and disproportionate punishment, it is the duty of the government to restrain the cruelties which the country members, in reward for their assiduous loyalty, have been allowed to introduce into the game laws.

The plan of the new bill (long since anticipated, in all its provisions, by the acute author of the pamphlet before us), is, that the public at large should be supplied by persons licensed by magistrates, and that all qualified persons should be permitted to sell their game to these licensed distributors; and there seems a fair chance that such a plan would succeed. The questions are, Would sufficient game come

into the hands of the licensed salesman? Would the
licensed salesman confine himself to the purchase of game
from qualified persons? Would buyers of game purchase
elsewhere than from the licensed salesman? Would the
poacher be undersold by the honest dealer? Would game
remain in the same plenty as before? It is understood
that the game laws are to remain as they are; with this
only difference, that the qualified man can sell to the
licensed man, and the licentiate to the public.

It seems probable to us, that vast quantities of game
would, after a little time, find their way into the hands of
licensed poulterers. Great people are very often half eaten
up by their establishments. The quantity of game killed
in a large shooting party is very great: to eat it is impossible,
and to dispose of it in presents very troublesome. The
preservation of game is very expensive; and, when it could
be bought, it would be no more a compliment to send it
as a present than it would be to send geese and fowls. If
game were sold, very large shooting establishments might
be made to pay their own expenses. The shame is made
by the law; there is a disgrace in being detected and fined.
If that barrier were removed, superfluous partridges would
go to the poulterers as readily as superfluous venison does
to the venison butcher—or as a gentleman sells the corn
and mutton off his farm which he cannot consume. For
these reasons, we do not doubt that the shops of licensed
poulterers would be full of game in the season; and this
part of the argument, we think, the arch-enemy, Sir John
Shelley, himself would concede to us.

The next question is, From whence they would procure
it? A licence for selling game, granted by country magistrates, would, from their jealousy upon these subjects, be
granted only to persons of some respectability and property.
The purchase of game from unqualified persons would, of
course, be guarded against by very heavy penalties, both
personal and pecuniary; and these penalties would be
inflicted, because opinion would go with them. "Here
is a respectable tradesman," it would be said, "who might
have bought as much game as he pleased in a lawful manner,
but who, in order to increase his profits by buying it a
little cheaper, has encouraged a poacher to steal it."
Public opinion, therefore, would certainly be in favour of a

very strong punishment; and a licensed vendor of game, who exposed himself to these risks, would expose himself to the loss of liberty, property, character, and licence. The persons interested to put a stop to such a practice, would not be the paid agents of Government, as in cases of smuggling; but all the gentlemen of the country, the customers of the tradesman for fish, poultry, or whatever else he dealt in, would have an interest in putting down the practice. In all probability, the practice would become disreputable, like the purchase of stolen poultry; and this would be a stronger barrier than the strongest laws. There would, of course, be some exceptions to this statement. A few shabby people would, for the chance of gaining sixpence, incur the risk of ruin and disgrace; but it is probable that the general practice would be otherwise.

For the same reasons, the consumers of game would rather give a little more for it to a licensed poulterer, than expose themselves to severe penalties by purchasing from poachers. The great mass of London consumers are supplied now, not from shabby people, in whom they can have no confidence—not from hawkers and porters, but from respectable tradesmen, in whose probity they have the most perfect confidence. Men will brave the law for pheasants, but not for sixpence or a shilling; and the law itself is much more difficult to be braved, when it allows pheasants to be bought at some price, than when it endeavours to render them utterly inaccessible to wealth. All the licensed salesmen, too, would have a direct interest in stopping the contraband trade of game. They would lose no character in doing so; their informations would be reasonable and respectable.

If all this be true, the poacher would have to compete with a great mass of game fairly and honestly poured into the market. He would be selling with a rope about his neck, to a person who bought with a rope about his neck; his description of customers would be much the same as the customers for stolen poultry, and his profits would be very materially abridged. At present, the poacher is in the same situation as the smuggler would be, if rum and brandy could not be purchased of any fair trader. The great check to the profits of the smuggler are, that, if you want his commodities, and will pay a higher price, you may have them elsewhere without the risk of disgrace. But forbid the purchase of these luxuries at any price. Shut up the shop of the brandy merchant, and you render the trade of the smuggler of incalculable value. The object of the intended bill is, to raise up precisely the same competition to the trade of the poacher, by giving the public an opportunity of buying lawfully and honestly the tempting articles in which he now deals exclusively. Such an improvement would not, perhaps, altogether annihilate his trade; but it would, in all probability, act as a very material check upon it.

The predominant argument against all this is, that the existing prohibition against buying game, though partially violated, does deter many persons from coming into the market; that if this prohibition were removed, the demand for game would be increased, the legal supply would be insufficient, and the residue would, and must be, supplied by the poacher, whose trade would, for these reasons, be as lucrative and flourishing as before. But it is only a few years since the purchase of game has been made illegal; and the market does not appear to have been at all narrowed by the prohibition; not one head of game the less has been sold by the poulterers; and scarcely one single conviction has taken place under that law. How, then, would the removal of the prohibition, and the alteration of the law, extend the market, and increase the demand, when the enactment of the prohibition has had no effect in narrowing it? But if the demand increases, why not the legal supply also? Game is increased upon an estate by feeding them in winter, by making some abatement to the tenants for guarding against depredations, by a large apparatus of gamekeepers and spies—in short by expense. But if this pleasure of shooting, so natural to country gentlemen, be made to pay its own expenses, by sending superfluous game to market, more men, it is reasonable to suppose, will thus preserve and augment their game. The love of pleasure and amusement will produce in the owners of game that desire to multiply game, which the love of gain does in the farmer to multiply poultry. Many gentlemen of small fortune will remember, that they cannot enjoy to any extent this pleasure without this resource; that the legal sale of poultry will discountenance poaching; and they will open an account with the poulterer, not to get richer, but to enjoy a great pleasure without an expense, in which, upon other terms, they could not honourably and conscientiously indulge. If country gentlemen of moderate fortune will do this (and we think after a little time they will do it), game may be multiplied and legally supplied to any extent. Another keeper, and another bean-stack, will produce their proportional supply of pheasants. The only reason why the great lord has more game per acre than the little squire is, that he spends more money per acre to preserve it.

For these reasons, we think the experiment of legalising the sale of game ought to be tried. The game laws have been carried to a pitch of oppression which is a disgrace to the country. The prisons are half filled with peasants shut up for the irregular slaughter of rabbits and birds —a sufficient reason for killing a weasel, but not for imprisoning a man. Something should be done; it is disgraceful to a Government to stand by, and see such enormous evils without interference. It is true, they are not connected with the struggles of party: but still, the happiness of the common people, whatever gentlemen may say, ought every now and then to be considered.

CHARACTERS OF FOX[1]

THIS singular work consists of a collection of all the panegyrics passed upon Mr. Fox, after his decease, in periodical publications, speeches, sermons, or elsewhere,—in a panegyric upon Mr. Fox, by Philopatris[2] himself,—and in a volume of notes by the said Philopatris upon the said panegyric.

Of the panegyrics, that by Sir James Mackintosh appears to us to be by far the best. It is remarkable for good sense, acting upon a perfect knowledge of his subject, for simplicity, and for feeling. Amid the languid or turgid efforts of mediocrity, it is delightful to notice the skill, attention, and resources of a superior man,—of a man, too, who seems to feel what he writes,—who does not aim at conveying his meaning in rhetorical and ornamented phrases, but who uses plain words to express strong sensations. We cannot help wishing, indeed, that Sir James Mackintosh had been more diffuse upon the political character of Mr. Fox, the great feature of whose life was the long and unwearied opposition which he made to the low cunning, the profligate extravagance, the sycophant mediocrity, and the stupid obstinacy of the English Court.

To estimate the merit, and the difficulty, of this opposition, we must remember the enormous influence which the Crown, through the medium of its patronage, exercises in the remotest corners of the kingdom,—the number of subjects whom it pays,—the much greater number whom it keeps in a state of expectation,—and the ferocious turpitude of those mercenaries whose present profits and future hopes are threatened by honest, and exposed by eloquent men. It is the easiest of all things, too, in this country, to make Englishmen believe that those who oppose the Government wish to ruin the country. The English are a very busy people; and, with all the faults of their governors, they are still a very happy people. They have, as they ought to have, a perfect confidence in the

[1] See p. 295.   [2] Dr. Samuel Parr.

administration of justice. The rights which the different classes of mankind exercise the one over the other are arranged upon equitable principles. Life, liberty, and property are protected from the violence and caprice of power. The visible and immediate stake, therefore, for which English politicians play, is not large enough to attract the notice of the people, and to call them off from their daily occupations, to investigate thoroughly the characters and motives of men engaged in the business of legislation. The people can only understand, and attend to, the last results of a long series of measures. They are impatient of the details which lead to these results; and it is the easiest of all things to make them believe that those who insist upon such details are actuated only by factious motives. We are all now groaning under the weight of taxes: but how often was Mr. Fox followed by the curses of his country for protesting against the two wars which have loaded us with these taxes?—the one of which wars has made America independent, and the other rendered France omnipotent. The case is the same with all the branches of public liberty. If the broad and palpable question were, whether every book which issues from the press should be subjected to the licence of a general censor, it would be impossible to blacken the character of any man who, so called upon, defended the liberty of publishing opinions. But, when the Attorney-General for the time being ingratiates himself with the Court, by nibbling at this valuable privilege of the people, it is very easy to treat hostility to his measures as a minute and frivolous opposition to the Government, and to persuade the mass of mankind that it is so. In fact, when a nation has become free, it is extremely difficult to persuade them that their freedom is only to be preserved by perpetual and minute jealousy. They do not observe that there is a constant, perhaps an unconscious, effort on the part of their governors to diminish, and so ultimately to destroy, that freedom. They stupidly imagine that what is, will always be; and, contented with the good they have already gained, are easily persuaded to suspect and vilify those friends— the object of whose life it is to preserve that good, and to increase it.

It was the lot of Mr. Fox to fight this battle for the greater

part of his life; in the course of which time he never was
seduced, by the love of power, wealth, nor popularity, to
sacrifice the happiness of the many to the interests of the
few. He rightly thought, that kings and all public officers
were instituted only for the good of those over whom they
preside; and he acted as if this conviction was always
present to his mind; disdaining and withstanding that
idolatrous tendency of mankind, by which they so often
not only suffer, but invite, ruin from that power which
they themselves have wisely created for their own happiness. He loved, too, the happiness of his countrymen
more than their favour; and while others were exhausting
the resources by flattering the ignorant prejudices and
foolish passions of the country, Mr. Fox was content to
be odious to the people, so long as he could be useful also.
It will be long before we witness again such pertinacious
opposition to the alarming power of the Crown, and to the
follies of our public measures, the necessary consequence
of that power. That such opposition should ever be united
again with such extraordinary talents, it is, perhaps, in
vain to hope.

One little exception to the eulogium of Sir James Mackintosh upon Mr. Fox, we cannot help making. We are
no admirers of Mr. Fox's poetry. His *Vers de Société*
appears to us flat and insipid. To write verses was the
only thing which Mr. Fox ever attempted to do without
doing it well. In that single instance he seems to have
mistaken his talent.

Immediately after the collection of panegyrics which
these volumes contain, follows the eulogium of Mr. Fox
by Philopatris himself; and then a volume of notes upon a
variety of topics which this eulogium has suggested.

It is impossible to read this singular book without being
everywhere struck with the lofty and honourable feelings,
the enlightened benevolence, and sterling honesty with
which it abounds. Its author is everywhere the circum-
spect friend of those moral and religious principles upon
which the happiness of society rests. Though he is never
timid, nor prejudiced, nor bigoted, his piety, not prudish
and full of antiquated and affected tricks, presents itself
with an earnest aspect, and in a manly form; obedient to
reason, prone to investigation, and dedicated to honest

purposes. The writer, a clergyman, speaks of himself as a very independent man, who has always expressed his opinions without any fear of consequences, or any hope of bettering his condition. We sincerely believe he speaks the truth; and revere him for the life which he has led. Political independence—discouraged enough in these times among all classes of men—is sure, in the timid profession of the church, to doom a man to eternal poverty and obscurity.

There are occasionally, in Philopatris, a great vigour of style, and felicity of expression. His display of classical learning is quite unrivalled—his reading various and good; and we may observe, at intervals, a talent for wit, of which he might have availed himself to excellent purpose, had it been compatible with the dignified style in which he generally conveys his sentiments. With all these excellent qualities of head and heart, we have seldom met with a writer more full of faults than Philopatris. There is an event recorded in the Bible, which men who write books should keep constantly in their remembrance. It is there set forth, that, many centuries ago, the earth was covered with a great flood, by which the whole of the human race, with the exception of one family, were destroyed. It appears, also, that from thence a great alteration was made in the longevity of mankind, who, from a range of seven or eight hundred years, which they enjoyed before the flood, were confined to their present period of seventy or eighty years. This epoch in the history of man gave birth to the two-fold division of the antediluvian and the postdiluvian style of writing; the latter of which naturally contracted itself into those inferior limits which were better accommodated to the abridged duration of human life and literary labour. Now, to forget this event,—to write without the fear of the deluge before his eyes, and to handle a subject as if mankind could lounge over a pamphlet for ten years, as before their submersion,—is to be guilty of the most grievous error into which a writer can possibly fall. The author of this book should call in the aid of some brilliant pencil, and cause the distressing scenes of the deluge to be portrayed in the most lively colours for his use. He should gaze at Noah, and be brief. The ark should constantly remind him of the little time there is left for reading; and he should learn, as they did in the ark, to crowd a great deal of matter into a very little compass.

Philopatris must not only condense what he says in a narrower compass, but he must say it in a more natural manner. Some persons can neither stir hand nor foot without making it clear that they are thinking of themselves, and laying little traps for approbation. In the course of two long volumes, the Patriot of Warwick is perpetually studying modes and postures:—the subject is the second consideration, and the mode of expression the first. Indeed, whole pages together seem to be mere exercises upon the English language, to evince the copiousness of our synonymes, and to show the various methods in which the parts of speech can be marshalled and arrayed. This, which would be tiresome in the ephemeral productions of a newspaper, is intolerable in two closely printed volumes.

Again: strange as it may appear to this author to say so, he must not fall into the frequent mistake of rural politicians, by supposing that the understandings of all Europe are occupied with him and his opinions. His ludicrous self-importance is perpetually destroying the effect of virtuous feeling and just observation, leaving his readers with a disposition to laugh, where they might otherwise learn and admire.

I have been asked, why, after pointing out by name the persons who seemed to me most qualified for reforming our Penal Code, I declined mentioning such ecclesiastics as might with propriety be employed in preparing for the use of the churches a grave and impressive discourse on the authority of human laws; and as other men may ask the same question which my friend did, I have determined, after some deliberation, to insert the substance of my answer in this place.

If the public service of our church should ever be directly employed in giving effect to the sanctions of our Penal Code, the office of drawing up such a discourse as I have ventured to recommend would, I suppose, be assigned to more than one person. My ecclesiastical superiors will, I am sure, make a wise choice. But they will hardly condemn me for saying, that the best sense expressed in the best language may be expected from the Bishops of Llandaff, Lincoln, St. David's, Cloyne and Norwich, the Dean of Christchurch, and the President of Magdalen College, Oxford. I mean not to throw the slightest reproach upon other dignitaries whom I have not mentioned. But I should imagine that few of my enlightened contemporaries hold an opinion different from my own upon the masculine understanding of a Watson, the sound judgment of a Tomline, the extensive erudition of a Burgess, the exquisite taste and good nature of a Bennet, the calm and enlightened benevolence of a Bathurst, the various and valuable attainments of a Cyril Jackson, or the learning, wisdom, integrity and piety of a Martin Routh.—(pp. 524, 525.)

In the name of common modesty, what could it have signified whether this author had given a list of ecclesiastics whom he thought qualified to preach about human laws? what is his opinion worth? who called for it? who wanted it? how many millions will be influenced by it? and who, oh gracious Heaven! who are a Burgess,— a Tomline,—a Bennet,—a Cyril Jackson,—a Martin Routh?—A *Tom,*—a *Jack,*—a Harry,—a Peter?—All good men enough in their generation, doubtless they are. But what have they done for the broad a? what has anyone of them perpetrated which will make him be remembered out of the sphere of his private virtues six months after his decease? Surely, scholars and gentlemen can drink tea with each other, and eat bread and butter, without all this laudatory cackling!

Philopatris has employed a great deal of time upon the subject of capital punishments, and has evinced a great deal of very laudable tenderness and humanity in discussing it. We are scarcely, however, converts to that system which would totally abolish the punishment of death. That it is much too frequently inflicted in this country, we readily admit; but we suspect it will be always necessary to reserve it for the most pernicious crimes. Death is the most terrible punishment to the common people, and therefore the most preventive. It does not perpetually outrage the feelings of those who are innocent, and likely to remain innocent, as would be the case from the spectacle of convicts working in the high roads and public places. Death is the most irrevocable punishment, which is in some sense a good; for, however necessary it might be to inflict labour and imprisonment for life, it would never be done. Kings and Legislatures would take pity after a great lapse of years; the punishment would be remitted, and its preventive efficacy, therefore, destroyed.

We agree with Philopatris, that the executions should be more solemn; but still the English are not of a very dramatic turn, and the thing must not be got up too finely. Philopatris, and Mr. Jeremy Bentham before him, lay a vast stress upon the promulgation of laws, and treat the inattention of the English Government to this point as a serious evil. It may be so—but we do not happen to remember any man punished for an offence which he did not know to be an offence; though he might not know exactly the degree in which it was punishable. Who are to read the laws to the people? who would listen to them if they were read? who would comprehend them if they listened? In a science like law there must be technical phrases, known only to professional men: business could not be carried on without them: and of what avail would it be to repeat such phrases to the people? Again, what laws are to be repeated, and in what places? Is a law respecting the number of threads on the shuttle of a Spital-fields weaver to be read to the corn-growers of the Isle of Thanet? If not, who is to make the selection? If the law cannot be comprehended by listening to the *viva voce* repetition, is the reader to explain it, and are there to be law lectures all over the kingdom? The fact is, that the evil does not exist. Those who are likely to commit the offence soon scent out the newly-devised punishments, and have been long thoroughly acquainted with the old ones. Of the nice applications of the law they are indeed ignorant; but they purchase the requisite skill of some man whose business it is to acquire it; and so they get into less mischief by trusting to others than they would do if they pretended to inform themselves. The people, it is true, are ignorant of the laws; but they are ignorant only of the laws which do not concern them. A poacher knows nothing of the penalties to which he exposes himself by stealing ten thousand pounds from the public. Commissioners of public boards are unacquainted with all the decretals of our ancestors respecting the wiring of hares; but the one pockets his extra percentage, and the other his leveret, with a perfect knowledge of the laws—the particular laws which it is his business to elude. Philopatris will excuse us for differing from him upon a subject where he seems to entertain such strong opinions. We have a real respect for all his opinions:—no man could form them who had not a good heart and a sound understanding. If we have been severe upon his style of writing, it is because we know his weight in the commonwealth: and we wish that the many young persons who justly admire and imitate him should be turned to the difficult task of imitating his many excellences, rather than the useless and easy one of copying his few defects.

o

CHIMNEY SWEEPERS [1]

An excellent and well-arranged dinner is a most pleasing occurrence, and a great triumph of civilised life. It is not only the descending morsel, and the enveloping sauce —but the rank, wealth, wit, and beauty which surround the meats—the learned management of light and heat— the silent and rapid services of the attendants—the smiling and sedulous host, proffering gusts and relishes—the exotic bottles—the embossed plate—the pleasant remarks —the handsome dresses—the cunning artifices in fruit and farina! The hour of dinner, in short, includes every thing of sensual and intellectual gratification which a great nation glories in producing.

In the midst of all this, who knows that the kitchen chimney caught fire half an hour before dinner!—and that a poor little wretch of six or seven years old, was sent up in the midst of the flames to put it out? We could not, previous to reading this evidence, have formed a conception of the miseries of these poor wretches, or that there should exist, in a civilised country, a class of human beings destined to such extreme and varied distress. We will give a short epitome of what is developed in the evidence before the two Houses of Parliament.

Boys are made chimney sweepers at the early age of five or six.

Little boys for small flues, is a common phrase in the cards left at the door by itinerant chimney sweepers. Flues made to ovens and coppers are often less than nine inches square; and it may be easily conceived, how slender the frame of that human body must be, which can force itself through such an aperture.

What is the age of the youngest boys who have been employed in this trade, to your knowledge? About five years of age: I know one now between five and six years old; it is the man's own son in the Strand: now there is another at Somers Town, I think, said he was between four and five, or about

[1] See p. 295.

five; Jack Hall, a little lad, takes him about.—Did you ever know any female children employed? Yes, I know one now. About two years ago there was a woman told me she had climbed scores of times, and there is one at Paddington now whose father taught her to climb; but I have often heard talk of them when I was apprentice, in different places.—What is the smallest-sized flue you have ever met with in the course of your experience? About eight inches by nine; these they are always obliged to climb in this posture (*describing it*), keeping the arms up straight; if they slip their arms down, they get jammed in; unless they get their arms close over their head they cannot climb.—(*Lords' Minutes*, No. 1, p. 8.)

The following is a specimen of the manner in which they are taught this art of climbing chimneys.

Do you remember being taught to climb chimneys? Yes.— What did you feel upon the first attempt to climb a chimney? The first chimney I went up, they told me there was some plum-pudding and money up at the top of it, and that is the way they enticed me up; and when I got up, I would not let the other boy get from under me to get at it, I thought he would get it; I could not get up, and shoved the pot and half the chimney down into the yard.—Did you experience any inconvenience to your knees, or your elbows? Yes, the skin was off my knees and elbows too, in climbing up the new chimneys they forced me up.—How did they force you up? When I got up, I cried out about my sore knees.—Were you beat or compelled to go up by any violent means? Yes, when I went to a narrow chimney, if I could not do it, I durst not go home; when I used to come down, my master would well beat me with the brush; and not only my master, but when we used to go with the journeymen, if we could not do it, they used to hit us three or four times with the brush.—(*Lords' Minutes*, No. 1, p. 5.)

In practising the art of climbing, they are often crippled.

You talked of the pargetting of chimneys; are many chimneys pargetted? There used to be more than are now; we used to have to go and sit all a-twist to parge them, according to the floors, to keep the smoke from coming out; then I could not straighten my legs; and that is the reason that many are cripples,—from parging and stopping the holes.—(*Lords' Minutes*, No. 1, p. 17.)

They are often stuck fast in a chimney, and, after remaining there many hours, are cut out.

Have you known, in the course of your practice, boys stick in chimneys at all? Yes, frequently.—Did you ever know an instance of a boy being suffocated to death? No; I do not recollect any one at present, but I have assisted in taking boys out when they have been nearly exhausted.—Did you ever know an instance of its being necessary to break open a chimney to take the boy out? O yes.—*Frequently? Monthly I might say ;* it is done with a cloak, if possible, that it should not be discovered: a master in general wishes it not to be known, and therefore speaks to the people belonging to the house not to mention it, for it was merely the boy's neglect; they often say it was the boy's neglect.—Why do they say that? The boy's climbing shirt is often very bad; the boy coming down, if the chimney be very narrow, and numbers of them are only nine inches, gets his shirt rumpled underneath him, and he has no power after he is fixed in that way (*with his hand up*).—Does a boy frequently stick in the chimney? Yes; I have known more instances of that the last twelve-month than before.—Do you ever have to break open in the inside of a room? Yes, I have helped to break through into a kitchen chimney in a dining room.—(*Lords' Minutes*, p. 34.)

To the same effect is the evidence of John Daniels (*Minutes*, p. 100), and of James Ludford (*Lords' Minutes*, p. 147).

You have swept the Penitentiary? I have.—Did you ever know a boy stick in any of the chimneys there? Yes, I have. —Was it one of your boys? It was.—Was there one or two that stuck? Two of them.—How long did they stick there? Two hours.—How were they got out? They were cut out.— Was there any danger while they were in that situation? It was the core from the pargetting of the chimney, and the rubbish that the labourers had thrown down, that stopped them, and when they got it aside them, they could not pass. —They both stuck together? Yes.—(*Lords' Minutes*, p. 147.)

One more instance we shall give, from the Evidence before the Commons.

Have you heard of any accidents that have recently happened to climbing boys in the small flues? Yes; I have *often* met with accidents myself when I was a boy; there was lately one in Mary-le-bone where the boy *lost his life* in a flue, a boy of the name of Tinsey (his father was of the same trade); that boy I think was about eleven or twelve years old.—Was there a coroner's inquest sat on the body of that boy you mentioned? Yes, there was; he was an apprentice of a man of the name of Gay. How many accidents do you recollect, which were attended with loss of life to the climbing boys? I have heard talk of many more than I know of; I never knew of more than three since I have been at the trade, but I have heard talk of many more.—Of twenty or thirty? I cannot say; I have been near losing my own life several times.— (*Commons' Report*, p. 53.)

We come now to burning little chimney sweepers. A large party are invited to dinner—a great display is to be made;—and about an hour before dinner, there is an alarm that the kitchen chimney is on fire! It is impossible to put off the distinguished personages who are expected. It gets very late for the soup and fish, the cook is frantic —all eyes are turned upon the sable consolation of the master chimney sweeper—and up into the midst of the burning chimney is sent one of the miserable little infants of the brush! There is a positive prohibition of this practice, and an enactment of penalties in one of the Acts of Parliament which respect chimney sweepers. But what matter Acts of Parliament, when the pleasures of genteel people are concerned? Or what is a toasted child, compared to the agonies of the mistress of the house with a deranged dinner?

Did you ever know a boy get burnt up a chimney? Yes. —Is that usual? Yes, I have been burnt myself, and have got the scars on my legs; a year ago I was up a chimney in Liquor Pond Street; I have been up *more than forty chimneys where I have been burnt.*—Did your master or the journeymen ever direct you to go up a chimney that is on fire? Yes, it is a general case.—Do they compel you to go up a chimney that is on fire? Oh yes, it was the general practice for two of us to stop at home on Sunday to be ready in case of a chimney being a-fire.—You say it is general to compel the boys to go up chimneys on fire? Yes, boys get very ill treated if they do not go up.—(*Lords' Minutes*, p. 34.)

Were you ever forced up a chimney on fire? Yes, I was forced up one once, and, because I could not do it, I was taken home and well hided with a brush by the journeyman.—Have you frequently been burnt in ascending chimneys on fire? Three times.—Are such hardships as you have described common in the trade with other boys? Yes, they are.— (Ibid., p. 100.)

What is the price for sending a boy up a chimney badly on fire? The price allowed is five shillings, but most of them charge half a guinea.—Is any part of that given to the boy? No, but very often the boy gets half a crown; and then the journeyman has half, and his mistress takes the other part to take care of against Sunday.—Have you never seen water thrown down from the top of a chimney when it is on fire?

Yes.—Is not that generally done? Yes; I have seen that done twenty times, and the boy in the chimney; at the time when the boy has hallooed out, "It is so hot I cannot go any further"; and then the expression is, with an oath, "Stop, and I will heave a pail of water down."—(Ibid., p. 39.)

Chimney sweepers are subject to a peculiar sort of cancer, which often brings them to a premature death.

He appeared perfectly willing to try the machines everywhere? I must say the man appeared perfectly willing; he had a fear that he and his family would be ruined by them; but I must say of him, that he is very different from other sweeps I have seen; he attends very much to his own business; he was as black as any boy he had got, and unfortunately in the course of conversation he told me he had got a cancer; he was a fine healthy strong-looking man; he told me he dreaded having an operation performed, but his father died of the same complaint, and that his father was sweeper to King George the Second.—(*Lords' Minutes*, p. 84.)

What is the nature of the particular disease? The diseases that we particularly noticed, to which they were subject, were of a cancerous description.—In what part? The scrotum in particular, etc.—Did you ever hear of cases of that description that were fatal? No, I do not think them as being altogether fatal, unless they will not submit to the operation; they have such a dread of the operation that they will not submit to it, and if they do not let it be perfectly removed, they will be liable to the return of it.—To what cause do you attribute that disease? I think it begins from a want of care; the scrotum being in so many folds or crevices, the soot lodges in them and creates an itching, and I conceive that, by scratching it and tearing it, the soot gets in and creates the irritability; which disease we know by the name of the chimney sweeper's cancer, and is always lectured upon separately as a distinct disease. —Then the Committee understands that the physicians who are entrusted with the care and management of those hospitals think that disease of such common occurrence, that it is necessary to make it a part of surgical education? Most assuredly; I remember Mr. Cline and Mr. Cooper were particular on that subject.—Without an operation there is no cure? I conceive not; I conceive without the operation it is death; for cancers are of that nature that unless you extirpate them entirely, they will never be cured.—(*Commons' Report*, pp. 60, 61.)

In addition to the life they lead as chimney sweepers, is superadded the occupation of nightmen.

(*By a Lord.*) Is it generally the custom that many masters are likewise nightmen? Yes; I forgot that circumstance, which is very grievous; I have been tied round the middle and let down several privies, for the purpose of fetching watches and such things; it is generally made the practice to take the smallest boy, to let him through the hole without taking up the seat, and to paddle about there until he finds it; they do not take a big boy, because it disturbs the seat.—(*Lords' Minutes*, p. 38.)

The bed of these poor little wretches is often the soot they have swept in the day.

How are the boys generally lodged; where do they sleep at night? Some masters may be better than others, but I know I have slept on the soot that was gathered in the day myself.— Where do boys generally sleep? Never on a bed; I never slept on a bed myself while I was apprentice.—Do they sleep in cellars? Yes, very often; I have slept in the cellar myself on the sacks I took out.—What had you to cover you? The same.—Had you any pillow? No further than my breeches and jacket under my head.—How were you clothed? When I was apprentice we had a pair of leather breeches and a small flannel jacket.—Any shoes and stockings? Oh dear no; no stockings.—Had you any other clothes for Sunday? Sometimes we had an old bit of a jacket, that we might wash out ourselves, and a shirt.—(*Lords' Minutes*, p. 40.)

Girls are occasionally employed as chimney sweepers.

Another circumstance, which has not been mentioned to the Committee, is, that there are several little girls employed; there are two of the name of Morgan at Windsor, daughters of the chimney sweeper who is employed to sweep the chimneys of the Castle; another instance at Uxbridge, and at Brighton, and at Whitechapel (which was some years ago), and at Hadley near Barnet, and Witham in Essex, and elsewhere. —(*Commons' Report*, p. 71.)

Another peculiar danger to which chimney sweepers are exposed, is the rottenness of the pots at the top of chimneys; —for they must ascend to the very summit, and show their brushes above them, or there is no proof that the work is properly completed. These chimney-pots, from their exposed situation, are very subject to decay; and when the poor little wretch has worked his way up to the top, pot and boy give way together, and are both shivered to atoms. There are many instances of this in the evidence before both Houses. When they outgrow the power of going up a chimney, they are fit for nothing else. The miseries they have suffered lead to nothing. They are not only enormous, but unprofitable; having suffered, in what is called the happiest part of life, every misery which a human being can suffer, they are then cast out to rob and steal, and given up to the law.

Not the least of their miseries, while their trial endures, is their exposure to cold. It will easily be believed that much money is not expended on the clothes of a poor boy stolen from his parents, or sold by them for a few shillings, and constantly occupied in dirty work. Yet the nature of their occupations renders chimney sweepers peculiarly susceptible of cold. And as chimneys must be swept very early, at four or five o'clock of a winter morning, the poor boys are shivering at the door, and attempting by repeated ringings to rouse the profligate footman; but the more they ring, the more the footman does not come.

Do they go out in the winter time without stockings? Oh yes.—Always? I never saw one go out *with* stockings; I have known masters make their boys pull off their leggings, and cut off the feet, to keep their feet warm when they have chilblains. —Are chimney sweepers' boys peculiarly subject to chilblains? Yes; I believe it is owing to the weather: they often go out at two or three in the morning, and their shoes are generally very bad.—Do they go out at that hour at Christmas? Yes; a man will have twenty jobs at four, and twenty more at five or six.—Are chimneys generally swept much about Christmas time? Yes; they are in general; it is left to the Christmas week.—Do you suppose it is frequent that, in the Christmas week, boys are out from three o'clock in the morning to nine or ten? Yes, further than that; I have known that a boy has been only in and out again directly all day till five o'clock in the evening.—Do you consider the journeymen and masters treat those boys generally with greater cruelty than other apprentices in other trades are treated? They do, most horrid and shocking.—(*Lords' Minutes*, p. 33.)

The following is the reluctant evidence of a master.

At what hour in the morning did your boys go out upon their employment? According to orders.—At any time? To be sure; suppose a nobleman wished to have his chimney done before four or five o'clock in the morning, it was done, or how were the servants to get their things done?—Supposing you had an order to attend at four o'clock in the morning in the month of December, you sent your boy? I was generally with him, or had a careful follower with him.—Do you think those early hours beneficial for him? I do: and I have heard that "early to bed and early to rise, is the way to be healthy, wealthy, and wise."—Did they always get in as soon as they knocked? No; it would be pleasant to the profession if they could.—How long did they wait? *Till the servants please to rise.*—How long might that be? According how heavy they were to sleep.—How long was that? It is impossible to say; ten minutes at one house, and twenty at another.—Perhaps half an hour? *We cannot see in the dark how the minutes go.* —Do you think it healthy to let them stand there twenty minutes at four o'clock in the morning in the winter time? He has a cloth to wrap himself in like a mantle, and keep himself warm.—(*Lords' Minutes,* pp. 138, 139.)

We must not forget sore eyes. Soot lodges on their eyelids, produces irritability, which requires friction; and the friction of dirty hands of course increases the disease. The greater proportion of chimney sweepers are in consequence blear-eyed. The boys are very small, but they are compelled to carry heavy loads of soot.

Are you at all lame yourself? No; but I am "knapped-kneed" with carrying heavy loads when I was an apprentice. —That was the occasion of it? It was.—In general, are persons employed in your trade either stunted or knock-kneed by carrying heavy loads during their childhood? It is owing to their masters a great deal; and when they climb a great deal it makes them weak.—(*Commons' Report,* p. 58.)

In climbing a chimney, the great hold is by the knees and elbows. A young child of six or seven years old, working with knees and elbows against hard bricks, soon rubs off the skin from these bony projections, and is forced to climb high chimneys with raw and bloody knees and elbows.

Are the boys' knees and elbows rendered sore when they first begin to learn to climb? Yes, they are, and pieces out of them.—Is that almost generally the case? It is; *there is not one out of twenty who is not;* and they are sure to take the scars to their grave: I have some now.—Are they usually compelled to continue climbing while those sores are open? *Yes;* the way they use to make them hard is that way.—Might not this severity be obviated by the use of pads in learning to climb? Yes; but they consider in the business, learning a boy, that he is never thoroughly learned until the boy's knees are hard after being sore; then they consider it necessary to put a pad on, from seeing the boys have bad knees; the children generally walk stiff-kneed.—Is it usual among the chimney sweepers to teach their boys to learn by means of pads? No; they learn them with nearly naked knees.—Is it done in one instance in twenty? No, nor one in fifty.— (*Lords' Minutes*, p. 32.)

According to the humanity of the master, the soot remains upon the bodies of the children, unwashed off, for any time from a week to a year.

Are the boys generally washed regularly? No, unless they wash themselves.—Did not your master take care you were washed? No.—Not once in three months? No, *not once a year.*—Did not he find you soap? No; I can take my oath on the Bible that he never found me one piece of soap during the time I was apprentice.—(*Lords' Minutes*, p. 41.)

The life of these poor little wretches is so miserable, that they often lie sulking in the flues, unwilling to come out.

Did you ever see severity used to boys that were not obstinate and perverse? Yes.—Very often? Yes, very often. The boys are rather obstinate; some of them are; some of them will get half-way up the chimney, and will not go any further, and then the journeyman will swear at them to come down, or go on; but the boys are too frightened to come down; they halloo out, we cannot get up, and they are afraid to come down; sometimes they will send for another boy, and drag them down; sometimes get up to the top of the chimney, and throw down water, and drive them down; then, when they get them down, they will begin to drag, or beat, or kick them about the house; then, when they get home, the master will beat them all round the kitchen afterwards, and give them no breakfast perhaps.—(*Lords' Minutes*, pp. 9, 10.)

When a chimney boy has done sufficient work for the master, he must work for the man; and he thus becomes for several hours after his morning's work a perquisite to the journeyman.

It is frequently the perquisite of the journeyman, when the first labour of the day on account of the master is finished, to "call the streets," in search of employment on their own account, with the apprentices, whose labour is thus unreasonably extended, and whose limbs are weakened and distorted by the weights which they have to carry, and by the distance which they have to walk. John Lawless says, "I have known a boy to climb from twenty to thirty chimneys for his master in the morning; he has then been sent out instantly with the journeyman, who has kept him out till three or four o'clock, till he has accumulated from six to eight bushels of soot."— (*Lords' Report*, p. 24.)

The sight of a little chimney sweeper often excites pity; and they have small presents made to them at the houses where they sweep. These benevolent alms are disposed of in the following manner:—

Do the boys receive little presents of money from people often in your trade? Yes, it is in general the custom.—Are they allowed to keep that for their own use? Not the whole of it,—the journeymen take what they think proper. The journeymen *are entitled to half* by the master's orders; and whatever a boy may get, if two boys and one journeyman are sent to a large house to sweep a number of chimneys, and after they have done, there should be a shilling, or eighteenpence given to the boys, the journeyman has his full half, and the two boys in general have the other.—Is it usual or customary for the journeyman to play at chuck farthing or other games with the boys? Frequently.—Do they win the money from the boys? Frequently; the children give their money to the journeymen to screen for them.—What do you mean by screening? Such a thing as sifting the soot. The child is tired, and he says, " Jem, I will give you twopence if you will sift my share of the soot"; there is sometimes twenty or thirty bushels to sift.—Do you think the boys retain one quarter of that given them for their own use? No.—(*Lords' Minutes,* p. 35.)

To this most horrible list of calamities is to be added the dreadful deaths by which chimney sweepers are often destroyed. Of these we once thought of giving two examples; one from London, the other from our own town of Edinburgh; but we confine ourselves to the latter.

James Thompson, chimney sweeper.—One day in the beginning of June, witness and panel (that is, the master, the party accused) had been sweeping vents together. About *four* o'clock in the afternoon, the panel proposed to go to Albany Street, where the panel's brother was cleaning a vent, with the assistance of Fraser, whom he had borrowed from the panel for the occasion. When witness and panel got to the house in Albany Street, they found Fraser, who had gone up the vent, *between eleven and twelve* o'clock, not yet come down. On entering the house they found a mason making a hole in the wall. Panel said, what was he doing? I suppose he has taken a lazy fit. The panel called to the boy, "What are you doing? what's keeping you?" The boy answered that he could not come. The panel worked a long while, sometimes persuading him, sometimes threatening and swearing at the boy, to get him down. Panel then said, "I will go to a hardware shop and get a barrel of gunpowder, and blow you

and the vent to the devil, if you do not come down." Panel
then began to slap at the wall—witness then went up a ladder,
and spoke to the boy through a small hole in the wall previously
made by the mason—but the boy did not answer. Panel's
brother told witness to come down, as the boy's master knew
best how to manage him. Witness then threw off his jacket,
and put a handkerchief about his head, and said to the panel,
"Let me go up the chimney to see what's keeping him."
The panel made no answer, but pushed witness away from
the chimney, and continued bullying the boy. At this time
the panel was standing on the grate, so that witness could not
go up the chimney; witness then said to panel's brother,
"There is no use for me here," meaning that panel would not
permit him to use his services. He prevented the mason
making the hole larger, saying, Stop, and I'll bring him down
in five minutes' time. Witness then put on his jacket, and
continued an hour in the room, *during all which time the panel
continued bullying the boy*. Panel then desired witness to go
to Reid's house to get the loan of his boy Alison. Witness went
to Reid's house and asked Reid to come and speak to panel's
brother. Reid asked if panel was there? Witness answered
he was; Reid said he would send his boy to the panel, but not
to the panel's brother. Witness and Reid went to Albany
Street; and when they got into the room, panel took his head
out of the chimney and asked Reid if he would lend him his
boy; Reid agreed; witness then returned to Reid's house for
his boy, and Reid called after him, "Fetch down a set of ropes
with you." By this time witness had been ten minutes in
the room, during which time panel was swearing, and asking
"What's keeping you, you scoundrel?" When witness returned with the boy and ropes, Reid took hold of the rope, and,
having loosed it, gave Alison one end, and directed him to
go up the chimney, saying, "Do not go farther than his feet,
and when you get there fasten it to his foot." Panel said
nothing all this time. Alison went up, and having fastened
the rope, Reid desired him to come down; Reid took the rope
and pulled, but did not bring down the boy; the rope broke!
Alison was sent up again with the other end of the rope, which
was fastened to the boy's foot. When Reid was pulling the
rope, panel said, "You have not the strength of a cat"; he
took the rope into his own hands, *pulling as strong as he could*.
Having pulled *about a quarter of an hour*, panel and Reid
fastened the rope round a crow bar, which they applied to
the wall as a lever, and both *pulled with all their strength for
about a quarter of an hour longer*, when it broke. During this
time witness heard the boy cry, and say, "My God Almighty!"
Panel said, "If I had you here, I would God Almighty you."
Witness thought the cries were in agony. The master of the
house brought a new piece of rope, and the panel's brother

spliced an eye on it. Reid expressed a wish to have it fastened on both thighs, to have greater purchase. Alison was sent up for this purpose, but came down, and said he could not get it fastened. Panel then began to slap at the wall. After striking a long while at the wall he got out a large stone; he then put in his head and called to Fraser, "Do you hear, you sir?" but got no answer: he then put in his hands, and drew down deceased's breeches. He then came down from the ladder. At this time the panel was in a state of perspiration: he sat down on a stool, and the master of the house gave him a dram. Witness did not hear panel make any remarks as to the situation of the boy Fraser. Witness thinks, that, from panel's appearance, he knew the boy was dead. —(*Commons' Report*, pp. 136–8.)

We have been thus particular in stating the case of the chimney sweepers, and in founding it upon the basis of facts, that we may make an answer to those profligate persons who are always ready to fling an air of ridicule upon the labours of humanity, because they are desirous that what they have not virtue to do themselves, should appear to be foolish and romantic when done by others. A still higher degree of depravity than this, is to want every sort of compassion for human misery, when it is accompanied by filth, poverty, and ignorance,—to regulate humanity by the income tax, and to deem the bodily wretchedness and the dirty tears of the poor a fit subject for pleasantry and contempt. We should have been loth to believe, that such deep-seated and disgusting immorality existed in these days; but the notice of it is forced upon us. Nor must we pass over a set of marvellously weak gentlemen, who discover democracy and revolution in every effort to improve the condition of the lower orders, and to take off a little of the load of misery from those points where it presses the hardest. Such are the men into whose heart Mrs. Fry has struck the deepest terror, —who abhor Mr. Bentham and his penitentiary; Mr. Bennet and his hulks; Sir James Mackintosh and his bloodless assizes; Mr. Tooke and his sweeping machines, —and every other human being who is great and good enough to sacrifice his quiet to his love for his fellow-creatures. Certainly we admit that humanity is sometimes the veil of ambition or of faction; but we have no doubt that there are a great many excellent persons to whom it is misery to see misery, and pleasure to lessen it; and who, by calling the public attention to the worst cases, and by giving birth to judicious legislative enactments for their improvement, have made, and are making, the world somewhat happier than they found it. Upon these principles we join hands with the friends of the chimney sweepers, and most heartily wish for the diminution of their numbers, and the limitation of their trade.

We are thoroughly convinced there are many respectable master chimney sweepers; though we suspect their numbers have been increased by the alarm which their former tyranny excited, and by the severe laws made for their coercion: but even with good masters the trade is miserable, —with bad ones it is not to be endured; and the evidence already quoted shows us how many of that character are to be met with in the occupation of sweeping chimneys.

After all, we must own that it was quite right to throw out the bill for prohibiting the sweeping of chimneys by boys—because humanity is a modern invention; and there are many chimneys in old houses which cannot possibly be swept in any other manner. But the construction of chimneys should be attended to in some new building act; and the treatment of boys be watched over with the most severe jealousy of the law. Above all, those who have chimneys accessible to machinery, should encourage the use of machines,* and not think it beneath their dignity to take a little trouble, in order to do a great deal of good. We should have been very glad to have seconded the views of the Climbing Society, and to have pleaded for the complete abolition of climbing boys, if we could conscientiously have done so. But such a measure, we are convinced from the evidence, could not be carried into execution without great injury to property, and great increased risk of fire. The Lords have investigated the matter with the greatest patience, humanity, and good sense; and they do not venture, in their Report, to recommend to the House the abolition of climbing boys.

* The price of a machine is fifteen shillings.

THE SOCIETY FOR THE SUPPRESSION OF VICE [1]

A SOCIETY, that holds out as its object the suppression of vice, must at first sight conciliate the favour of every respectable person; and he who objects to an institution calculated apparently to do so much good, is bound to give very clear and satisfactory reasons for his dissent from so popular an opinion. We certainly have, for a long time, had doubts of its utility; and now think ourselves called upon to state the grounds of our distrust.

Though it were clear that individual informers are useful auxiliaries to the administration of the laws, it would by no means follow that these informers should be allowed to combine,—to form themselves into a body,—to make a public purse,—and to prosecute under a common name. An informer, whether he is paid by the week, like the agents of this society—or by the crime, as in common cases,—is, in general, a man of a very indifferent character. So much fraud and deception are necessary for carrying on his trade—it is so odious to his fellow-subjects,—that no man of respectability will ever undertake it. It is evidently impossible to make such a character otherwise than odious. A man who receives weekly pay for prying into the transgressions of mankind, and bringing them to consequent punishment, will always be hated by mankind; and the office must fall to the lot of some man of desperate fortunes and ambiguous character. The multiplication, therefore, of such officers, and the extensive patronage of such characters, may, by the management of large and opulent societies, become an evil nearly as great as the evils they would suppress. The alarm which a private and disguised accuser occasions in a neighbourhood, is known to be prodigious, not only to the guilty, but to those who may be at once innocent, and ignorant, and timid. The destruction of social confidence is another evil, the consequence of information. An informer gets access to my house or family,—worms my secret out of me,—and

[1] See p. 296.

then betrays me to the magistrate. Now, all these evils may be tolerated in a small degree, while, in a greater degree, they would be perfectly intolerable. Thirty or forty informers roaming about the metropolis, may frighten the mass of offenders a little, and do some good: ten thousand informers would either create an insurrection, or totally destroy the confidence and cheerfulness of private life. Whatever may be said, therefore, of the single and insulated informer, it is quite a new question when we come to a corporation of informers supported by large contributions. The one may be a good, the other a very serious evil; the one legal, the other wholly out of the contemplation of law,—which often, and very wisely, allows individuals to do, what it forbids to many individuals assembled.

If once combination is allowed for the suppression of vice, where are its limits to be? Its capital may as well consist of £100,000 *per annum*, as of a thousand: its numbers may increase from a thousand subscribers, which this society, it seems, had reached in its second year, to twenty thousand: and in that case, what accused person of an inferior condition of life would have the temerity to stand against such a society? Their mandates would very soon be law; and there is no compliance into which they might not frighten the common people, and the lower orders of tradesmen. The idea of a society of gentlemen, calling themselves an Association for the Suppression of Vice, would alarm any small offender, to a degree that would make him prefer any submission to any resistance. He would consider the very fact of being accused by them as almost sufficient to ruin him.

An individual accuser accuses at his own expense; and the risk he runs is a good security that the subject will not be harassed by needless accusations,—a security which, of course, he cannot have against such a society as this, to whom pecuniary loss is an object of such little consequence. It must never be forgotten, that this is not a society for *punishing* people who have been found to transgress the law, but for *accusing* persons of transgressing the law; and that, before trial, the accused person is to be considered as innocent, and is to have every fair chance of establishing his innocence. He must be no

common defendant, however, who does not contend
against such a society with very fearful odds;—the best
counsel engaged for his opponents,—great practice in the
particular court and particular species of cause,—witnesses
thoroughly hackneyed in a court of justice,—and an
unlimited command of money. It by no means follows,
that the legislature, in allowing individuals to be informers,
meant to subject the accused person to the superior weight
and power of such societies. The very influence of names
must have a considerable weight with the jury. Lord
Dartmouth, Lord Radstock, and the Bishop of Durham,
versus a Whitechapel butcher or a publican! Is this a
fair contest before a jury? It is not so even in London;
and what must it be in the country, where a society for
the suppression of vice may consist of all the principal
persons in the neighbourhood? These societies are now
established in York, in Reading, and in many other large
towns. Wherever this is the case, it is far from improbable
that the same persons, at the Quarter or Town Sessions,
may be both judges and accusers; and still more fatally
so, if the offence is tried by a special jury. This is already
most notoriously the case in societies for the preservation
of game. They prosecute a poacher;—the jury is special;
and the poor wretch is found guilty by the very same
persons who have accused him.

If it be lawful for respectable men to combine for the
purpose of turning informers, it is lawful for the lowest
and most despicable race of informers to do the same
thing; and then it is quite clear that every species of
wickedness and extortion would be the consequence. We
are rather surprised that no society of perjured attorneys
and fraudulent bankrupts has risen up in this metropolis
for the suppression of vice. A chairman, deputy-chairman,
subscriptions, and an annual sermon, would give great
dignity to their proceedings; and they would soon begin
to take some rank in the world.

It is true that it is the duty of grand juries to inform
against vice; but the law knows the probable number
of grand jurymen, the times of their meeting, and the
description of persons of whom they consist. Of voluntary societies it can know nothing, — their numbers,
their wealth, or the character of their members. It may

P

therefore trust to a grand jury what it would by no means trust to an unknown combination. A vast distinction is to be made, too, between official duties and voluntary duties. The first are commonly carried on with calmness and moderation; the latter often characterised, in their execution, by rash and intemperate zeal.

The present Society receives no members but those who are of the Church of England. As we are now arguing the question generally, we have a right to make any supposition. It is equally free, therefore, upon general principles, for a society of sectarians to combine and exclude members of the Church of England; and the suppression of vice may thus come in aid of Methodism, Jacobinism, or of any set of principles, however perilous, either to Church or State. The present Society may perhaps consist of persons whose sentiments on these points are rational and respectable. Combinations, however, of this sort may give birth to something far different; and such a supposition is the fair way of trying the question.

We doubt if there be not some mischief in averting the fears and hopes of the people from the known and constituted authorities of the country to those self-created powers;—a Society that punishes in the Strand, another which rewards at Lloyd's Coffee-house! If these things get to any great height, they throw an air of insignificance over those branches of the government to whom these cares properly devolve, and whose authority is by these means assisted, till it is superseded. It is supposed that a project must necessarily be good, because it is intended for the aid of law and government. At this rate, there should be a society in aid of the government, for procuring intelligence from foreign parts, with accredited agents all over Europe. There should be a voluntary transport board, and a gratuitous victualling office. There should be a duplicate, in short, of every department of the State, —the one appointed by the King, and the other by itself. There should be a real Lord Glenbervie in the woods and forests,—and with him a monster, a voluntary Lord Glenbervie, serving without pay, and guiding *gratis*, with secret counsel, the axe of his prototype. If it be asked, who are the constituted authorities who are legally appointed to watch over morals, and whose functions the Society usurp?

our answer is, that there are in England about twelve thousand clergy, not unhandsomely paid for persuading the people, and about four thousand justices, thirty grand juries, and forty thousand constables, whose duty and whose inclination it is to compel them to do right. Under such circumstances, a voluntary moral society does indeed seem to be the purest result of volition; for there certainly is not the smallest particle of necessity mingled with its existence.

It is hardly possible that a society for the suppression of vice can ever be kept within the bounds of good sense and moderation. If there are many members who have really become so from a feeling of duty, there will necessarily be some who enter the Society to hide a bad character, and others whose object it is to recommend themselves to their betters by a sedulous and bustling inquisition into the immoralities of the public. The loudest and noisiest suppressors will always carry it against the more prudent part of the community; the most violent will be considered as the most moral; and those who see the absurdity will, from the fear of being thought to encourage vice, be reluctant to oppose it.

It is of great importance to keep public opinion on the side of virtue. To their authorised and legal correctors, mankind are, on common occasions, ready enough to submit; but there is something in the self-erection of a voluntary magistracy which creates so much disgust that it almost renders vice popular, and puts the offence at a premium. We have no doubt but that the immediate effect of a voluntary combination for the suppression of vice, is an involuntary combination in favour of the vices to be suppressed; and this is a very serious drawback from any good of which such societies may be the occasion; for the state of morals, at any one period, depends much more upon opinion than law; and to bring odious and disgusting auxiliaries to the aid of virtue, is to do the utmost possible good to the cause of vice. We regret that mankind are as they are; and we sincerely wish that the species at large were as completely devoid of every vice and infirmity as the President, Vice-President, and Committee of the Suppressing Society; but, till they are thus regenerated, it is of the greatest consequence to teach them virtue and religion in a manner which will not make them hate both the one and the other. The greatest delicacy is required in the application of violence to moral and religious sentiment. We forget, that the object is, not to produce the outward compliance, but to raise up the inward feeling, which secures the outward compliance. You may drag men into church by main force, and prosecute them for buying a pot of beer,—and cut them off from the enjoyment of a leg of mutton;—and you may do all this, till you make the common people hate Sunday, and the clergy, and religion, and everything which relates to such subjects. There are many crimes, indeed, where persuasion cannot be waited for, and where the untaught feelings of all men go along with the violence of the law. A robber and a murderer must be knocked on the head like mad dogs; but we have no great opinion of the possibility of indicting men into piety, or of calling in the Quarter Sessions to the aid of religion. You may produce outward conformity by these means; but you are so far from producing (the only thing worth producing) the inward feeling, that you incur a great risk of giving birth to a totally opposite sentiment.

The violent modes of making men good, just alluded to, have been resorted to at periods when the science of legislation was not so well understood as it now is; or when the manners of the age have been peculiarly gloomy or fanatical. The improved knowledge, and the improved temper of later times, push such laws into the background, and silently repeal them. A Suppressing Society, hunting everywhere for penalty and information, has a direct tendency to revive ancient ignorance and fanaticism,— and to re-enact laws which, if ever they ought to have existed at all, were certainly calculated for a very different style of manners, and a very different degree of information. To compel men to go to church under a penalty appears to us to be absolutely absurd. The bitterest enemy of religion will necessarily be that person who is driven to a compliance with its outward ceremonies, by informers and justices of the peace. In the same manner, any constable who hears another swear an oath has a right to seize him, and carry him before a magistrate, where he is to be fined so much for each execration. It is impossible to carry

such laws into execution; and it is lucky that it is impossible,
—for their execution would create an infinitely greater
evil than it attempted to remedy. The common sense,
and common feeling of mankind, if left to themselves,
would silently repeal such laws; and it is one of the evils
of these societies, that they render absurdity eternal, and
ignorance indestructible. Do not let us be misunderstood:
upon the object to be accomplished, there can be but one
opinion;—it is only upon the means employed, that there
can be the slightest difference of sentiment. To go to
church is a duty of the greatest possible importance; and
on the blasphemy and vulgarity of swearing, there can be
but one opinion. But such duties are not the objects of
legislation; they must be left to the general state of public
sentiment; which sentiment must be influenced by example,
by the exertions of the pulpit and the press, and, above all,
by education. The fear of God can never be taught by
constables, nor the pleasures of religion be learnt from a
common informer.

Beginning with the best intentions in the world, such
societies must in all probability degenerate into a receptacle
for every species of tittle-tattle, impertinence, and malice.
Men, whose trade is rat-catching, love to catch rats; the
bug-destroyer seizes on his bug with delight; and the
suppressor is gratified by finding his vice. The last soon
becomes a mere tradesman like the others; none of them
moralise, or lament that their respective evils should exist
in the world. The public feeling is swallowed up in the
pursuit of a daily occupation, and in the display of a
technical skill. Here, then, is a society of men, who invite
accusation,—who receive it (almost unknown to themselves) with pleasure,—and who, if they hate dulness and
inoccupation, can have very little pleasure in the innocence
of their fellow-creatures. The natural consequence of
all this is, that (besides that portion of rumour which
every member contributes at the weekly meeting) their
table must be covered with anonymous lies against the
characters of individuals. Every servant discharged from
his master's service,—every villain who hates the man he
has injured,—every cowardly assassin of character,—now
knows where his accusations will be received, and where
they cannot fail to produce some portion of the mischievous

effects which he wishes. The very first step of such a Society should be, to declare, in the plainest manner, that they would never receive any anonymous accusation. This would be the only security to the public, that they were not degrading themselves into a receptacle for malice and falsehood. Such a declaration would inspire some species of confidence; and make us believe that their object was neither the love of power, nor the gratification of uncharitable feelings. The Society for the Suppression, however, have done no such thing. They request, indeed, the signature of the informers whom they invite; but they do not (as they ought) make that signature an indispensable condition.

Nothing has disgusted us so much in the proceedings of this Society, as the control which they exercise over the amusements of the poor. One of the specious titles under which this legal meanness is gratified is, *Prevention of Cruelty to Animals*.

Of cruelty to animals, let the reader take the following specimens:—

Running an iron hook in the intestines of an animal; presenting this first animal to another as his food; and then pulling this second creature up and suspending him by the barb in his stomach.

Riding a horse till he drops, in order to see an innocent animal torn to pieces by dogs.

Keeping a poor animal upright for many weeks, to communicate a peculiar hardness to his flesh.

Making deep incisions into the flesh of another animal while living, in order to make the muscles more firm.

Immersing another animal, while living, in hot water.

Now we do fairly admit, that such abominable cruelties as these are worthy the interference of the law: and that the Society should have punished them, cannot be matter of surprise to any feeling mind.—But stop, gentle reader! these cruelties are the cruelties of the Suppressing Committee, not of the poor. You must not think of punishing these.—The first of these cruelties passes under the pretty name of *angling*;—and therefore there can be no harm in it—the more particularly as the President himself has one of the best preserved trout streams in England.—The next is *hunting*;—and as many of the Vice-Presidents and of the Committee hunt, it is not possible there can be any cruelty in hunting.[1] The next is, a process for making *brawn*—a dish never tasted by the poor, and therefore not to be disturbed by indictment. The fourth is the mode of *crimping* cod; and the fifth, of boiling lobsters; all high-life cruelties, with which a justice of the peace has no business to meddle. The real thing which calls forth the sympathies, and harrows up the soul, is to see a number of boisterous artisans baiting a bull, or a bear; not a savage hare, or a carnivorous stag,—but a poor, innocent, timid bear; — not pursued by magistrates, and deputy lieutenants, and men of education,—but by those who must necessarily seek their relaxation in noise and tumultuous merriment,—by men whose feelings are blunted, and whose understanding is wholly devoid of refinement. The Society detail, with symptoms of great complacency, their detection of a bear-baiting in Blackboy Alley, Chick Lane, and the prosecution of the offenders before a magistrate. It appears to us, that nothing can be more partial and unjust than this kind of proceedings. A man of ten thousand a year may worry a fox as much as he pleases,—may encourage the breed of a mischievous animal on purpose to worry it; and a poor labourer is carried before a magistrate for paying sixpence to see an exhibition of courage between a dog and a bear! Any cruelty may be practised to gorge the stomachs of the rich,—none to enliven the holidays of the poor. We venerate those feelings which really protect creatures susceptible of pain, and incapable of complaint. But heaven-born pity, now-a-days, calls for the income-tax, and the court guide; and ascertains the rank and fortune of the tormentor before she weeps for the pain of the sufferer. It is astonishing how the

[1] "How reasonable creatures," says the Society, "can enjoy a pastime which is the cause of such sufferings to brute animals, or how they can consider themselves entitled, for their own amusement, to stimulate those animals, by means of the antipathies which Providence has thought proper to place between them, to worry and tear, and often to destroy each other, it is difficult to conceive. So inhuman a practice, by a retribution peculiarly just, tends obviously to render the human character brutal and ferocious," etc. etc. (*Address*, pp. 71, 72). We take it for granted that the reader sees clearly that no part of this description can possibly apply to the case of *hunting*.

natural feelings of mankind are distorted by false theories. Nothing can be more mischievous than to say, that the pain inflicted by the dog of a man of quality is not (when the strength of the two animals is the same) equal to that produced by the cur of a butcher. Haller, in his *Pathology*, expressly says, *that the animal bitten knows no difference in the quality of the biting animal's master*; and it is now the universal opinion among all enlightened men, that the misery of the brawner would be very little diminished, if he could be made sensible that he was to be eaten up only by persons of the first fashion. The contrary supposition seems to us to be absolute nonsense; it is the desertion of the true *Baconian* philosophy, and the substitution of mere unsupported conjecture in its place. The trespass, however, which calls forth all the energies of a suppresser, is the sound of a fiddle. That the common people are really enjoying themselves, is now beyond all doubt: and away rush Secretary, President, and Committee, to clap the cotillon into the Compter, and to bring back the life of the poor to its regular standard of decorous gloom. The gambling houses of St. James's remain untouched. The peer ruins himself and his family with impunity; while the Irish labourer is privately whipped for not making a better use of the excellent moral and religious education which he has received in the days of his youth!

It is not true, as urged by the Society, that the vices of the poor are carried on in houses of public resort, and those of the rich in their own houses. The Society cannot be ignorant of the innumerable gambling houses resorted to by men of fashion. Is there one they have suppressed, or attempted to suppress? Can anything be more despicable than such distinctions as these? Those who make them seem to have for other persons' vices all the rigour of the ancient Puritans—without a particle of their honesty or their courage. To suppose that any society will ever attack the vices of people of fashion, is wholly out of the question. If the Society consisted of tradesmen, they would infallibly be turned off by the vicious customers whose pleasures they interrupted: and what gentleman so fond of suppressing, as to interfere with the vices of good company, and inform against persons who were really genteel? He knows very well that the consequence of such interference would be a complete exclusion from elegant society; that the upper classes could not, and would not, endure it; and that he must immediately lose his rank in the world, if his zeal subjected fashionable offenders to the slightest inconvenience from the law. Nothing, therefore, remains, but to rage against the Sunday dinners of the poor, and to prevent a bricklayer's labourer from losing, on the seventh day, that beard which has been augmenting the other six. We see at the head of this Society the names of several noblemen, and of other persons moving in the fashionable world. Is it possible they can be ignorant of the innumerable offences against the law and morality which are committed by their own acquaintances and connections? Is there one single instance where they have directed the attention of the Society to this higher species of suppression, and sacrificed men of consideration to that zeal for virtue which watches so acutely over the vices of the poor? It would give us very little pleasure to see a duchess sent to the Poultry Compter; but if we saw the Society flying at such high game, we should at least say they were honest and courageous, whatever judgment we might form of their good sense. At present they should denominate themselves a Society for suppressing the vices of persons whose income does not exceed £500 *per annum*; and then, to put all classes upon an equal footing, there must be another society of barbers, butchers, and bakers, to return to the higher classes that moral character, by which they are so highly benefited.

To show how impossible it is to keep such societies within any kind of bounds, we shall quote a passage respecting circulating libraries, from their *Proceedings*.

Your Committee have good reasons for believing, that the circulation of their notices among the printsellers, warning them against the sale or exhibition of indecent representations, has produced, and continues to produce, the best effects. But they have to lament that the extended establishments of circulating libraries, however useful they may be, in a variety of respects, to the easy and general diffusion of knowledge, are extremely injurious to morals and religion, by the indiscriminate admission which they give to works of a prurient and immoral nature. It is a toilsome task to any virtuous and enlightened mind, to wade through the catalogues of these collections, and much more to select such books from them as have only an apparent bad tendency. But your Committee being convinced that their attention ought to be directed to those institutions which possess such powerful and numerous means of poisoning the minds of young persons, and especially of the female youth, have therefore begun to make some endeavours towards their better regulation.— (*Statement of the Proceedings for* 1804, pp. 11, 12.)

In the same spirit we see them writing to a country magistrate in Devonshire, respecting a wake advertised in the public papers. Nothing can be more presumptuous than such conduct, or produce, in the minds of impartial men, a more decisive impression against the Society.

The natural answer from the members of the Society (the only answer they have ever made to the enemies of their institution) will be, that we are lovers of vice,— desirous of promoting indecency, of destroying the Sabbath, and of leaving mankind to the unrestrained gratification of their passions. We have only very calmly to reply, that we are neither so stupid nor so wicked as not to concur in every scheme which has for its object the preservation of rational religion and sound morality;—but the scheme must be well concerted,—and those who are to carry it into execution must deserve our confidence, from their talents and their character. Upon religion and morals depends the happiness of mankind;—but the fortune of knaves and the power of fools is sometimes made to rest on the same apparent basis; and we will never (if we can help it) allow a rogue to get rich, or a blockhead to get powerful, under the sanction of these awful words. We do not by any means intend to apply these contemptuous epithets to the Society for the Suppression. That there are among their numbers some very odious hypocrites, is not impossible; that many men who believe they come there from the love of virtue, do really join the Society from the love of power, we do not doubt: but we see no reason to doubt that the great mass of subscribers consists of persons who have very sincere intentions of doing good. That they have, in some instances, done a great deal of good, we admit with the greatest pleasure. We believe, that in the hands of truly honest, intrepid, and, above all, discreet men, such a society might become a valuable institution, improve in some degree the public morals, and increase the public happiness. So many qualities, however, are required to carry it on well,—the temptations to absurdity and impertinence are so very great,—that we ever despair of seeing our wishes upon this subject realised. In the present instance, our object has been to suppress the arrogance of suppressors,—to keep them within due bounds,—to show them that to do good requires a little more talent and reflection than they are aware of, —and, above all, to impress upon them that true zeal for virtue knows no distinction between the rich and the poor; and that the cowardly and the mean can never be the true friends of morality, and the promoters of human happiness. If they attend to these rough doctrines they will ever find in the writers of this Journal their warmest admirers, and their most sincere advocates and friends.

SERMONS

I publish this Sermon (or rather allow others to publish it), because many persons, who know the city of Bristol better than I do, have earnestly solicited me to do so, and are convinced it will do good. It is not without reluctance (as far as I myself am concerned) that I send to the Press such plain rudiments of common charity and common sense.

SYDNEY SMITH.

Nov. 8, 1828.

ON THE RULES OF CHRISTIAN CHARITY

PREACHED AT BRISTOL ON GUY FAWKES DAY, 1828.

[You will be amused by hearing that I am to preach the 5th November sermon at Bristol, and to dine at the 5th November dinner with the Mayor and Corporation of Bristol. All sorts of bad theology are preached at the Cathedral on that day, and all sorts of bad toasts drunk at the Mansion House. I will do neither the one nor the other, nor bow the knee in the house of Rimmon.—*Letter to Henry Howard, Esq.*]

COL. III. 12, 13

Put on, as the elect of God, kindness, humbleness of mind, meekness, long-suffering; forbearing one another, and forgiving one another.

THE Church of England, in its wisdom and piety, has very properly ordained that a day of thanksgiving should be set apart, in which we may return thanks to Almighty God, for the mercies vouchsafed to this nation in their escape from the dreadful plot planned for the destruction of the Sovereign and his Parliament,—the forerunner, no doubt, of such sanguinary scenes as were suited to the manners of that age, and must have proved the inevitable consequence of such enormous wickedness and cruelty. Such an escape is a fair and lawful foundation for national piety. And it is a comely and Christian sight to see the magistrates and high authorities of the land obedient to the ordinances of the Church, and holding forth to their fellow-subjects a wise example of national gratitude and serious devotion. This use of this day is deserving of every commendation. The idea that Almighty God does sometimes exercise a special providence for the preservation of a whole people is justified by Scripture, is not repugnant to reason, and can produce nothing but feelings and opinions favourable to virtue and religion.

Another wise and lawful use of this day is an honest self-congratulation that we have burst through those bands which the Roman Catholic priesthood would impose upon human judgment; that the Protestant Church not only permits, but exhorts, every man to appeal from human authority to the Scriptures; that it makes of the clergy guides and advisers, not masters and oracles; that it discourages vain and idle ceremonies, unmeaning observances, and hypocritical pomp; and encourages freedom in thinking upon religion, and simplicity in religious forms. It is impossible that any candid man should not observe the marked superiority of the Protestant over the Catholic faith in these particulars; and difficult that any pious man should not feel grateful to Almighty Providence for escape from danger which would have plunged this country afresh into so many errors and so many absurdities.

I hope, in this condemnation of the Catholic religion (in which I most sincerely join its bitterest enemies), I shall not be so far mistaken as to have it supposed that I would convey the slightest approbation of any laws which disqualify or incapacitate any class of men from civil offices on account of religious opinions. I regard all such laws as fatal and lamentable mistakes in legislation; they are mistakes of troubled times and half-barbarous ages. All Europe is gradually emerging from their influence. This country has lately, with the entire consent of its Prelates, made a noble and successful effort, by the abolition of some of the most obnoxious laws of this class. In proportion as such example is followed, the enemies of Church and State will be diminished, and the foundation of peace, order, and happiness be strengthened. These are my opinions, which I mention, not to convert you, but to guard myself from misrepresentation. It is my duty,—it is my wish,—it is the subject of this day to point out those evils of the Catholic religion from which we have escaped; but I should be to the last degree concerned, if a condemnation of theological errors were to be construed into an approbation of laws which I cannot but consider as deeply marked by a spirit of intolerance. I therefore beg you to remember, that I record these opinions, not for the purpose of converting anyone to them, which would be an abuse of the privilege of addressing you from the pulpit; not that I attach the slightest degree of importance to them because they are mine; but merely to guard myself from misrepresentation upon a point on which all men's passions are, at this moment, so powerfully excited.

I have said that, at this moment, all men's passions are powerfully excited on this subject. If this be true, it points out to me my line of duty. I must use my endeavours to guard against the abuse of this day; to take care that the principles of sound reason are not lost sight of; and that such excitement, instead of rising into dangerous vehemence, is calmed into active and useful investigation on the subject.

I shall, therefore, on the present occasion, not investigate generally the duties of charity and forbearance, but of charity and forbearance in religious matters; of that Christian meekness and humility which prevent the intrusion of bad passions into religious concerns, and keep calm and pure the mind intent upon eternity. And remember, I beg of you, that the rules I shall offer you for the observation of Christian charity are general, and of universal application. What you choose to do, and which way you incline upon any particular question, are, and can be, no concern of mine. It would be the height of arrogance and presumption in me, or in any other minister of God's word, to interfere on such points; I only endeavour to teach that spirit of forbearance and charity, which (though it cannot always prevent differences upon religious points) will ensure that these differences are carried on with Christian gentleness. I have endeavoured to lay down these rules for difference with care and moderation; and if you will attend to them patiently I think you will agree with me, that however the practice of them may be forgotten, the propriety of them cannot be denied.

It would always be easier to fall in with human passions than to resist them; but the ministers of God must do their duty through evil report, and through good report; neither prevented nor excited by the interests of the present day. They must teach those general truths which the Christian religion has committed to their care, and upon which the happiness and peace of the world depend.

In pressing upon you the great duty of religious charity, the inutility of the opposite defect of religious violence first offers itself to, and indeed obtrudes itself upon, my notice. The evil of difference of opinion must exist; it admits of no cure. The wildest visionary does not now hope he can bring his fellow-creatures to one standard of

Q

faith. If history has taught us any one thing, it is that mankind, on such sort of subjects, will form their own opinions. Therefore to want charity in religious matters is at least useless; it hardens error, and provokes recrimination: but it does not enlighten those whom we wish to reclaim, nor does it extend doctrines which to us appear so clear and indisputable. But to do wrong, and to gain nothing by it, is surely to add folly to fault, and to proclaim an understanding not led by the rule of reason, as well as a disposition unregulated by the Christian faith.

Religious charity requires that we should not judge any sect of Christians by the representations of their enemies alone, without hearing and reading what they have to say in their own defence; it requires only, of course, to state such a rule to procure for it general admission. No man can pretend to say that such a rule is not founded upon the plainest principles of justice—upon those plain principles of justice which no one thinks of violating in the ordinary concerns of life; and yet I fear that rule is not always very strictly adhered to in religious animosities. Religious hatred is often founded on tradition, often on hearsay, often on the misrepresentations of notorious enemies; without inquiry, without the slightest examination of opposite reasons and authorities, or consideration of that which the accused party has to offer for defence or explanation. It is impossible, I admit, to examine everything; many have not talents, many have not leisure, for such pursuits; many must be contented with the faith in which they have been brought up, and must think it the best modification of the Christian faith, because they are told it is so. But this imperfect acquaintance with religious controversy, though not blameable when it proceeds from want of power, and want of opportunity, can be no possible justification of violent and acrimonious opinions. I would say to the ignorant man, "It is not your ignorance I blame; you have had no means perhaps of acquiring knowledge: the circumstances of your life have not led to it—may have prevented it; but then I must tell you, if you have not had leisure to inquire, you have no right to accuse. If you are unacquainted with the opposite arguments,—or, knowing, cannot balance them, it is not upon you the task devolves of exposing the errors, and impugning the opinions of other sects." If charity be ever necessary, it is in those who know accurately neither the accusation nor the defence. If invectives,—if rooted antipathy, in religious opinions be ever a breach of Christian rules, it is so in those who, not being able to become wise, are not willing to become charitable and modest.

Any candid man acquainted with religious controversy, will, I think, admit that he has frequently, in the course of his studies, been astonished by the force of arguments with which that cause has been defended which he at first thought to be incapable of any defence at all. Some accusations he has found to be utterly groundless; in others the facts and arguments have been mis-stated: in other instances the accusation has been retorted: in many cases the tenets have been defended by strong arguments and honest appeal to Scripture, in many with consummate acuteness and deep learning. So that religious studies often teach to opponents a greater respect for each other's talents, motives, and acquirements; exhibit the real difficulties of the subject; lessen the surprise and anger which are apt to be excited by opposition; and by these means, promote that forgiving one another, and forbearing one another, which are so powerfully recommended by the words of my text.

A great deal of mischief is done by not attending to the limits of interference with each other's religious opinions, —by not leaving to the power and wisdom of God, that which belongs to God alone. Our holy religion consists of some doctrines which influence practice, and of others which are purely speculative. If religious errors be of the former description, they may, perhaps, be fair objects of human interference; but if the opinion be merely theological and speculative, there the right of human interference seems to end, because the necessity for such interference does not exist. Any error of this nature is between the Creator and the creature,—between the Redeemer and the redeemed. If such opinions are not the best opinions which can be found, God Almighty will punish the error, if mere error seemeth to the Almighty a fit object of punishment. Why may not man wait if God waits? Where are we called upon in Scripture to pursue men for errors purely speculative?—to assist Heaven in punishing those offences which belong only to Heaven?—in fighting unasked for what we deem to be the battles of God,—of that patient and merciful God, who pities the frailties we do not pity —who forgives the errors we do not forgive,—who sends rain upon the just and the unjust, and maketh his sun to shine upon the evil and the good.

Another canon of religious charity is to revise, at long intervals, the bad opinions we have been compelled, or rather our forefathers have been compelled, to form of other Christian sects; to see whether the different bias of the age, the more general diffusion of intelligence, do not render those tenets less pernicious: that which might prove a very great evil under other circumstances, and in other times, may, perhaps, however weak and erroneous, be harmless in these times, and under these circumstances. We must be aware, too, that we do not mistake recollections for apprehensions, and confound together what has passed with what is to come,—history with futurity. For instance, it would be the most enormous abuse of this religious institution to imagine that such dreadful scenes of wickedness are to be apprehended from the Catholics of the present day, because the annals of this country were disgraced by such an event two hundred years ago. It would be an enormous abuse of this day to extend the crimes of a few desperate wretches to a whole sect; to fix the passions of dark ages upon times of refinement and civilisation. All these are mistakes and abuses of this day, which violate every principle of Christian charity, endanger the peace of society, and give life and perpetuity to hatreds, which must perish at one time or another, and had better, for the peace of society, perish now.

It would be religiously charitable, also, to consider whether the objectionable tenets, which different sects profess, are in their hearts as well as in their books. There is unfortunately so much pride where there ought to be so much humility, that it is difficult, if not almost impossible, to make religious sects abjure or recant the doctrines they have once professed. It is not in this manner, I fear, that the best and purest churches are ever reformed. But the doctrine gradually becomes obsolete; and, though not disowned, ceases in fact to be a distinguishing characteristic of the sect which professes it. These modes of reformation,—

this silent antiquation of doctrines,—this real improvement, which the parties themselves are too wise not to feel, though not wise enough to own, must, I am afraid, be generally conceded to human infirmity. They are indulgences not unnecessary to many sects of Christians. The more generous method would be to admit error where error exists, to say these were the tenets and interpretations of dark and ignorant ages; wider inquiry, fresh discussion, superior intelligence have convinced us we are wrong; we will act in future upon better and wiser principles. This is what men do in laws, arts, and sciences; and happy for them would it be if they used the same modest docility in the highest of all concerns. But it is, I fear, more than experience will allow us to expect; and therefore the kindest and most charitable method is to allow religious sects silently to improve without reminding them of, and taunting them with, the improvement; without bringing them to the humiliation of formal disavowal, or the still more pernicious practice of defending what they know to be indefensible. The triumphs which proceed from the neglect of these principles are not (what they pretend to be) the triumphs of religion, but the triumphs of personal vanity. The object is not to extinguish dangerous error with as little pain and degradation as possible to him who has fallen into the error: but the object is to exalt ourselves, and to depreciate our theological opponents, as much as possible, at any expense to God's service, and to the real interests of truth and religion.

There is another practice not less common than this, and equally uncharitable; and that is, to represent the opinions of the most violent and eager persons who can be met with, as the common and received opinions of the whole sect. There are, in every denomination of Christians, individuals, by whose opinion or by whose conduct the great body would very reluctantly be judged. Some men aim at attracting notice by singularity; some are deficient in temper; some in learning; some push every principle to the extreme; distort, overstate, pervert; fill every one to whom their cause is dear with concern that it should have been committed to such rash and intemperate advocates. If you wish to gain a victory over your antagonists, these are the men whose writings you should study, whose

opinions you should dwell on, and should carefully bring
forward to notice; but if you wish, as the elect of God, to
put on kindness and humbleness, meekness and long-
suffering,—if you wish to forbear and to forgive, it will
then occur to you that you should seek the true opinions
of any sect from those only who are approved of, and
reverenced by that sect; to whose authority that sect
defer, and by whose arguments they consider their tenets
to be properly defended. This may not suit your purpose
if you are combating for victory; but it is your duty if you
are combating for truth; it is the safe, honest, and splendid
conduct of him, who never writes nor speaks on religious
subjects, but that he may diffuse the real blessings of
religion among his fellow-creatures, and restrain the
bitterness of controversy by the feelings of Christian
charity and forbearance.

Let us also ask ourselves, when we are sitting in severe
judgment upon the faults, follies, and errors of other
Christian sects, whether it be not barely possible that we
have fallen into some mistakes and misrepresentations?
Let us ask ourselves, honestly and fairly, whether we are
wholly exempt from prejudice, from pride, from obstinate
adhesion to what candour calls upon us to alter, and to
yield? Are there no violent and mistaken members of
our own community, by whose conduct we should be loth
to be guided,—by whose tenets we should not choose our
faith should be judged? Has time, that improves all,
found nothing in us to change for the better? Amid all
the manifold divisions of the Christian world, are we the
only Christians who, without having anything to learn
from the knowledge and civilisation of the last three
centuries, have started up, without infancy, and without
error, into consummate wisdom and spotless perfection?

To listen to enemies as well as friends is a rule which
not only increases sense in common life, but is highly
favourable to the increase of religious candour. You find
that you are not so free from faults as your friends suppose,
nor so full of faults as your enemies suppose. You begin
to think it not impossible that you may be as unjust to
others as they are to you; and that the wisest and most
Christian scheme is that of mutual indulgence; that it is
better to put on, as the elect of God, kindness, humbleness

of mind, meekness, long-suffering, forbearing one another, and forgiving one another.

Some men cannot understand how they are to be zealous if they are candid in religious matters; how the energy, necessary for the one virtue, is compatible with the calmness which the other requires. But remember that the Scriptures carefully distinguish between laudable zeal and indiscreet zeal; that the apostles and epistolary writers knew they had as much to fear from the over-excitement of some men, as from the supineness of others; and in nothing have they laboured more than in preventing religion from arming human passions, instead of allaying them, and rendering those principles a source of mutual jealousy and hatred which were intended for universal peace. I admit that indifference sometimes puts on the appearance of candour; but though there is a counterfeit, yet there is a reality; and the imitation proves the value of the original, because men only attempt to multiply the appearances of useful and important things. The object is to be at the same time pious to God and charitable to man; to render your own faith as pure and perfect as possible, not only without hatred of those who differ from you, but with a constant recollection that it is possible, in spite of thought and study, that you may have been mistaken,—that other sects may be right,—and that a zeal in his service, which God does not want, is a very bad excuse for those bad passions which his sacred word condemns.

Lastly, I would suggest that many differences between sects are of less importance than the furious zeal of many men would make them. Are the tenets of any sect of such a description that we believe they will be saved under the Christian faith? Do they fulfil the common duties of life? Do they respect property? Are they obedient to the laws? Do they speak the truth? If all these things be right, the violence of hostility may surely submit to some little softness and relaxation; honest difference of opinion cannot call for such entire separation and complete antipathy; such zeal as this, if it *be* zeal, and not something worse, is not surely zeal according to discretion.

The arguments, then, which I have adduced in support of the great principles of religious charity are, that violence

upon such subjects is rarely or ever found to be useful;
but generally to produce effects opposite to those which
are intended.   I have observed that religious sects are not
to be judged from the representations of their enemies;
but that they are to be heard for themselves, in the pleadings of their best writers, not in the representations of
those whose intemperate zeal is a misfortune to the sect
to which they belong.   If you will study the principles of
your religious opponents, you will often find your contempt
and hatred lessened in proportion as you are better acquainted with what you despise.   Many religious opinions,
which are purely speculative, are without the limits of
human interference.   In the numerous sects of Christianity,
interpreting our religion in very opposite manners, all
cannot be right.   Imitate the forbearance and long-
suffering of God, who throws the mantle of his mercy
over all, and who will probably save, on the last day, the
piously right and the piously wrong, seeking Jesus in
humbleness of mind.   Do not drive religious sects to the
disgrace (or to what they foolishly think the disgrace) of
formally disavowing tenets they once professed, but concede
something to human weakness; and when the tenet is
virtually given up, treat it as if it were actually given up;
and always consider it to be very possible that you yourself may have made mistakes, and fallen into erroneous
opinions, as well as any other sect to which you are opposed.
If you put on these dispositions, and this tenor of mind,
you cannot be guilty of any religious fault, take what part
you will in the religious disputes which appear to be coming
on the world.   If you choose to perpetuate the restrictions
upon your fellow-creatures, no one has a right to call you
bigoted; if you choose to do them away, no one has any
right to call you lax and indifferent: you have done your
utmost to do right, and whether you err, or do not err,
in your mode of interpreting the Christian religion, you
show at least that you have caught its heavenly spirit,—
that you have put on, as the elect of God, kindness, humbleness of mind, meekness, long-suffering, forbearing one
another, and forgiving one another.

I have thus endeavoured to lay before you the uses and
abuses of this day; and, having stated the great mercy of
God's interference, and the blessings this country has

secured to itself in resisting the errors and follies, and superstitions of the Catholic Church, I have endeavoured that this just sense of our own superiority should not militate against the sacred principles of Christian charity. That charity which I ask of others, I ask also for myself. I am sure I am preaching before those who will think (whether they agree with me or not) that I have spoken conscientiously, and from good motives, and from honest feelings, on a very difficult subject,—not sought for by me, but devolving upon me in the course of duty;—in which I should have been heartily ashamed of myself (as you would have been ashamed of me), if I had thought only how to flatter and please, or thought of anything but what I hope I always do think of in the pulpit,—that I am placed here by God to tell truth, and to do good.

I shall conclude my sermon (extended, I am afraid, already to an unreasonable length), by reciting to you a very short and beautiful apologue, taken from the Rabbinical writers. It is, I believe, quoted by Bishop Taylor in his *Holy Living and Dying*. I have not now access to that book, but I quote it to you from memory, and should be made truly happy if you would quote it to others from memory also.

"As Abraham was sitting in the door of his tent, there came unto him a wayfaring man; and Abraham gave him water for his feet, and set bread before him. And Abraham said unto him, 'Let us now worship the Lord our God before we eat of this bread.' And the wayfaring man said unto Abraham, 'I will not worship the Lord thy God, for thy God is not my God; but I will worship my God, even the God of my fathers.' But Abraham was exceeding wroth; and he rose up to put the wayfaring man forth from the door of his tent. And the voice of the Lord was heard in the tent,—Abraham! Abraham! have I borne with this man for three score and ten years, and canst not thou bear with him for one hour?"

[To-day I have preached an honest sermon (5th of November) before the Mayor and Corporation, in the Cathedral;—the most Protestant Corporation in England! They stared at me with all their eyes. Several of them could not keep the turtle on their stomachs. *Letter to Lord Holland.*]

"ON THE IMMORTALITY OF THE SOUL"

1 Cor. xv. 35–38

But some man will say, how are the dead raised up. And with what body do they come? Thou fool! that which thou sowest is not quickened except it die; and that which thou sowest, thou sowest not that body which shall be, but bare grain, it may chance of wheat, or some other grain; but God giveth it a body as it hath pleased him—and to every seed his own body.

He who looks at any object of matter, can scarcely be said to know at what it is he does look if he confines himself only to its present qualities, and neglects the indications of its future existence.

Look at the seed; does it move? Is there in it the slightest sign of life? Could any man conjecture, previous to experience, that it would not always remain what it now is? Yet of that seed comes the green herb; man gathers of it his daily bread; or if such be its body, it riseth up to be the strength and beauty of the forest.

The principle of change is indeed widely diffused over the works of Providence; few things are in that state now in which they are hereafter to remain; the bird destined for the air, sleeps in his shell; the beautiful insect that is to flutter in the sun, crawls in the earth till the season of his glory is come: the child that requires the hand of a parent to give him food, may soon be changed into a saint or a sage. So also (says the great apostle) is it with the soul of man; this is not its resting-place; it was never intended to remain here and to be always as it now is; it will be changed as the seed is changed; the corruptible will put on incorruption; the mortal, immortality; the object for which it is created will be made manifest; at the very moment that it seems to perish, it is passing into a higher order of creatures and getting hold of a better life.

This comparison between the outward world and the changes of the soul, set on foot by the holy apostle, may perhaps be carried one step farther.

As we are admonished, by experience, of this propensity to change in all the objects we behold, we accustom ourselves to look out with eagerness and attention for the signs of these changes; we say of the seed when it begins to burst, this part will become the branch, and from hence the root will grow; we trace out in the shell the organs of the perfect animal: and we say with certainty, these operations are for a future existence; to this perishing seed, to this inanimate shell, they are useless; but the seed will grow, and the shell will live; these are the signs in them of a second state, they have other appearances to put on and other objects to accomplish, to which their present being is entirely subordinate and ministerial. This also is true of the soul of man. It does not do all here that it was intended to do. It was never modelled for this world alone. There are in it qualities utterly useless here, qualities which carry about with them the signs of preparation as if the soul was to undergo a great change, surviving the body and living for ever before God.

There cannot be a more awful speculation than to follow out this train of thought and to endeavour to find what those qualities of our minds are which appear to have a reference to some future scene of existence which, by shewing us that we are intended for another and a better world, add the natural evidence for immortality to that which is derived from Christian revelation.

First, it must be observed, man in every stage of society, civilised or savage, has universally believed that he is to live hereafter. We have no sooner become acquainted with the opinions of any new people, however barbarous their condition, however remote and insulated their situation, but we immediately discover among them this sacred notion of a second life—discover it obscured by foolish inventions, disgraced by superstition, but still discover it shining through the dross and betraying its excellent nature. Why then has the Almighty God, who in all other creations is acknowledged to do nothing in vain, who could have pinioned down the mind within any limits, given it such a range that its thoughts reach up to

Heaven, where it can never dwell? Why is it enabled to discover a God, if that God is to doom it to annihilation? Why has it the power to draw a never-ending scene of happiness, if it has but a few wretched years to live? What advantageth us, says the apostle, if the dead rise not at all? let us eat and drink, for to-morrow we die. But alas, the mind of man is not so constituted, the death of to-morrow ruins the appetite of to-day; the beast that perishes, he only is pleased to the last and is never troubled by that futurity by which he is never to be blest. Believing that God exists, that God is our maker, that God is just, we cannot believe that he has given us minds capable of forming the notion of immortality, but unworthy of enjoying immortality itself. Therefore, this universal belief in a future state is one sign of change, one proof that the soul is not now in its last stage of being, that the change which it undergoes is merely change and not destruction.

If we had been destined for this world alone it is probable we should have been contented with what this world affords; the excellence we saw and felt would have been the only excellence we could conceive. But now man always imagines something better than he sees. No grandeur and no beauty which he beholds are equal to the grandeur and the beauty which he conceives. Something tells him this is human, that elsewhere there are fairer and better things than these. In all times man has delighted to draw a natural and moral world after his own fancy, a land without storm and tempest, a people without violence and injustice living in perpetual peace and exercising unwearied benevolence. This discontent of present things is made a part of man's nature to remind him that present things are not always to endure. He is swift to conceive better things to inure him to that perfection which must infinitely exceed even his imagination. If man is to live again, the object of such a provision is easy to be comprehended and worthy of Almighty wisdom. But why is it given if all ends here? Why are we so keen to discern the imperfections of this our first and last and only home? A being of this world has no need of it. It is a mark of futurity, the forerunner of another world, the strong evidence of an immortal being.

To exist in this world seems to be the only purpose for which the brute creation was intended. They eat and drink, and perish. Nor does it appear that they have any superfluous faculties, any portion of understanding greater than what is necessary for the preservation of their brief existence. If they have lived a few years and given birth to other beings like themselves, they appear to have done all that Providence ever intended them to do. If man, like these, had only talents to gather his support and defeat the hostile animals which surrounded him no hope of immortality could be gathered from a condition like this; man would be of the earth, earthy; destined to live in this world with qualities fitted for this world and to all appearance limited to it. But in speaking of the mind of man we forget and we leap over all those faculties which are sufficient for the preservation of life. We do not wonder at man because he is cunning in procuring his food, but we are amazed with the variety, the superfluity, the immensity of human talents. We are astonished that he should have found his way over the seas and numbered the stars, and called by its name every earth and stone and plant and creeping reptile that the Almighty hath made. We see him gathered together in great cities, guided by laws, disciplined by instruction, softened by fine arts, and sanctified by solemn worship. We count over the pious spirit of the world, the beautiful writers, the great statesmen, all who have invented subtlely, who have thought deeply, who have executed wisely. All these are proofs that we are destined for a second life. It is not possible to believe that this redundant vigour, this lavish and excessive power was given for the mere gathering of meat and drink. If the only object is present existence such faculties are cruel, are misplaced, are useless. They all shew us that there is something great awaiting us, that the soul is now young, and infantine springing up into a more perfect life when the body falls into dust.

Then why is it that there is always a progress from one novelty to another? Why does happiness recede before us as we advance? Why is man driven by the present moment to a future which, when it comes, still beckons him to a future beyond? In boyhood it is to be youth, in youth it is to be manhood, in manhood it is to be old age.

But in youth pleasure wearies, in manhood power fatigues, in old age sadness and weakness oppress—till man is wearied out by the long delusion and sees at last if he would reach that happiness he has so long pursued, he must follow it over the great gulph across which Dives called to Lazarus for aid.

God would not have so framed the heart of man if that heart is perishable and mortal. It is not one God that has made the invisible spirit and another God that has made all the objects we can see and touch. But one Omnipotence and one Omniscience has acted throughout in forming the most stupendous mind and in completing the minutest insect. If this incessant change be then the quality of a soul which is to suffer death, if our desires can here find no resting place and are not to exist anywhere but here, where is there besides such an inconsistency in all the other works of God? No animal has wings that is not destined to fly; every creature that swims in the deep has all the organs and instruments necessary for that kind of life. When we look at the courageous animals we are well aware that they must live by their courage. Of the timid we do not doubt but that they owe their safety to their circumspection. We always assign to Providence a purpose. We cannot look upon a bodily organ or witness a mental quality without assigning to them a particular use. If the present use is not obvious the creature is to undergo some change that will justify the work of God and bring that organ or that quality into action. This half-living reptile that is now crawling on the earth will not end in this state; those rudiments of wings will expand and he will become an inhabitant of the air. Thus we reason of all nature, and thus we should reason also of the soul of man. This eternal change, this sickness of present things, this appetite for the future, these are the marks of the wings and the signs of the great flight. This is not the world to which they belong, but they are the instruments and the organs which enable us to detach ourselves from this world, and to spring up into greater purity and freedom.

Of the other qualities of the mind there is no one who doubts. The connection they have with this life cannot be mistaken. Resentment is given us for protection, fear for preservation, hope for comfort, compassion for mutual aid, gratitude for the encouragement of mutual benevolence. All these are present qualities, some beautiful, some bad, but all calculated for the present scene, all bearing upon our immediate destiny, all connected with this world. But the knowledge of God and his attributes, the ungratified notions of excellence, the impatience of present things, the unwearied appetite for change, the lavish variety and splendour of the human faculties—all these things are not to be explained but by believing the soul to be immortal or the God that made it to be unjust.

There is one other, and an almost universal passion in human nature which appears to be planted in us to excite and to cherish the feeling of the immortality of the soul— the desire of being remembered and honoured after death, or, as it is commonly denominated, the love of posthumous fame. All men feel it. It would overwhelm any of us here present with the deepest affliction to believe that we were utterly forgotten when we ceased to live. After religion, the great soother and comforter in death is to believe that we shall survive in the memory of those whom we leave behind. If this passion was a passion only of the rich and great, it might proceed from a reluctance to quit those enjoyments which are said by the son of Sirach to make death so terrible. But all men have it. The poor wish to live in the memory of the poor, the wretched to be remembered even by the wretched—anything but to be forgotten and blotted out, than which there is nothing more awful to the mind of man. For what purpose is it then that our wishes shoot out beyond our endurance, and that we have such an irresistible tendency to paint ourselves as conscious of honour or of shame after the outward and visible man has perished away? This universal feeling was not given in mockery and derision of mankind. He is surely not allowed for the sport of some higher order of beings to hope so strongly that which is impossible. This peculiarity of his nature is not accidental. It was not overlooked in the structure of his mind, but it was placed there with design and placed there with benevolence— with design because nothing in this world is done without design, with benevolence because man wanted this glimpse of another life for his happiness and he wanted it for his elevation, to give him courage under all the evils of the world, and to whisper into his inward soul that he only is unchangeable amid vicissitude and imperishable amid decay.

It is a science not unworthy of time and attention to find out what the qualities of our minds are and for what purposes they were intended. But it is impossible in the prosecution of this study not to perceive that the mind with all its worldly attributes has some qualities entirely destined for futurity, arranged for a totally separate order of things, doing within us the service of Heaven and watching carefully over the ark of God which every man carries in his heart. Therefore do not answer me with saying all this perishes to the eye, it seems as if the soul were dead. I reply with the holy apostle, it is the great law of nature, that which thou sowest is not quickened except it die, and that which thou sowest thou sowest, not that body which shall be, but God giveth it a body as it hath pleased Him, and to every seed its own body.

The season is now come when those changes to which the apostle alludes begin to take place. The sower has deposited the seed in the ground, and to the outward eye it seems to perish. Yet ere long it will be green with life, and God will give to every seed the body which hath pleased Him. Let it be our care, then, to derive from the changes of nature a lesson of religious wisdom, and beholding the decay and the resurrection of the outward world to remember before it is too late that we also must die and rise again.

SPEECHES

ON THE REJECTION OF THE REFORM BILL

SPEECH AT TAUNTON [1]

MR. BAILIFF, I have spoken so often on this subject, that I am sure both you and the gentlemen here present will be obliged to me for saying but little, and that favour I am as willing to confer, as you can be to receive it. I feel most deeply the event which has taken place, because, by putting the two Houses of Parliament in collision with each other, it will impede the public business, and diminish the public prosperity. I feel it as a churchman, because I cannot but blush to see so many dignitaries of the Church arrayed against the wishes and happiness of the people. I feel it more than all, because I believe it will sow the seeds of deadly hatred between the aristocracy and the great mass of the people. The loss of the bill I do not feel, and for the best of all possible reasons—because I have not the slightest idea that it *is* lost. I have no more doubt, before the expiration of the winter, that this bill will pass, than I have that the annual tax bills will pass, and greater certainty than this no man can have, for Franklin tells us, there are but two things certain in this world—death and taxes. As for the possibility of the House of Lords preventing ere long a reform of Parliament, I hold it to be the most absurd notion that ever entered into human imagination. I do not mean to be disrespectful, but the attempt of the Lords to stop the progress of reform, reminds me very forcibly of the great storm of Sidmouth, and of the conduct of the excellent Mrs. Partington [2] on that occasion. In the winter of 1824, there set in a great flood upon that town—the tide rose to an incredible height— the waves rushed in upon the houses, and everything was threatened with destruction. In the midst of this sublime and terrible storm, Dame Partington, who lived upon the beach, was seen at the door of her house with mop and pattens, trundling her mop, squeezing out the sea-water,

[1] See p. 296.   [2] See p. 296.

and vigorously pushing away the Atlantic Ocean. The
Atlantic was roused. Mrs. Partington's spirit was up;
but I need not tell you that the contest was unequal.
The Atlantic Ocean beat Mrs. Partington. She was
excellent at a slop, or a puddle, but she should not have
meddled with a tempest. Gentlemen, be at your ease—
be quiet and steady. You will beat Mrs. Partington.

They tell you, gentlemen, in the debates by which we
have been lately occupied, that the bill is not justified by
experience. I do not think this true; but if it were true,
nations are sometimes compelled to act without experience
for their guide, and to trust to their own sagacity for
the anticipation of consequences. The instances where
this country has been compelled thus to act have been so
eminently successful, that I see no cause for fear, even if
we were acting in the manner imputed to us by our enemies.
What precedents and what experience were there at the
Reformation, when the country, with one unanimous effort,
pushed out the Pope, and his grasping and ambitious
clergy?—What experience, when at the Revolution we
drove away our ancient race of kings, and chose another
family, more congenial to our free principles?—And yet
to those two events, contrary to experience, and unguided
by precedents, we owe all our domestic happiness, and
civil and religious freedom—and having got rid of corrupt
priests and despotic kings, by our sense and our courage,
are we now to be intimidated by the awful danger of
extinguishing Boroughmongers, and shaking from our neck
the ignominious yoke which their baseness has imposed
upon it? Go on, they say, as you have done for these
hundred years last past. I answer it is impossible: five
hundred people now write and read, where one hundred
wrote and read fifty years ago. The iniquities and enormities of the borough system are now known to the meanest
of the people. You have a different sort of men to deal
with—you must change because the beings whom you
govern are changed. After all, and to be short, I must
say that it has always appeared to me to be the most
absolute nonsense that we cannot be a great, or a rich and
happy nation, without suffering ourselves to be bought
and sold every five years like a pack of negro slaves. I
hope I am not a very rash man, but I would launch boldly

into this experiment without any fear of consequences, and I believe there is not a man here present who would not cheerfully embark with me. As to the enemies of the bill, who pretend to be reformers, I know them, I believe, better than you do, and I earnestly caution you against them. You will have no more of reform than they are compelled to grant—you will have no reform at all, if they can avoid it—you will be hurried into a war to turn your attention from reform. They do not understand you—they will not believe in the improvement you have made—they think the English of the present day are as the English of the times of Queen Anne or George the First. They know no more of the present state of their own country, than of the state of the Esquimaux Indians. Gentlemen, I view the ignorance of the present state of the country with the most serious concern, and I believe they will one day or another waken into conviction with horror and dismay. I will omit no means of rousing them to a sense of their danger;—for this object, I cheerfully sign the petition proposed by Dr. Kinglake, which I consider to be the wisest and most moderate of the two.

ON THE REFORM BILL

STICK to the Bill—it is your Magna Charta, and your Runnymede. King John made a present to the Barons. King William has made a similar present to you. Never mind; common qualities good in common times. If a man does not vote for the Bill, he is unclean—the plague-spot is upon him—push him into the lazaretto of the last century, with Wetherell and Sadler—purify the air before you approach him—bathe your hands in Chloride of Lime, if you have been contaminated by his touch.

So far from its being a merely theoretical improvement, I put it to any man, who is himself embarked in a profession, or has sons in the same situation, if the unfair influence of Boroughmongers has not perpetually thwarted him in his lawful career of ambition and professional emolument? "I have been in three general engagements at sea," said an old sailor—"have been twice wounded; —I commanded the boats when the French frigate, the ASTROLABE, was cut out so gallantly." "Then you are made a Post Captain?" "No. I was very near it; but— Lieutenant Thompson cut me out, as I cut out the French frigate; his father is Town Clerk of the Borough for which Lord F—— is Member, and there my chance was finished." In the same manner, all over England, you will find great scholars rotting on curacies — brave captains starving in garrets—profound lawyers decayed and mouldering in the Inns of Court, because the parsons, warriors, and advocates of Boroughmongers must be crammed to saturation, before there is a morsel of bread for the man who does not sell his votes, and put his country up to auction; and though this is of every day occurrence, the Borough system, we are told, is no practical evil.

Who can bear to walk through a slaughter-house? blood, garbage, stomachs, entrails, legs, tails, kidneys, horrors—I often walk a mile about to avoid it. What a scene of disgust and horror is an election—the base and infamous traffic of principles—a candidate of high character reduced to such means—the perjury and evasion of agents—the detestable rapacity of voters—the ten days' dominion of mammon, and Belial. The Bill lessens it—begins the destruction of such practices—affords some chance, and some means of turning public opinion against bribery, and of rendering it infamous.

But the thing I cannot, and will not bear, is this;—what right has *this* Lord, or *that* Marquis, to buy ten seats in Parliament, in the shape of Boroughs, and then to make laws to govern me? And how are these masses of power re-distributed? The eldest son of my Lord is just come from Eton—he knows a good deal about Æneas and Dido, Apollo and Daphne—and that is all; and to this boy his father gives a six-hundredth part of the power of making laws, as he would give him a horse or a double-barrelled gun. Then Vellum, the steward, is put in—an admirable man;—he has raised the estates—watched the progress of the family Road and Canal Bills—and Vellum shall help to rule over the people of Israel. A neighbouring country gentleman, Mr. Plumpkin, hunts with my Lord—opens him a gate or two, while the hounds are running—dines with my Lord—agrees with my Lord—wishes he could rival the South-Down sheep of my Lord—and upon Plumpkin is conferred a portion of the government. Then there is a distant relation of the same name, in the County Militia, with white teeth, who calls up the carriage at the Opera, and is always wishing O'Connell was hanged, drawn, and quartered—then a barrister, who has written an article in the *Quarterly*, and is very likely to speak, and refute M'Culloch; and these five people, in whose nomination I have no more agency than I have in the nomination of the toll-keepers of the Bosphorus, are to make laws for me and my family—to put their hands in my purse, and to sway the future destinies of this country; and when the neighbours step in, and beg permission to say a few words before these persons are chosen, there is an universal cry of ruin, confusion, and destruction;—we have become a great people under Vellum and Plumpkin—under Vellum and Plumpkin our ships have covered the ocean—under Vellum and Plumpkin our armies have secured the strength of the Hills—to turn out Vellum and Plumpkin is not Reform, but Revolution.

Was there ever such a Ministry? Was there ever before a real Ministry of the people? Look at the condition of the country when it was placed in their hands: the state of the house when the incoming tenant took possession: windows broken, chimneys on fire, mobs round the house threatening to pull it down, roof tumbling, rain pouring in. It was courage to occupy it; it was a miracle to save it; it will be the glory of glories to enlarge and expand it, and to make it the eternal palace of wise and temperate freedom.

Proper examples have been made among the unhappy and misguided disciples of Swing: a rope has been carried round O'Connell's legs, and a ring inserted in Cobbett's nose. Then the Game Laws!!! Was ever conduct so shabby as that of the two or three governments which preceded that of Lord Grey? The cruelties and enormities of this code had been thoroughly exposed; and a general conviction existed of the necessity of a change. Bills were brought in by various gentlemen, containing some trifling alteration in this abominable code, and even these were sacrificed to the tricks and manœuvres of some noble Nimrod, who availed himself of the emptiness of the town in July, and flung out the Bill. Government never stirred a step. The fulness of the prisons, the wretchedness and demoralisation of the poor, never came across them. The humane and considerate Peel never once offered to extend his ægis over them. It had nothing to do with the state of party; and some of their double-barrelled voters might be offended. In the meantime, for every ten pheasants which fluttered in the wood, one English peasant was rotting in gaol. No sooner is Lord Althorp Chancellor of the Exchequer, than he turns out of the house a trumpery and (perhaps) an insidious Bill for the improvement of the Game Laws; and in an instant offers the assistance of Government for the abolition of the whole code.

Then look at the gigantic Brougham, sworn in at twelve o'clock, and before six has a bill on the table, abolishing the abuses of a Court which has been the curse of the people of England for centuries. For twenty-five long years did Lord Eldon sit in that Court, surrounded with misery and sorrow, which he never held up a finger to alleviate. The widow and the orphan cried to him as

vainly as the town crier cries when he offers a small reward
for a full purse; the bankrupt of the Court became the
lunatic of the Court, estates mouldered away, and mansions
fell down; but the fees came in, and all was well. But
in an instant the iron mace of Brougham shivered to atoms
this house of fraud and of delay; and this is the man who
will help to govern you; who bottoms his reputation on
doing good to you; who knows, that to reform abuses is
the safest basis of fame, and the surest instrument of
power; who uses the highest gifts of reason, and the most
splendid efforts of genius, to rectify those abuses, which
all the genius and talent of the profession [1] have hitherto
been employed to justify, and to protect. Look to
Brougham, and turn you to that side where he waves his
long and lean finger; and mark well that face which nature
has marked so forcibly—which dissolves pensions—turns
jobbers into honest men—scares away the plunderer of
the public—and is a terror to him who doeth evil to the
people. But, above all, look to the Northern Earl, victim,
before this honest and manly reign, of the spitefulness of
the Court. You may now, for the first time, learn to trust
in the professions of a Minister; you are directed by a man
who prefers character to place, and who has given such
unequivocal proofs of honesty and patriotism, that his
image ought to be amongst your household gods, and his
name to be lisped by your children: two thousand years
hence it will be a legend like the fable of Perseus and
Andromeda: Britannia chained to a mountain—two
hundred rotten animals menacing her destruction, till a
tall Earl, armed with Schedule A., and followed by his
page Russell, drives them into the deep, and delivers
over Britannia in safety to crowds of ten-pound renters,
who deafen the air with their acclamations. Forthwith,
Latin verses upon this—school exercises—boys whipt, and
all the usual absurdities of education. Don't part with
the Administration composed of Lord Grey and Lord
Brougham; and not only these, but look at them all—the
mild wisdom of Lansdowne—the genius and extensive
knowledge of Holland, in whose bold and honest life there
is no varying nor shadow of change—the unexpected and

[1] Lord Lyndhurst is an exception; I firmly believe he had no
wish to perpetuate the abuses of the Court of Chancery.

exemplary activity of Lord Melbourne—and the rising parliamentary talents of Stanley. You are ignorant of your best interests, if every vote you can bestow is not given to such a ministry as this.

You will soon find an alteration of behaviour in the upper orders when elections become real. You will find that you are raised to the importance to which you ought to be raised. The merciless ejector, the rural tyrant, will be restrained within the limits of decency and humanity, and will improve their own characters, at the same time that they better your condition.

It is not the power of aristocracy that will be destroyed by these measures, but the *unfair* power. If the Duke of Newcastle is kind and obliging to his neighbours, he will probably lead his neighbours; if he is a man of sense, he will lead them more certainly, and to a better purpose. All this is as it should be; but the Duke of Newcastle, at present, by buying certain old houses, could govern his neighbours and legislate for them, even if he had not five grains of understanding, and if he were the most churlish and brutal man under heaven. The present state of things renders unnecessary all those important virtues, which rich and well-born men, under a better system, would exercise for the public good. The Duke of Newcastle (I mention him only as an instance), Lord Exeter will do as well, but either of those noblemen, depending not upon walls, arches, and abutments, for their power—but upon mercy, charity, forbearance, indulgence, and example— would pay this price, and lead the people by their affections; one would be the God of Stamford, and the other of Newark. This union of the great with the many is the real healthy state of a country; such a country is strong to invincibility —and this strength the Borough system entirely destroys.

Cant words creep in, and affect quarrels; the changes are rung between Revolution and Reform; but, first settle whether a wise government ought to attempt the measure —whether anything is wanted—whether less would do— and, having settled this, mere nomenclature becomes of very little consequence. But, after all, if it be Revolution, and not Reform, it will only induce me to receive an old political toast in a twofold meaning, and with twofold pleasure. When King William and the great and glorious

Revolution are given, I shall think not only of escape from
bigotry, but exemption from corruption; and I shall thank
Providence, which has given us a second King William
for the destruction of vice, as the other of that name was
given us for the conservation of freedom.

All former political changes, proposed by these very men,
it is said, were mild and gentle, compared to this: true,
but are you on Saturday night to seize your apothecary
by the throat, and to say to him, "Subtle compounder,
fraudulent posologist, did not you order me a drachm of
this medicine on Monday morning, and now you declare,
that nothing short of an ounce can do me any good?"
"True enough," would he of the phials reply, "*but you
did not take the drachm on Monday morning*—that makes
all the difference, my dear Sir; if you had done as I advised
you at first, the small quantity of medicine would have
sufficed; and, instead of being in a night-gown and slippers
upstairs, you would have been walking vigorously in
Piccadilly. Do as you please—and die if you please; but
don't blame me because you despised my advice, and by
your own ignorance and obstinacy have entailed upon
yourself tenfold rhubarb and unlimited infusion of senna."

Now see the consequences of having a manly Leader,
and a manly Cabinet. Suppose they had come out with
a little ill-fashioned seven months' reform; what would
have been the consequence? The same opposition from
the Tories—that would have been quite certain—and not
a single Reformer in England satisfied with the measure.
You have now a real Reform, and a fair share of power
delegated to the people.

The Anti-Reformers cite the increased power of the press
—this is the very reason why I want an increased power
in the House of Commons. The *Times, Herald, Advertiser,
Globe, Sun, Courier,* and *Chronicle,* are a heptarchy, which
govern this country, and govern it because the people
are so badly represented. I am perfectly satisfied, that
with a fair and honest House of Commons the power of
the press would diminish—and that the greatest authority
would centre in the highest place.

Is it possible for a gentleman to get into Parliament,
at present, without doing things he is utterly ashamed of
—without mixing himself up with the lowest and basest

of mankind? Hands, accustomed to the scented lubricity of soap, are defiled with pitch, and contaminated with filth. Is there not some inherent vice in a Government, which cannot be carried on but with such abominable wickedness, in which no gentleman can mingle without moral degradation, and the practice of crimes, the very imputation of which, on other occasions, he would repel at the hazard of his life?

What signifies a small majority in the House? The miracle is, that there should have been any majority at all; that there was not an immense majority on the other side. It was a very long period before the Courts of Justice in Jersey could put down smuggling; and why? The Judges, Counsel, Attorneys, Crier of the Court, Grand and Petty Jurymen, were all smugglers, and the High Sheriff and Constables were running goods every moonlight night.

How are you to do without a government? And what other government, if this Bill be ultimately lost, could possibly be found? How could any country defray the ruinous expense of protecting, with troops and constables, the Duke of Wellington and Sir Robert Peel, who literally would not be able to walk from the Horse Guards to Grosvenor Square, without two or three regiments of foot to screen them from the mob; and in these hollow squares the Hero of Waterloo would have to spend his political life? By the whole exercise of his splendid military talents, by strong batteries, at Bootle's and White's, he might, on nights of great debate, reach the House of Lords; but Sir Robert would probably be cut off, and nothing could save Twiss and Lewis.

The great majority of persons returned by the new Boroughs would either be men of high reputation for talents, or persons of fortune known in the neighbourhood; they have property and character to lose. Why are they to plunge into mad and revolutionary projects of pillaging the public creditor? It is not the interest of any such man to do it; he would lose more by the destruction of public credit than he would gain by a remission of what he paid for the interest of the public debt. And if it is not the interest of anyone to act in this manner, it is not the interest of the mass. How many, also, of these new legislators would there be, who were not themselves creditors of the State? Is it the interest of such men to create a revolution, by destroying the constitutional power of the House of Lords, or of the King? Does there exist in persons of that class any disposition for such changes? Are not all their feelings, and opinions, and prejudices, on the opposite side? The majority of the new members will be landed gentlemen: their genus is utterly distinct from the revolutionary tribe; they have Molar teeth; they are destitute of the carnivorous and incisive jaws of political adventurers.

There will be mistakes at first, as there are in all changes. All young Ladies will imagine (as soon as this Bill is carried) that they will be instantly married. Schoolboys believe that Gerunds and Supines will be abolished, and that Currant Tarts must ultimately come down in price; the Corporal and Sergeant are sure of double pay; bad Poets will expect a demand for their Epics; Fools will be disappointed, as they always are; reasonable men, who know what to expect, will find that a very serious good has been obtained.

What good to the hewer of wood and the drawer of water? How is he benefited, if Old Sarum is abolished and Birmingham Members created? But if you ask this question of Reform, you must ask it of a great number of other great measures. How is he benefited by Catholic Emancipation, by the repeal of the Corporation and Test Acts, by the Revolution of 1688, by any great political change? by a good government? In the first place, if many are benefited, and the lower orders are not injured, this alone is reason enough for the change. But the hewer of wood and the drawer of water *are* benefited by reform. Reform will produce economy and investigation; there will be fewer jobs, and a less lavish expenditure; wars will not be persevered in for years after the people are tired of them; taxes will be taken off the poor, and laid upon the rich; demotic habits will be more common in a country where the rich are forced to court the poor for political power; cruel and oppressive punishments (such as those for night poaching) will be abolished. If you steal a pheasant you will be punished as you ought to be, but not sent away from your wife and children for seven years. Tobacco

will be 2d. per lb. cheaper. Candles will fall in price.
These last results of an improved government will be felt.
We do not pretend to abolish poverty, or to prevent
wretchedness; but if peace, economy, and justice, are the
results of Reform, a number of small benefits, or rather of
benefits which appear small to us, but not to them, will
accrue to millions of the people; and the connection between
the existence of John Russell, and the reduced price of
bread and cheese, will be as clear as it has been the object
of his honest, wise, and useful life to make it.

Don't be led away by such nonsense; all things are
dearer under a bad government, and cheaper under a good
one. The real question they ask you is, What difference
can any change of government make to you? They want
to keep the bees from buzzing and stinging, in order that
they may rob the hive in peace.

Work well! How does it work well, when every human
being in-doors and out (with the exception of the Duke of
Wellington) says it must be made to work better, or it
will soon cease to work at all? It is little short of absolute
nonsense to call a government good, which the great mass
of Englishmen would, before twenty years were elapsed,
if Reform were denied, rise up and destroy. Of what
use have all the cruel laws been of Perceval, Eldon, and
Castlereagh, to extinguish Reform? Lord John Russell,
and his abettors, would have been committed to gaol
twenty years ago for half only of his present Reform; and
now relays of the people would drag them from London to
Edinburgh; at which latter city we are told, by Mr. Dundas,
that there is no eagerness for Reform. Five minutes before
Moses struck the rock, this gentleman would have said
that there was no eagerness for water.

There are two methods of making alterations: the one
is to despise the applicants, to begin with refusing every
concession, then to relax by making concessions which are
always too late; by offering in 1831 what is then too late,
but would have been cheerfully accepted in 1830—gradually
to O'Connellise the country, till at last, after this process
has gone on for some time, the alarm becomes too great,
and every thing is conceded in hurry and confusion. In
the meantime fresh conspiracies have been hatched by
the long delay, and no gratitude is expressed for what

has been extorted by fear. In this way peace was concluded with America, and Emancipation granted to the Catholics; and in this way the war of complexion will be finished in the West Indies. The other method is, to see at a distance that the thing must be done, and to do it effectually, *and at once*; to take it out of the hands of the common people, and to carry the measure in a manly liberal manner, so as to satisfy the great majority. The merit of this belongs to the Administration of Lord Grey. He is the only Minister I know of who has begun a great measure in good time, conceded at the beginning of twenty years what would have been extorted at the end of it, and prevented that folly, violence, and ignorance, which emanate from a long denial and extorted concession of justice to great masses of human beings. I believe the Question of Reform, or any dangerous agitation of it, is set at rest for thirty or forty years; and this is an eternity in politics.

Boroughs are not the power proceeding from wealth. Many men who have no Boroughs are infinitely richer than those who have—but it is the artifice of wealth in seizing hold of certain localities. The Boroughmonger is like rheumatism, which owes its power, not so much to the intensity of the pain as to its peculiar position; a little higher up, or a little lower down, the same pain would be trifling; but it fixes in the joints, and gets into the headquarters of motion and activity. The Boroughmonger knows the importance of arthritic positions; he disdains muscle, gets into the joints, and lords it over the whole machine by felicity of place. Other men are as rich—but those riches are not fixed in the critical spot.

I live a good deal with all ranks and descriptions of people; I am thoroughly convinced that the party of Democrats and Republicans is very small and contemptible; that the English love their institutions—that they love not only this King, (who would not love him?) but the kingly office—that they have no hatred to the Aristocracy. I am not afraid of trusting English happiness to English Gentlemen. I believe that the half million of new voters will choose much better for the public, than the twenty or thirty Peers, to whose usurped power they succeed.

If any man doubt of the power of Reform, let him take these two memorable proofs of its omnipotence. First, but for the declaration against it, I believe the Duke of Wellington might this day have been in office; and, secondly, in the whole course of the debates at County Meetings and in Parliament, there are not twenty men who have declared against Reform. Some advance an inch, some a foot, some a yard—but nobody stands still—nobody says, We ought to remain just where we were—everybody discovers that he is a Reformer, and has long been so—and appears infinitely delighted with this new view of himself. Nobody appears without the cockade—bigger or less—but always the cockade.

An exact and elaborate census is called for—vast information should have been laid upon the table of the House —great time should have been given for deliberation. All these objections, being turned into English, simply mean, that the chances of another year should have been given for defeating the Bill. In that time the Poles may be crushed, the Belgians organised, Louis Philip dethroned; war may rage all over Europe—the popular spirit may be diverted to other objects. It is certainly provoking that the Ministry foresaw all these possibilities, and determined to model the iron while it was red and glowing.

It is not enough that a political institution works well practically: it must be defensible; it must be such as will bear discussion, and not excite ridicule and contempt. It might work well for aught I know, if, like the savages of Onelashka, we sent out to catch a king: but who could defend a coronation by chase? who can defend the payment of £40,000 for the three-hundredth part of the power of Parliament, and the resale of this power to Government for places to the Lord Williams and Lord Charles's, and others of the Anglophagi? Teach a million of the common people to read—and such a government (work it ever so well) must perish in twenty years. It is impossible to persuade the mass of mankind that there are not other and better methods of governing a country. It is so complicated, so wicked, such envy and hatred accumulate against the gentlemen who have fixed themselves on the joints, that it cannot fail to perish, and to be driven, as it *is* driven, from the country by a general burst of hatred and detestation. I meant, gentlemen, to have spoken for another half hour, but I am old and tired. Thank me for ending—but, gentlemen, bear with me for another moment; one word before I end. I am old, but I thank God I have lived to see more than my observations on human nature taught me I had any right to expect. I have lived to see an honest King, in whose word his Ministers can trust; who disdains to deceive those men whom he has called to the public service, but makes common cause with them for the common good; and exercises the highest powers of a ruler for the dearest interests of the State. I have lived to see a King with a good heart, who, surrounded by Nobles, thinks of common men; who loves the great mass of English people, and wishes to be loved by them; who knows that his real power, as he feels that his happiness, is founded on their affection. I have lived to see a King, who, without pretending to the pomp of superior intellect, has the wisdom to see, that the decayed institutions of human policy require amendment; and who, in spite of clamour, interest, prejudice, and fear, has the manliness to carry these wise changes into immediate execution. Gentlemen, farewell: shout for the King!

S

LETTERS TO THE PRESS

PETITION TO THE HOUSE OF CONGRESS AT WASHINGTON ON AMERICAN DEBTS

THE HUMBLE PETITION *of the* REV. SYDNEY SMITH *to the* HOUSE OF CONGRESS *at* WASHINGTON.

I PETITION your honourable House to institute some measures for the restoration of American credit, and for the repayment of debts incurred and repudiated by several of the States. Your Petitioner lent to the State of Pennsylvania a sum of money, for the purpose of some public improvement. The amount, though small, is to him important, and is a saving from a life income, made with difficulty and privation. If their refusal to pay (from which a very large number of English families are suffering) had been the result of war, produced by the unjust aggression of powerful enemies; if it had arisen from civil discord; if it had proceeded from an improvident application of means in the first years of self-government: if it were the act of a poor State struggling against the barrenness of nature—every friend of America would have been contented to wait for better times; but the fraud is committed in the profound peace of Pennsylvania, by the richest State in the Union, after the wise investment of the borrowed money in roads and canals, of which the repudiators are every day reaping the advantage. It is an act of bad faith which (all its circumstances considered) has no parallel, and no excuse.

Nor is it only the loss of property which your Petitioner laments; he laments still more that immense power which the bad faith of America has given to aristocratical opinions, and to the enemies of free institutions, in the old world. It is in vain any longer to appeal to history, and to point out the wrongs which the many have received from the few. The Americans, who boast to have improved the institutions of the old world, have at least equalled its crimes. A great nation, after trampling under foot all earthly tyranny, has been guilty of a fraud as enormous as ever disgraced the worst king of the most degraded nation of Europe.

It is most painful to your Petitioner to see that American citizens excite, wherever they may go, the recollection that they belong to a dishonest people, who pride themselves on having tricked and pillaged Europe; and this mark is fixed by their faithless legislators on some of the best and most honourable men in the world, whom every Englishman has been eager to see and proud to receive.

It is a subject of serious concern to your Petitioner that you are losing all that power which the friends of freedom rejoiced that you possessed, looking upon you as the ark of human happiness, and the most splendid picture of justice and of wisdom that the world had yet seen. Little did the friends of America expect it, and sad is the spectacle to see you rejected by every State in Europe, as a nation with whom no contract can be made, because none will be kept; unstable in the very foundations of social life, deficient in the elements of good faith, men who prefer any load of infamy however great, to any pressure of taxation however light.

Nor is it only this gigantic bankruptcy for so many degrees of longitude and latitude which your Petitioner deplores, but he is alarmed also by that total want of shame with which these things have been done; the callous immorality with which Europe has been plundered, that deadness of the moral sense which seems to preclude all return to honesty, to perpetuate this new infamy, and to threaten its extension over every State of the Union.

To any man of real philanthropy, who receives pleasure from the improvements of the world, the repudiation of the public debts of America, and the shameless manner in which it has been talked of and done, is the most melancholy event which has happened during the existence of the present generation. Your Petitioner sincerely prays that the great and good men still existing among you may, by teaching to the United States the deep disgrace they have incurred in the whole world, restore them to moral health, to that high position they have lost, and which, for the happiness of mankind, it is so important they should ever maintain; for the United States are now working out the greatest of all political problems, and upon that confederacy the eyes of thinking men are intensely fixed, to see how far the mass of mankind can be trusted with the management of their own affairs, and the establishment of their own happiness.

May 18, 1843.

ON THE AMERICAN DEBTS[1]

To the Editor of the " Morning Chronicle"

SIR,

Having been unwell for some days past, I have had no opportunity of paying my respects to General Duff Green, who (whatever be his other merits) has certainly not shown himself a Washington in defence of his country. The General demands, with a beautiful simplicity, *"Whence this morbid hatred of America?"* But this question, all-affecting as it is, is stolen from Pilpay's fables:—"A fox," says Pilpay, "caught by the leg in a trap near the farm-yard, uttered the most piercing cries of distress: forthwith all the birds of the yard gathered round him, and seemed to delight in his misfortune; hens chuckled, geese hissed, ducks quacked, and chanticleer with shrill cockadoodles rent the air. 'Whence,' said the fox, limping forward with infinite gravity, 'whence this morbid hatred of the fox? What have I done? Whom have I injured? I am overwhelmed with astonishment at these symptoms of aversion.' 'Oh! you old villain,' the poultry exclaimed, 'Where are our ducklings? Where are our goslings? Did not I see you running away yesterday with my mother in your mouth? Did you not eat up all my relations last week? You ought to die the worst of deaths—to be pecked into a thousand pieces.'" Now hence, General Green, comes the morbid hatred of America, as you term it—because her conduct has been predatory—because she has ruined so many helpless children, so many miserable women, so many aged men—because she has disturbed the order of the world, and rifled those sacred treasures which human virtue had hoarded for human misery. Why is such hatred morbid? Why, is it not just, inevitable, innate? Why, is it not disgraceful to want it? Why, is it not honourable to feel it?

Hate America!!! I have loved and honoured America all my life; and in the *Edinburgh Review*, and at all oppor-

[1] See p. 296.

tunities which my trumpery sphere of action has afforded, I have never ceased to praise and defend the United States; and to every American to whom I have had the good fortune to be introduced, I have proffered all the hospitality in my power. But I cannot shut my eyes to enormous dishonesty; nor, remembering their former state, can I restrain myself from calling on them (though I copy Satan) to spring up from the gulf of infamy in which they are rolling,—

Awake, arise, or be for ever fallen.

I am astonished that the honest States of America do not draw a *cordon sanitaire* round their unpaying brethren —that the truly mercantile New Yorkers, and the thoroughly honest people of Massachusetts, do not in their European visits wear an uniform with "S. S., or Solvent States," worked in gold letters upon the coat, and receipts in full of all demands tamboured on their waistcoats, and "our own property" figured on their pantaloons.

But the General seemed shocked that I should say the Americans cannot go to war without money: but what do I mean by war? Not irruptions into Canada—not the embodying of militia in Oregon; but a long, tedious, maritime war of four or five years' duration. Is any man so foolish as to suppose that Rothschild has nothing to do with such wars as these? and that a bankrupt State, without the power of borrowing a shilling in the world, may not be crippled in such a contest? We all know that the Americans can fight. Nobody doubts their courage. I see now in my mind's eye a whole army on the plains of Pennsylvania in battle array, immense corps of insolvent light infantry, regiments of heavy horse debtors, battalions of repudiators, brigades of bankrupts, with *Vivre sans payer, ou mourir*, on their banners, and *ære alieno* on their trumpets: all these desperate debtors would fight to the death for their country, and probably drive into the sea their invading creditors. Of their courage, I repeat again, I have no doubt. I wish I had the same confidence in their wisdom. But I believe they will become intoxicated by the flattery of unprincipled orators; and, instead of entering with us into a noble competition in making calico (the great object for which the Anglo-Saxon race appears to have been created), they will waste their happiness and their money (if they can get any) in years of silly, bloody, foolish, and accursed war, to prove to the world that Perkins is a real fine gentleman, and that the carronades of the Washington steamer will carry further than those of the Britisher Victoria, or the Robert Peel vessel of war.

I am accused of applying the epithet repudiation to States which have not repudiated. Perhaps so; but then these latter states have not paid. But what is the difference between a man who says, "I don't owe you anything, and will not pay you," and another who says, "I do owe you a sum," and who, having admitted the debt, never pays it? There seems in the first to be some slight colour of right; but the second is broad, blazing, refulgent, meridian fraud.

It may be very true that rich and educated men in Pennsylvania wish to pay the debt, and that the real objectors are the Dutch and German agriculturists, who cannot be made to understand the effect of character upon clover. All this may be very true, but it is a domestic quarrel. Their churchwardens of reputation must make a private rate of infamy for themselves—we have nothing to do with this rate. The real quarrel is the Unpaid World *versus* the State of Pennsylvania.

And now, dear Jonathan, let me beg of you to follow the advice of a real friend, who will say to you what Wat Tyler had not the virtue to say, and what all speakers in the eleven recent Pennsylvanian elections have cautiously abstained from saying,—"Make a great effort; book up at once, and pay." You have no conception of the obloquy and contempt to which you are exposing yourselves all over Europe. Bull is naturally disposed to love you, but he loves nobody who does not pay him. His imaginary paradise is some planet of punctual payment, where ready money prevails, and where debt and discount are unknown. As for me, as soon as I hear that the last farthing is paid to the last creditor, I will appear on my knees at the bar of the Pennsylvanian Senate in the plumeopicean robe of American controversy. Each Conscript Jonathan shall trickle over me a few drops of tar, and help to decorate me with those penal plumes in which the vanquished reasoner of the transatlantic world does homage to the physical superiority of his opponents. And now, having eased my soul of its indignation, and sold my stock at forty per cent. discount, I sulkily retire from the subject, with a fixed intention of lending no more money to free and enlightened republics, but of employing my money henceforth in buying up Abyssinian bonds, and purchasing into the Turkish Fours, or the Tunis Three-and-a-half per Cent. funds.

SYDNEY SMITH.

November 22, 1843.

"LOCKING IN" ON RAILWAYS [1]

To the Editor of the "Morning Chronicle"

SIR,

It falls to my lot to travel frequently on the Great Western Railway, and I request permission, through the medium of your able and honest journal, to make a complaint against the directors of that company.

It is the custom on that railway to lock the passengers in on both sides—a custom which, in spite of the dreadful example at Paris, I have every reason to believe they mean to continue without any relaxation.

In the course of a long life I have no recollection of any accident so shocking as that on the Paris railway—a massacre so sudden, so full of torment—death at the moment of pleasure—death aggravated by all the amazement, fear, and pain which can be condensed into the last moments of existence.

Who can say that the same scene may not be acted over again on the Great Western Railroad? That in the midst of their tunnel of three miles' length the same scene of slaughter and combustion may not scatter dismay and alarm over the whole country?

It seems to me perfectly monstrous that a board of ten or twelve monopolists can read such a description, and say to the public, "You must run your chance of being burnt or mutilated. We have arranged our plan upon the locking-in system, and we shall not incur the risk and expense of changing it."

The plea is, that rash or drunken people will attempt to get out of the carriages which are not locked, and that this measure really originates from attention to the safety of the public; so that the lives of two hundred persons who are not drunk and are not rash, are to be endangered for the half-yearly preservation of some idiot, upon whose

[1] See p. 296.

body the coroner is to sit, and over whom the sudden-death man is to deliver his sermon against the directors.

The very fact of locking the doors will be a frequent source of accidents. Mankind, whatever the directors may think of that process, are impatient of combustion. The Paris accident will never be forgotten. The passengers will attempt to escape through the windows, and ten times more of mischief will be done than if they had been left to escape by the doors in the usual manner.

It is not only the locking of the doors which is to be deprecated; but the effects which it has upon the imagination. Women, old people, and the sick, are all forced to travel by the railroad; and for two hundred miles they live under the recollection not only of impending danger, but under the knowledge that escape is impossible—a journey comes to be contemplated with horror. Men cannot persuade the females of their family to travel by the railroad; it is inseparably connected with abominable tyranny and perilous imprisonment.

Why does the necessity of locking both doors exist only on the Great Western? Why is one of the doors left open on all other railways?

The public have a right to every advantage under permitted monopoly which they would enjoy under free competition; and they are unjust to themselves if they do not insist upon this right. If there were two parallel railways, the one locking you in, and the other not, is there the smallest doubt which would carry away all the business? Can there be any hesitation in which timid women, drunken men, sages, philosophers, bishops, and all combustible beings, would place themselves?

I very much doubt the legality of locking doors, and refusing to open them. I arrive at a station where others are admitted; but I am not suffered to get out, though perhaps at the point of death. In all other positions of life there is egress where there is ingress. Man is universally the master of his own body, except he chooses to go from Paddington to Bridgewater: there only the Habeas Corpus is refused.

Nothing, in fact, can be more utterly silly or mistaken than this over-officious care of the public; as if every man who was not a railway director was a child or a fool. But why stop here? Why are not strait-waistcoats used? Why is not the accidental traveller strapped down? Why do contusion and fracture still remain physically possible?

Is not this extreme care of the public new? When first mail coaches began to travel twelve miles an hour, the *outsides* (if I remember rightly) were never tied to the roof. In packets, landsmen are not locked into the cabin to prevent them from tumbling overboard. This affectionate nonsense prevails only on the Great Western. It is there only that men, women, and children (seeking the only mode of transit which remains) are by these tender-hearted monopolists immediately committed to their locomotive prisons. Nothing can, in fact, be so absurd as all this officious zeal. It is the duty of the directors to take all reasonable precautions to warn the public of danger—to make it clear that there is no negligence on the part of the railroad directors; and then, this done, if a fool-hardy person choose to expose himself to danger, so be it. Fools there will be on roads of iron and on roads of gravel, and they must suffer for their folly; but why are Socrates, Solon, and Solomon to be locked up?

But is all this, which appears so philanthropical, mere philanthropy? Does not the locking of the doors save servants and policemen? Does not economy mingle with these benevolent feelings? Is it to save a few fellow-creatures, or a few pounds, that the children of the West are to be hermetically sealed in the locomotives? I do not say it is so; but I say it deserves a very serious examination whether it be so or not. Great and heavy is the sin of the directors of this huge monopoly, if they repeat upon their own iron the tragedy of Paris, in order to increase their dividends a few shillings per cent.

The country has (perhaps inevitably) given way to this great monopoly. Nothing can make it tolerable for a moment but the most severe and watchful jealousy of the manner in which its powers are exercised. We shall have tyrannical rules, vexatious rules, ill temper, pure folly, and meddling and impertinent paternity. It is the absolute duty of Lord Ripon and Mr. Gladstone (if the directors prove themselves to be so inadequate to the new situation in which they are placed) to restrain and direct them by law; and if these two gentlemen are afraid of the responsibility of such laws, they are deficient in the moral courage which their office requires, and the most important interests of the public are neglected.

I am, Sir, your obedient servant,

SYDNEY SMITH.

May 21, 1842.

THIRD LETTER TO ARCHDEACON SINGLETON

MY DEAR SIR,

I hope this is the last letter you will receive from me on Church matters. I am tired of the subject; so are you; so is everybody. In spite of many Bishops' charges, I am unbroken; and remain entirely of the same opinion as I was two or three years since—that the mutilation of Deans and Chapters is a rash, foolish, and imprudent measure.

I do not think the charge of the Bishop of London successful, in combating those arguments which have been used against the impending Dean and Chapter Bill; but it is quiet, gentlemanlike, temperate, and written in a manner which entirely becomes the high office and character which he bears.

I agree with him in saying that the Plurality and Residence Bill is, upon the whole, a very good Bill;—nobody, however, knows better than the Bishop of London the various changes it has undergone, and the improvements it has received. I could point out fourteen or fifteen very material alterations for the better since it came out of the hands of the Commission, and all *bearing materially upon the happiness and comfort of the parochial Clergy*. I will mention only a few:—the Bill, as originally introduced, gave the Bishop a power, when he considered the duties of the parish to be improperly performed, to suspend the Clergyman and appoint a Curate with a salary. Some impious person thought it not impossible that occasionally such a power might be maliciously and vindictively exercised, and that some check to it should be admitted into the Bill; accordingly, under the existing act, an Ecclesiastical Jury is to be summoned, and into that jury the defendant Clergyman may introduce a friend of his own.

If a Clergyman, from illness or any other overwhelming necessity, were prevented from having two services, he was exposed to an information, and penalty. In answering the Bishop, he was subjected to two opposite sets of penal-

256

ties—the one for saying *Yes*; the other for saying *No*: he was amenable to the needless and impertinent scrutiny of a Rural Dean before he was exposed to the scrutiny of a Bishop. Curates might be forced upon him by subscribing parishioners, and the certainty of a schism established in the parish; a Curate might have been forced upon *present* incumbents by the Bishop without any complaint made; upon men who took, or, perhaps, bought, their livings under very different laws;—all these acts of injustice are done away with, but it is not to the *credit* of the framers of the Bill that they were ever admitted, and they completely justify the opposition with which the Bill was received by me and by others. I add, however, with great pleasure, that when these and other objections were made, they were heard with candour, and promised to be remedied by the Archbishop of Canterbury and the Bishop of London and Lord John Russell.

I have spoken of the power to issue a Commission to inquire into the wellbeing of any parish: a vindictive and malicious Bishop might, it is true, convert this, which was intended for the protection, to the oppression of the Clergy —afraid to dispossess a Clergyman of his own authority, he might attempt to do the same thing under the cover of a jury of his ecclesiastical creatures. But I can hardly conceive such baseness in the prelate, or such infamous subserviency in the agents. An honest and respectable Bishop will remember that the very issue of such a Commission is a serious slur upon the character of a Clergyman; he will do all he can to prevent it by private monition and remonstrance; and if driven to such an act of power, he will of course state to the accused Clergyman the subjects of accusation, the names of his accusers, and give him ample time for his defence. If upon anonymous accusation he subjects a Clergyman to such an investigation, or refuses to him any advantage which the law gives to every accused person, he is an infamous, degraded, and scandalous tyrant: but I cannot believe there is such a man to be found upon the bench.

There is in this new Bill a very humane clause (though not introduced by the Commission), enabling the widow of the deceased clergyman to retain possession of the parsonage house for two months after the death of the

T

Incumbent. It ought, in fairness, to be extended to the heirs, executors, and administrators of the Incumbent. It is a great hardship that a family settled in a parish for fifty years perhaps, should be torn up by the roots in eight or ten days; and the interval of two months, allowing time for repairs, might put to rest many questions of dilapidation.

To the Bishop's power of intruding a Curate without any complaint on the part of the parish that the duty has been inadequately performed, I retain the same objections as before. It is a power which without this condition will be unfairly and partially exercised. The first object I admit is not the provision of the Clergyman, but the care of the parish: but one way of taking care of parishes is to take care that clergymen are not treated with tyranny, partiality, and injustice: and the best way of effecting this is to remember that their superiors have the same human passions as other people; and not to trust them with a power which may be so grossly abused, and which (incredible as the Bishop of London may deem it) *has been*, in some instances, grossly abused.

I cannot imagine what the Bishop means by saying, that the members of Cathedrals do not in virtue of their office bear any part in the parochial instruction of the people. This is a fine deceitful word, the word *parochial*, and eminently calculated to coax the public. If he means simply that Cathedrals do not belong to parishes, that St. Paul's is not the parish church of Upper Puddicomb, and that the Vicar of St. Fiddlefrid does not officiate in Westminster Abbey: all this is true enough, but do they not in the most material points instruct the people precisely in the same manner as the parochial Clergy? Are not prayers and sermons the most important means of spiritual instruction? And are there not eighteen or twenty services in every Cathedral for one which is heard in parish churches? I have very often counted in the afternoon of week days in St. Paul's one hundred and fifty people, and on Sundays it is full to suffocation. Is all this to go for nothing? and what right has the Bishop of London to suppose that there is not as much real piety in Cathedrals, as in the most roadless, postless, melancholy, sequestered hamlet, preached to by the most provincial, sequestered, bucolic Clergyman in the Queen's dominions?

A number of little children, it is true, do not repeat a catechism of which they do not comprehend a word; but it is rather rapid and wholesale to say, that the parochial Clergy are spiritual instructors of the people, and that the Cathedral Clergy are only so in a very restricted sense. I say that in the most material points and acts of instruction, they are much more laborious and incessant than any parochial Clergy. It might really be supposed from the Bishop of London's reasoning, that some other methods of instruction took place in Cathedrals than prayers and sermons can afford; that lectures were read on chemistry, or lessons given on dancing; or that it was a Mechanics' Institute, or a vast receptacle for hexameter and penta-meter boys. His own most respectable Chaplain, who is often there as a member of the body, will tell him that the prayers are strictly adhered to, according to the rubric, with the difference only that the service is beautifully chanted instead of being badly read; that instead of the atrocious bawling of parish Churches, the Anthems are sung with great taste and feeling; and if the preaching is not good, it is the fault of the Bishop of London, who has the whole range of London preachers from whom to make his selection. The real fact is, that, instead of being something materially different from the parochial Clergy, as the Commissioners wish to make them, the Cathedral Clergy are fellow-labourers with the parochial Clergy, outworking them ten to one; but the Commission having provided snugly for the Bishops, have by *the merest accident in the world* entangled themselves in this quarrel with Cathedrals.

"Had the question," says the Bishop, "been proposed to the religious part of the community, Whether, if no other means were to be found, the effective cure of souls should be provided for by the total suppression of those Ecclesiastical Corporations which have no cure of souls, nor bear any part in the parochial labours of the Clergy; that question, I verily believe, would have been carried in the affirmative by an immense majority of suffrages." But suppose no other means could be found for the effective cure of souls than the suppression of Bishops, does the Bishop of London imagine that the majority of suffrages would have been less immense? How idle to put such cases!

A pious man leaves a large sum of money in Catholic times for some purposes which are superstitious, and for others, such as preaching and reading prayers, which are applicable to all times; the superstitious usages are abolished, the pious usages remain: now the Bishop must admit, if you take half or any part of this money from Clergymen to whom it was given, and divide it for similar purposes among Clergy to whom it was not given, you deviate materially from the intentions of the founder. These foundations are made *in loco*; in many of them the *locus* was perhaps the original cause of the gift. A man who founds an alms-house at Edmonton does not mean that the poor of Tottenham should avail themselves of it; and if he could have anticipated such a consequence, he would not have endowed any alms-house at all. Such is the respect for property that the Court of Chancery, when it becomes impracticable to carry the will of the donor into execution, always attend to the *cy pres*, and apply the charitable fund to a purpose as germane as possible to the intention of the founder; but here, when men of Lincoln have left to Lincoln Cathedral, and men of Hereford, to Hereford, the Commissioners seize it all, melt it into a common mass, and disperse it over the kingdom. Surely the Bishop of London cannot contend that this is not a greater deviation from the will of the founder than if the same people remaining in the same place, receiving all the founder gave them, and doing all things not forbidden by the law, which the founder ordered, were to do something more than the founder ordered, were to become the guardians of education, the counsel to the Bishop, and the Curators of the Diocese in his old age and decay.

The public are greater robbers and plunderers than any one in the public; look at the whole transaction, it is a mixture of meanness and violence. The country choose to have an established religion, and a resident parochial Clergy, but they do not choose to build houses for their parochial Clergy, or to pay them in many instances more than a butler or a coachman receives. How is this deficiency to be supplied? The heads of the Church propose to this public to seize upon estates which never belonged to the public, and which were left for another purpose;

and by the seizure of these estates to save that which ought to come out of the public purse.

Suppose Parliament were to seize upon all the almshouses in England, and apply them to the diminution of the poor-rate, what a number of ingenious arguments might be pressed into the service of this robbery: "Can anything be more revolting than that the poor of Northumberland should be starving, while the poor of the suburban hamlets are dividing the benefactions of the pious dead? *'We want for these purposes all that we can obtain from whatever sources derived.'*" I do not deny the right of Parliament to do this, or anything else; but I deny that it would be expedient; because I think it better to make any sacrifices, and to endure any evil, than to gratify this rapacious spirit of plunder and confiscation. Suppose these Commissioner Prelates, firm and unmoved, when we were all alarmed, had told the public that the parochial Clergy were badly provided for, and that it was the duty of that public to provide a proper support for their Ministers;—suppose the Commissioners, instead of leading them on to confiscation, had warned their fellow-subjects against the base economy, and the perilous injustice of seizing on that which was not their own;— suppose they had called for water and washed their hands, and said, "We call you all to witness that we are innocent of this great ruin";—does the Bishop of London imagine that the Prelates who made such a stand would have gone down to posterity less respected and less revered than those men upon whose tombs it must (after all the enumeration of their virtues) be written, *that under their auspices and by their counsels the destruction of the English Church began*? Pity that the Archbishop of Canterbury had not retained those feelings, when, at the first meeting of Bishops, the Bishop of London proposed this *holy innovation* upon Cathedrals, and the head of our Church declared with vehemence and indignation that nothing in the earth would induce him to consent to it.

Si mens non læva fuisset,
Trojaque nunc stares, Priamique arx alta maneres.

"But," says the Lord Bishop of London, "you admit the principle of confiscation by proposing the confiscation and partition of Prebends in the possession of non-residents." I am thinking of something else, and I see all of a sudden a great blaze of light: I behold a great number of gentlemen in short aprons, neat purple coats, and gold buckles, rushing about with torches in their hands, calling each other "My Lord," and setting fire to all the rooms in the house, and the people below delighted with the combustion: finding it impossible to turn them from their purpose, and finding that they are all what they are, by divine permission; I endeavour to direct their *holy innovations* into another channel; and I say to them, "My Lords, had not you better set fire to the out of door offices, to the barns and stables, and spare this fine library and this noble drawing-room? Yonder are several cow-houses of which no use is made; pray direct your fury against them, and leave this beautiful and venerable mansion as you found it." If I address the divinely permitted in this manner, has the Bishop of London any right to call me a brother incendiary?

Our *holy innovator*, the Bishop of London, has drawn a very affecting picture of *sheep having no shepherd*, and of millions who have no *spiritual food*: our wants, he says, are most imperious; even if we were to tax large Livings we must still have the money of the Cathedrals: no plea will exempt you, nothing can stop us, for the formation of benefices, and the endowment of new ones. We want (and he prints it in italics) for these purposes *"all that we can obtain from whatever sources derived."* I never remember to have been more alarmed in my life than by this passage. I said to myself, the necessities of the Church have got such complete hold of the imagination of this energetic Prelate, who is so captivated by the holiness of his innovations, that all grades and orders of the Church and all present and future interests will be sacrificed to it. I immediately rushed to the acts of Parliament which I always have under my pillow to see at once the worst of what had happened. I found present revenues of the Bishops all safe; that is some comfort, I said to myself: Canterbury, £24,000 or £25,000 per annum; London, £18,000 or £20,000. I began to feel some comfort: "things are not so bad; the Bishops do not mean to sacrifice to *sheep and shepherd's money* their present revenues; the

Bishop of London is less violent and headstrong than I thought he would be." I looked a little further, and found that £15,000 per annum is allotted to the future Archbishop of Canterbury, £10,000 to the Bishop of London, £8000 to Durham, and £8000 each to Winchester and Ely. "Nothing of *sheep and shepherd* in all this," I exclaimed, and felt still more comforted. It was not till after the Bishops were taken care of, and the revenues of the Cathedrals came into full view, that I saw the perfect development of the *sheep and shepherd principle*, the deep and heartfelt compassion for spiritual labourers, and that inward groaning for the destitute state of the Church, and that firm purpose, printed in italics, of taking *for these purposes all that could be obtained from whatever source derived;* and even in this delicious rummage of Cathedral property, where all the fine church feelings of the Bishop's heart could be indulged without costing the poor sufferer a penny, stalls for Archdeacons in Lincoln and St. Paul's are, to the amount of £2000 per annum, taken from the *sheep and shepherd fund*, and the patronage of them divided between two commissioners, the Bishop of London and the Bishop of Lincoln, instead of being paid to additional *labourers in the Vineyard*.

Has there been any difficulty, I would ask, in procuring Archdeacons upon the very moderate pay they now receive? Can any Clergyman be more thoroughly respectable than the present Archdeacons in the see of London? but men bearing such an office in the Church, it may be said, should be highly paid, and Archbishops who could very well keep up their dignity upon £7000 per annum, are to be allowed £15,000. I make no objection to all this; but then what becomes of all these heart-rending phrases of *sheep and shepherd, and drooping vineyards, and flocks without spiritual consolation*? The Bishop's argument is, that the superfluous must give way to the necessary; but in fighting, the Bishop should take great care that his cannons are not seized, and turned against himself. He has awarded to the Bishops of England a superfluity as great as that which he intends to take from the Cathedrals; and then, when he legislates for an order to which he does not belong, begins to remember the distresses of the lower Clergy, paints them with all the colours of impassioned eloquence, and informs the Cathedral institutions that he must have *every farthing he can lay his hand upon.* Is not this as if one affected powerfully by a charity sermon were to put his hands in another man's pocket, and cast, from what he had extracted, a liberal contribution into the plate?

I beg not to be mistaken; I am very far from considering the Bishop of London as a sordid and interested person; but this is a complete instance of how the best of men deceive themselves, where their interests are concerned. I have no doubt the Bishop firmly imagined he was doing his duty; but there should have been men of all grades in the Commission, some one to say a word for Cathedrals and against Bishops.

The Bishop says, "his antagonists have allowed three Canons to be sufficient for St. Paul's, and therefore four must be sufficient for other Cathedrals." Sufficient to read the prayers and preach the sermons, certainly, and so would *one* be; but not sufficient to excite by the hope of increased rank and wealth eleven thousand parochial Clergy.

The most important and cogent arguments against the Dean and Chapter confiscations are passed over in silence in the Bishop's Charge. This, in reasoning, is always the wisest and most convenient plan, and which all young Bishops should imitate after the manner of this wary polemic. I object to the confiscation *because it will throw a great deal more of capital out of the parochial Church than it will bring into it.* I am very sorry to come forward with so homely an argument, which shocks so many Clergymen, and particularly those with the largest incomes, and the best Bishoprics; but the truth is, the greater number of Clergymen go into the Church in order that they may derive a comfortable income *from* the Church. Such men intend to do their duty, and they do it; but the duty is, however, not the motive, but the adjunct. If I were writing in gala and parade, I would not hold this language; but we are in earnest, and on business; and as very rash and hasty changes are founded upon contrary suppositions of the pure disinterestedness and perfect inattention to temporals in the Clergy, we must get down at once to the solid rock, without heeding how we disturb the turf and the flowers above. The parochial Clergy maintain their present decent appearance quite as much by their own capital as by the income they derive from the Church. I will now state the income and capital of seven Clergymen, taken promiscuously in this neighbourhood:—No. 1. Living £200, Capital £12,000; No. 2. Living £800, Capital £15,000; No. 3. Living £500, Capital £12,000; No. 4. Living £150, Capital £10,000; No. 5. Living £800, Capital £12,000; No. 6. Living £150, Capital £1000; No. 7. Living £600, Capital £16,000. I have diligently inquired into the circumstances of seven Unitarian and Wesleyan ministers, and I question much if the whole seven could make up £6000 between them; and the zeal of enthusiasm of this last division is certainly not inferior to that of the former. Now here is a capital of £72,000 carried into the Church, which the confiscations of the Commissioners would force out of it, by taking away the good things which were the temptation to its introduction. So that by the old plan of paying by lottery, instead of giving a proper competence to each, not only do you obtain a parochial Clergy upon much cheaper terms; but from the gambling propensities of human nature, and the irresistible tendency to hope that they shall gain the great prizes, you tempt men into your service who keep up their credit, and yours, not by your allowance, but by their own capital; and to destroy this wise and well-working arrangement, a great number of Bishops, Marquises, and John Russells, are huddled into a chamber, and after proposing a scheme which will turn the English Church into a collection of consecrated beggars, we are informed by the Bishop of London that it is a *Holy Innovation*.

I have no manner of doubt, that the immediate effect of passing the Dean and Chapter Bill will be, that a great number of fathers and uncles, judging, and properly judging, that the Church is a very altered and deteriorated profession, will turn the industry and capital of their *élèves* into another channel. My friend, Robert Eden, says, "This is of the earth earthy": be it so; I cannot help it, I paint mankind as I find them, and am not answerable for their defects. When an argument taken from real life, and the actual condition of the world, is brought among the shadowy discussions of Ecclesiastics, it always occasions terror and dismay; it is like Æneas stepping into Charon's boat, which carried only ghosts and spirits.

> Gemuit sub pondere cymba
> Sutilis.

The whole plan of the Bishop of London is a ptochogony —a generation of beggars. He purposes, out of the spoils of the Cathedral, to create a thousand livings, and to give to the thousand Clergymen £130 per annum each: a Christian Bishop proposing. in cold blood, to create a thousand livings of £130 per annum each;—to call into existence a thousand of the most unhappy men on the face of the earth,—the sons of the poor, without hope, without the assistance of private fortune, chained to the soil, ashamed to live with their inferiors, unfit for the society of the better classes, and dragging about the English curse of poverty, without the smallest hope that they can ever shake it off. At present such livings are filled by young men who have better hopes—who have reason to expect good property—who look forward to a college or a family living—who are the sons of men of some substance, and hope so to pass on to something better—who exist under the delusion of being hereafter Deans and Prebendaries —who are paid once by money, and three times by hope. Will the Bishop of London promise to the progeny of any of these thousand victims of the *Holy Innovation* that, if they behave well, one of them shall have his butler's place; another take care of the cedars and hyssops of his garden? Will he take their daughters for his nursery-maids? and may some of the sons of these "labourers of the vineyard" hope one day to ride the leaders from St. James's to Fulham? Here is hope—here is room for ambition—a field for genius, and a ray of amelioration! If these beautiful feelings of compassion are throbbing under the cassock of the Bishop, he ought in common justice to himself to make them known.

If it were a scheme for giving ease and independence to any large bodies of Clergymen, it might be listened to; but the revenues of the English Church are such as to render this wholly and entirely out of the question. If you place a man in a village in the country, require that he should be of good manners and well educated; that his habits and appearance should be above those of the farmers to whom he preaches, if he has nothing else to expect (as would be the case in a Church of equal division); and if upon his village income he is to support a wife and educate a family without any power of making himself known in a remote and solitary situation, such a person ought to receive £500 per annum, and be furnished with a house. There are about 10,700 parishes in England and Wales, whose average income is £285 per annum. Now, to provide these incumbents with decent houses, to keep them in repair, and to raise the income of the incumbent to £500 per annum, would require (if all the incomes of the Bishops, Deans and Chapters of separate dignitaries, of sinecure rectories, were confiscated, and if the excess of all the livings in England above £500 per annum were added to them) a sum of two millions and a half in addition to the present income of the whole Church; and no power on earth could persuade the present Parliament of Great Britain to grant a single shilling for that purpose. Now, is it possible to pay such a Church upon any other principle than that of unequal division? The proposed pillage of the Cathedral and College Churches (omitting all consideration of the separate estate of dignitaries) would amount, divided among all the Benefices in England, to about £5 12s. 6½d. per man: and this, which would not stop an hiatus in a cassock, and would drive out of the parochial Church ten times as much as it brought into it, is the panacea for pauperism recommended by Her Majesty's Commissioners.

But if this plan were to drive men of capital out of the Church, and to pauperise the English Clergy, where would the harm be? Could not all the duties of religion be performed as well by poor Clergymen as by men of good substance? My great and serious apprehension is, that such would not be the case. There would be the greatest risk that your Clergy would be fanatical, and ignorant; that their habits would be low and mean, and that they would be despised.

Then a picture is drawn of a Clergyman with £130 per annum, who combines all moral, physical, and intellectual advantages, a learned man, dedicating himself intensely to the care of his parish—of charming manners and dignified

deportment—six feet two inches high, beautifully pro-
portioned, with a magnificent countenance, expressive
of all the cardinal virtues and the Ten Commandments,
—and it is asked with an air of triumph if such a man as
this will fall into contempt on account of his poverty?
But substitute for him an average, ordinary, uninteresting
Minister; obese, dumpy, neither ill-natured nor good-
natured; neither learned, nor ignorant, striding over the
stiles to Church, with a second-rate wife—dusty and
deliquescent—and four parochial children, full of catechism
and bread and butter; or let him be seen in one of those
Shem-Ham-and-Japhet buggies—made on Mount Ararat
soon after the subsidence of the waters, driving in the
High Street of Edmonton [1];—among all his pecuniary,
saponaceous, oleaginous parishioners. Can any man of
common sense say that all these outward circumstances
of the Ministers of religion have no bearing on religion
itself?

I ask the Bishop of London, a man of honour and conscience as he is, if he thinks five years will elapse before
a second attack is made upon Deans and Chapters? Does
he think, after Reformers have tasted the flesh of the
Church, that they will put up with any other diet? Does
he forget that Deans and Chapters are but mock turtle—
that more delicious delicacies remain behind? Five
years hence he will attempt to make a stand, and he will
be laughed at and eaten up. In this very charge the
Bishop accuses the Lay Commissioners of another intended
attack upon the property of the Church, contrary to the
clearest and most explicit stipulations (as he says) with
the heads of the Establishment.

Much is said of the conduct of the Commissioners, but
that is of the least possible consequence. They may have
acted for the best, according to the then existing circumstances; they may seriously have intended to do their
duty to the country; and I am far from saying or thinking
they did not; but without the least reference to the Commissioners, the question is, Is it wise to pass this bill, and

---

[1] A parish which the Bishop of London has the greatest desire
to divide into little bits; but which appears quite as fit to preserve
its integrity as St. James's, St. George's, or Kensington, all in the
patronage of the Bishop.

to justify such an open and tremendous sacrifice of Church property? Does public opinion *now* call for any such measure? is it a wise distribution of the funds of an ill-paid Church? and will it not force more capital out of the parochial part of the Church than it brings into it? If the bill be bad, it is surely not to pass out of compliment to the feelings of the Archbishop of Canterbury. If the project be hasty, it is not to be adopted to gratify the Bishop of London. The mischief to the Church is surely a greater evil than the stultification of the Commissioners, etc. If the physician have prescribed hastily, is the medicine to be taken to the death or disease of the patient? If the judge have condemned improperly, is the criminal to be hung, that the wisdom of the magistrate may not be impugned? [1]

But, why are the Commissioners to be stultified by the rejection of the measure? The measure may have been very good when it was recommended, and very objectionable now. I thought, and many men thought, that the Church was going to pieces—that the affections of the common people were lost to the Establishment; and that large sacrifices must be instantly made, to avert the effects of this temporary madness; but those days are gone by— and with them ought to be put aside measures which might have been wise in those days, but are wise no longer.

After all, the Archbishop of Canterbury and the Bishop of London are good and placable men; and will ere long forget and forgive the successful efforts of their enemies in defeating this mis-ecclesiastic law.

Suppose the Commission were now beginning to sit for the first time, will any man living say that they would make such reports as they have made? and that they would seriously propose such a tremendous revolution in Church property? And if they would not, the inference is irresistible, that to consult the feelings of two or three churchmen, we are complimenting away the safety of the Church. Milton asked where the nymphs were when Lycidas perished? I ask where the Bishops are when

---

[1] "After the trouble the Commissioners have taken (says Sir Robert), after the obloquy they have incurred," etc. etc. etc.

the remorseless deep is closing over the head of their beloved Establishment? [1]

You must have read an attack upon me by the Bishop of Gloucester, in the course of which he says that I have not been appointed to my situation as Canon of St. Paul's for my piety and learning, but because I am a scoffer and a jester. Is not this rather strong for a Bishop, and does it not appear to you, Mr. Archdeacon, as rather too close an imitation of that language which is used in the apostolic occupation of trafficking in fish? Whether I have been appointed for my piety or not, must depend upon what this poor man means by piety. He means by that word, of course, a defence of all the tyrannical and oppressive abuses of the Church which have been swept away within the last fifteen or twenty years of my life; the Corporation and Test Acts; the Penal Laws against the Catholics; the Compulsory Marriages of Dissenters, and all those disabling and disqualifying laws which were the disgrace of our Church, and which he has always looked up to as the consummation of human wisdom. If piety consisted in the defence of these—if it was impious to struggle for their abrogation, I have indeed led an ungodly life.

There is nothing pompous gentlemen are so much afraid of as a little humour. It is like the objection of certain cephalic animalculæ to the use of small-tooth combs, "Finger and thumb, precipitate powder, or anything else you please; but for heaven's sake no small-tooth combs!" After all, I believe, Bishop Monk has been the cause of much more laughter than ever I have been; I cannot account for it, but I never see him enter a room without exciting a smile on every countenance within it.

Dr. Monk is furious at my attacking the heads of the Church; but how can I help it? If the heads of the Church are at the head of the Mob; if I find the best of men doing that, which has in all times drawn upon the worst enemies of the human race the bitterest curses of History, am I to stop because the motives of these men are pure, and their lives blameless? I wish I could find a blot in their lives,

[1] What is the use of publishing separate charges, as the Bishops of Winchester, Oxford, and Rochester have done? Why do not the dissentient Bishops form into a firm phalanx to save the Church and fling out the Bill?

or a vice in their motives. The whole power of the motion
is in the character of the movers: feeble friends, false
friends, and foolish friends, all cease to look into the
measure, and say, Would such a measure have been recommended by such men as the Prelates of Canterbury and
London, if it were not for the public advantage? And in
this way, the great good of a religious establishment, now
rendered moderate and compatible with all men's liberties
and rights, is sacrificed to names; and the Church destroyed
from good breeding and Etiquette! the real truth is, that
Canterbury and London have been frightened—they have
overlooked the effect of time and delay—they have been
betrayed into a fearful and ruinous mistake. Painful as
it is to teach men who ought to teach us, the legislature
ought, while there is yet time, to awake and read them
this lesson.

It is dangerous for a Prelate to write; and whoever does
it, ought to be a very wise one. He has speculated why I
was made a Canon of St. Paul's. Suppose I were to follow
his example, and, going through the bench of Bishops,
were to ask for what reason each man had been made a
Bishop; suppose I were to go into the county of Gloucester,
etc. etc. etc.!!!!!

I was afraid the Bishop would attribute my promotion
to the *Edinburgh Review*; but upon the subject of Promotion by Reviews he preserves an impenetrable silence.
If my excellent patron Earl Grey had any reasons of this
kind, he may at least be sure that the Reviews commonly
attributed to me were really written *by* me. I should
have considered myself as the lowest of created beings to
have disguised myself in another man's wit, and to have
received a reward to which I was not entitled.[1]

I presume that what has drawn upon me the indignation
of this Prelate, is the observations I have from time to
time made on the conduct of the Commissioners; of which

---

[1] I understand that the Bishop bursts into tears every now and
then, and says that I have set him the name of Simon, and that all
the Bishops now call him Simon. Simon of Gloucester, however,
after all, is a real writer, and how could I know that Dr. Monk's
name was Simon? When tutor in Lord Carrington's family, he
was called by the endearing though somewhat unmajestic name of
Dick; and if I had thought about his name at all, I should have
called him Richard of Gloucester.

he positively asserts himself to have been a member; but whether he was, or was not a member, I utterly acquit him of all possible blame, and of every species of imputation which may attach to the conduct of the Commission. In using that word, I have always meant the Archbishop of Canterbury, the Bishop of London, and Lord John Russell; and have, honestly speaking, given no more heed to the Bishop of Gloucester, than if he had been sitting in a Commission of Bonzes in the Court of Pekin.

To read, however, his Lordship a lesson of good manners, I had prepared for him a chastisement which would have been echoed from the *Seagrave* who banqueteth in the castle, to the idiot who spitteth over the bridge at Gloucester; but the following appeal struck my eye, and stopped my pen:—"Since that time my inadequate qualifications have sustained an appalling diminution by the affection of my eyes, which have impaired my vision, and the progress of which threatens to consign me to darkness: I beg the benefit of your prayers to the Father of all mercies, that he will restore to me the better use of the visual organs, to be employed on his service; or that he will inwardly illumine the intellectual vision, with a particle of that Divine ray, which his Holy Spirit can alone impart."

It might have been better taste, perhaps, if a mitred invalid, in describing his bodily infirmities before a church full of Clergymen, whose prayers he asked, had been a little more sparing in the abuse of his enemies; but a good deal must be forgiven to the sick. I wish that every Christian was as well aware as this poor Bishop of what he needed from Divine assistance; and in the supplication for the restoration of his sight and the improvement of his understanding, I most fervently and cordially join.

I was much amused with what old Hermann [1] says of the Bishop of London's Æschylus. "We find," he says, "*a great arbitrariness of proceeding, and much boldness of innovation, guided by no sure principle*"; here it is: *qualis ab incepto*. He begins with Æschylus, and ends with the Church of England; begins with profane, and ends with holy innovations—scratching out old readings which

[1] Ueber die Behandlung der Griechischen Dichter bei den Engländern. Von Gottfried Hermann. Wiemar Jahrbücher, vol. liv. 1831.

every commentator had sanctioned; abolishing ecclesiastical dignities which every reformer had spared; thrusting an anapæst into a verse, which will not bear it; and intruding a Canon into a Cathedral, which does not want it; and this is the Prelate by whom the proposed reform of the Church has been principally planned, and to whose practical wisdom the Legislature is called upon to defer. The Bishop of London is a man of very great ability, humane, placable, generous, munificent; very agreeable, but not to be trusted with great interests where calmness and judgment are required; unfortunately, my old and amiable schoolfellow, the Archbishop of Canterbury, has melted away before him, and sacrificed that wisdom on which we all founded our security.

Much writing and much talking are very tiresome; and, above all, they are so to men who, living in the world, arrive at those rapid and just conclusions which are only to be made by living in the world. This bill past, every man of sense acquainted with human affairs must see, that as far as the Church is concerned, the thing is at an end. From Lord John Russell, the present improver of the Church, we shall descend to Hume, from Hume to Roebuck, and after Roebuck we shall receive our last improvements from Dr. Wade: plunder will follow after plunder, degradation after degradation. The Church is gone, and what remains is not life, but sickness, spasm, and struggle.

Whatever happens, I am not to blame; I have fought my fight.—Farewell.

SYDNEY SMITH.

U

MISCELLANEA

MISCELLANEA

BERKELEY'S GROUSE!

HOWICK Sept. 9, 1808.

DEAR LADY HOLLAND,

I take the liberty to send you two brace of grouse,— curious, because killed by a Scotch metaphysician; in other and better language, they are mere ideas, shot by other ideas, out of a pure intellectual notion, called a gun.

I found a great number of philosophers in Edinburgh, in a high state of obscurity and metaphysics.

Dugald Stewart is extremely alarmed by the repeated assurances I made that he was the author of *Plymley's Letters*,—or generally considered so to be.

I have been staying here two days on my return and two days on my journey to Edinburgh. An excellent man, Lord Grey, and pleasant to be seen in the bosom of his family. I approve very highly also of his lady.

Ever most affectionately yours,
SYDNEY SMITH.

A CURE FOR LOW SPIRITS.

FOSTON, February 16th, 1820.

DEAR LADY GEORGIANA,

Nobody has suffered more from low spirits than I have done—so I feel for you. 1st. Live as well as you dare. 2nd. Go into the shower bath with a small quantity of water, at a temperature low enough to give you a slight sensation of cold, 75° or 80°. 3rd. Amusing books. 4th. Short views of human life—not further than dinner or tea. 5th. Be as busy as you can. 6th. See as much as you can of those friends who respect and like you. 7th. And of those acquaintances who amuse you. 8th. Make no secret of low spirits to your friends, but talk of them freely—they are always worse for dignified concealment. 9th. Attend to the effects tea and coffee produce upon you. 10th. Compare your lot with that of other people. 11th. Don't expect too much from human life

—a sorry business at the best. 12th. Avoid poetry, dramatic representations (except comedy), music, serious novels, melancholy, sentimental people, and everything likely to excite feeling or emotion, not ending in active benevolence. 13th. *Do good*, and endeavour to please everybody of every degree. 14th. Be as much as you can in the open air without fatigue. 15th. Make the room where you commonly sit, gay and pleasant. 16th. Struggle by little and little against idleness. 17th. Don't be too severe upon yourself, or underrate yourself, but do yourself justice. 18th. Keep good blazing fires. 19th. Be firm and constant in the exercise of rational religion. 20th. Believe me,

dear Lady Georgiana,
Very truly yours,
SYDNEY SMITH.

AN INDEPENDENT POET.

8 DOUGHTY STREET, BRUNSWICK SQUARE.

MY DEAR LADY HOLLAND,

I told the little poet,[1] after the proper softenings of wine, dinner, flattery, repeating his verses, etc. etc., that a friend of mine wished to lend him some money, and I begged him to take it. The poet said that he had a very sacred and serious notion of the duties of independence, that he thought he had no right to be burdensome to others from the mere apprehensions of evil, and that he was in no immediate want. If it was necessary, he would ask me hereafter for the money without scruple; and that the knowing he *had* such resources in reserve, was a great comfort to him. This was very sensible and very honourable to him, nor had he the slightest feeling of affront on the subject, but, on the contrary, of great gratitude to his benefactor, whose name I did not mention, as the money was not received. I therefore cancel your draft, and will call upon you, if he calls upon me. This, I presume, meets your approbation. I had a great deal of conversation with him, and he is a much more sensible man than I had any idea of. I have received this morning

[1] Thomas Campbell.

a very kind letter from Sir Francis Baring, almost amounting to a promise that I am to be a professor in his new institution.

I cannot conclude this letter without telling you, that you are a very good lady for what you have done; and that, for it, I give you my hearty benediction.

> Respectfully and sincerely yours,
> SYDNEY SMITH.

ON LIBEL.

I am exceedingly glad Lord Holland has taken up the business of libels; the punishment of late appears to me atrocious. If libels against the public are *very* bad, they become sedition or treason; new crimes may be punished as such; but as long as they are *only* libels, such punishments as have lately been inflicted are preposterous; and seem to proceed from that hatred which feeble and decorous persons always feel against those who disturb the repose of their minds, call their opinions in question, and compel them to think and reason. There should be a maximum of imprisonment for libel. . . . Libels are not so mischievous in a free country, as Mr. Justice Grose, in his very bad lectures, would make them out to be. Who would have mutinied for Cobbett's libel? or who would have risen up against the German soldiers? And how easily he might have been answered!

ON QUAKER BABIES.

Did you say, a Quaker baby? Impossible! there is no such thing; there never was; they are always born broad-brimmed and in full quake. . . . Well, all I can say is, I never saw one; and what is still more remarkable I never met with anyone who had. Do you believe in it? Lady Morley does not. Have you not heard the report that they are fed on drab-coloured pap? It must be this that gives them their beautiful complexion. I have a theory about them and bluecoat boys, which I will tell you some day.

DEAR LADY MORLEY,

Pray understand me rightly! I do not give the Bluecoat theory as an established fact, but as a highly probable conjecture; look at the circumstances. At a very early age young Quakers disappear, at a very early age the Coat-boys are seen; at the age of seventeen or eighteen young Quakers are again seen; at the same age the Coat-boys disappear: who has ever heard of a Coat-man? The thing is utterly unknown in natural history. Upon what other evidence does the migration of the grub into the aurelia rest? After a certain number of days the grub is no more seen, and the aurelia flutters over his relics. That such a prominent fact should have escaped our naturalists is truly astonishing; I had long suspected it, but was afraid to come out with a speculation so bold, and now mention it as protected and sanctioned by you.

Dissection would throw great light upon the question; and if our friend —— would receive two boys into his house about the time of their changing their coats, great service would be rendered to the cause.

Our friend, Lord Grey, not remarkable for his attention to natural history, was a good deal struck with the novelty and ingenuity of the hypothesis. I have ascertained that the young Bluecoat infants are fed with drab-coloured pap, which looks very suspicious. More hereafter on this interesting subject. Where real science is to be promoted I will make no apology to your ladyship for this intrusion.

ON SCOTCH SHEEP AND DRAUGHT OXEN.

It has been my lot to have passed the greater part of my life in cities.—About six or seven years ago, I was placed in the country, in a situation where I was under the necessity of becoming a farmer; and, amongst the many expensive blunders I have made, I warn those who may find themselves in similar situations against *Scotch Sheep* and *Oxen for ploughing*. I had heard a great deal of the fine flavour of Scotch mutton, and it was one of the great luxuries I promised myself in farming. A luxury it certainly is; but the price paid for it is such, that I would rather give up the use of animal food altogether, than obtain it by such a system of cares and anxieties. Ten times a day my men were called off from their work to hunt the Scotch sheep out of my own and my neighbours' wheat. They crawled through hedges where I should have thought a rabbit could hardly have found admission; and, where crawling would not do, they had recourse to leaping. Five or six times they all assembled in a body, and set out on their return to the North. My bailiff took a place in the mail, pursued, and overtook them halfway to Newcastle. Then it was quite impossible to get them fat. They consumed my turnips in winter, and my clover in the summer, without any apparent addition to their weight; ten or twelve per cent. always died of the rot; and more would have perished in the same manner, if they had not been prematurely eaten out of the way.

My ploughing oxen were the subject of an equal vexation. They had a constant purging upon them, which it was impossible to stop. They ate more than twice as much as the same number of horses. They did half as much work as the same number of horses. They could not bear hot weather, nor wet weather, nor go well down hill. It took five men to shoe an ox. They ran against my gate-posts, lay down in the cart whenever they were tired, and ran away at the sight of a stranger.

I have now got into a good breed of English sheep, and useful cart-horses, and am doing very well. I make this statement to guard young gentleman-farmers against listening to the pernicious nonsense of brother gentlemen, for whose advice I am at least poorer by £300 to £400.

To His Grandchild.

(On sending him a letter overweight)

Oh, you little wretch! Your letter cost me fourpence. I will pull all the plums out of your puddings; I will undress your dolls and steal their under petticoats; you shall have no currant-jelly to your rice; I will kiss you till you cannot see out of your eyes; when nobody else whips you, I will do so; I will fill you so full of sugar-plums that they shall run out of your nose and ears; lastly, your frocks shall be so short that they shall not come below your knees.

Your loving grandfather,
Sydney Smith.

A Winter Salad.

Two well-boiled potatoes, passed through a sieve; a teaspoonful of mustard; two teaspoonfuls of salt; one of essence of anchovy; about a quarter of a teaspoonful of very finely chopped onions, well fringed into the mixture; three tablespoonfuls of oil; one of vinegar; the yolk of two eggs, hard boiled. Stir up the salad immediately before dinner, and stir it up thoroughly.

N.B. As this salad is the result of great experience and reflection, it is hoped young salad-makers will not attempt to make any improvements upon it.

The Sovereign People.

The new Beer Bill has begun its operations. Everybody is drunk. Those who are not singing are sprawling. The sovereign people are in a beastly state.

On Liberty.

I love liberty, but I hope it can be so managed that I shall have soft beds, good dinners, fine linen, etc., for the rest of my life. I am too old to fight or to suffer.

An Embarrassment.

I dined with Lord Holland; there was at table Barras, the ex-director, in whose countenance I immediately discovered all the signs of blood and cruelty which distinguished his conduct. I found, however, at the end of dinner, that it was not Barras, but M. de Barante, an historian and man of letters, who, I believe, has never killed anything greater than a flea.

A Civil Philosopher.

Philosopher Malthus came here last week. I got an agreeable party for him of unmarried people. There was only one lady who had had a child; but he is a good-natured man, and, if there are no appearances of approaching fertility, is civil to every lady.

ON HIMSELF.

PARIS, *June 29th*, 1844.

SIR,

Your application to me does me honour, and requires, on your part, no sort of apology.

It is scarcely possible to speak much of self, and I have little or nothing to tell which has not been told before in my preface.

I am seventy-four years of age; and being Canon of St. Paul's in London, and a rector of a parish in the country, my time is divided equally between town and country. I am living amongst the best society in the metropolis, and at ease in my circumstances; in tolerable health, a mild Whig, a tolerating Churchman, and much given to talking, laughing, and noise. I dine with the rich in London, and physic the poor in the country; passing from the sauces of Dives to the sores of Lazarus. I am, upon the whole, a happy man; have found the world an entertaining world, and am thankful to providence for the part allotted to me in it. . . .

[*Letter to M. Eugène Robin.*]

September 22nd.

AN ENCLOSURE.

I am very much mortified that Lady Dufferin does not answer my letter. She has gone to Germany—she is sick —she has married Rogers—she . . . In short, all sorts of melancholy explanations came across me, till I found that the probable reason of her not answering my letter was, that she had not received it. I was strengthened in this belief from finding in my writing-desk the letter itself, which was written a month ago, and I conceived it to have been despatched the same day. I can write nothing better, for I can only repeat my admiration and regard.

[*In a letter to Lady Dufferin from Combe Florey, undated.*]

MY DEAR DICKENS,

I accept your obliging invitation conditionally. If I am invited by any man of greater genius than yourself, or one by whose works I have been more completely interested, I will repudiate you, and dine with the more splendid phenomenon of the two.

Ever yours sincerely,

SYDNEY SMITH.

NOTE TO MISS G. HARCOURT.

My dear G.,
The pain in my knee
Would not suffer me
To drink your bohea.
I can laugh and talk,
But I cannot walk;
And I thought his Grace would stare
If I put my leg on a chair.
And to give the knee its former power
It must be fomented for half-an-hour;
And in this very disagreeable state,
If I had come at all, I should have been too late.

Mar. 29, 1843.

Thy servant is threescore-and-ten years old; can he hear the sound of singing men and singing women? A Canon at the Opera! Where have you lived? In what habitations of the heathen? I thank you, shuddering; and am ever your unseducible friend,

SYDNEY SMITH.

[*To Mrs. Meynell, from Green St. June* 1840.]

AN INVITATION.

Pray lay an injunction on Tim Thompson, that he in nowise journey to or from the Metropolis without tarrying here.

Though you are absent, jokes shall never fail;
I'll kill the fatted calf, and tap the foaming ale;
We'll settle men and things by rule of thumb,
And break the lingering night with ancient rum.

A Maxim.

I mean to make some maxims, like Rochefoucauld, and to preserve them. My first is this: After having lived half their lives respectably, many men get tired of honesty and many women of propriety.

The Poetical Medicine Chest.

With store of powdered rhubarb we begin;
(To leave out powdered rhubarb were a sin)
Pack mild magnesia deep within the chest;
And glittering gum from Araby the blest;
And keep, oh lady, keep within thy reach
The slimy surgeon, blood-devouring leech.
Laurel-born camphor, opiate drugs prepare,
They banish pain, and calm consuming care.
Glauber and Epsom salts their aid combine,
Translucent streams of castor-oil be thine,
And gentle manna in thy bottles shine.
If morbid spot of septic sore invade,
By heaven-sent bark the morbid spot is stayed;
When with black bile hepatic regions swell,
With subtle calomel the plague expel.
Anise and mint with strong Æolian sway,
Intestine storms of flatulence allay,
And ipecachuana clears the way.
I know thee well, thou antimonial power,
And to thee fly in that heart-rending hour,
When feverish patients heave their laden breath
And all is sickness, agony, and death!
Soda and potash change the humours crude,
When hoven parsons swell with luscious food.
Spare not in eastern blasts when babies die,
The wholesale vigour of the Spanish fly.
From timely torture seek thy infant's rest,
And spread the poison on his labouring breast.
And so, fair lady, when in evil hour
Less prudent mothers mourn some faded flower,
Six Howards valiant and six Howards fair,
Shall live and love thee, and reward thy care.

REPLY TO AN INVITATION TO DINNER AT THE FISHMONGERS' HALL.

Much do I love, at civic treat,
The monsters of the deep to eat;
To see the rosy salmon lying,
By smelts encircled, born for frying;
And from the china boat to pour,
On flaky cod, the flavour'd shower.
Thee, above all, I much regard,
Flatter than Longman's flattest bard,
Much honour'd turbot!—sore I grieve
Thee and thy dainty friends to leave.
Far from ye all, in snuggest corner
I go to dine with little Horner:
He who, with philosophic eye,
Sat brooding o'er his Christmas pie:
Then firm resolved, with either thumb,
Tore forth the crust-enveloped plum,
And, mad with youthful dreams of future fame,
Proclaim'd the deathless glories of his name.

November 1842.

To MISS BERRY.

Where is Tittenhanger?
Is it near Bangor?
Is it in Scotland,
Or a more flat land?
Is it in Wales,
Or near Versailles?
Tell me, in the name of grace,
Why you go to such a place?
I do not know in what map to look,
And I can't find it in the road-book.
I always feel so sad and undone,
When you and Agnes go from London.
Your loving friend and plump divine
Accepts your kind commands to dine.
I will be certain to remember
The fifteenth day of this November.
There is a young Prince
Two days since——

But for fear I should be a bore,
I won't write you any more;
Indeed I've nothing else to tell
But that Monckton Milnes is well.

A POST-WAR SLUMP.

Commerce and manufactures are still in a frightful
state of stagnation.

No foreign barks in British ports are seen,
Stuff'd to the water's edge with velveteen,
Or bursting with big bales of bombazine;
No distant chimes demand our corduroy,
Unmatch'd habiliment for man and boy;
No fleets of fustian quit the British shore,
The cloth-creating engines cease to roar,
Still is that loom which breech'd the world before.

TO THE COUNTESS OF MORLEY.

I am always glad when London time arrives; it always
seems in the country as if Joshua were at work, and had
stopped the sun.   You, dear Lady Morley, have the reverse
of Joshua's talent, and accelerate the course of that
luminary:

By force prophetic Joshua stopp'd the sun,
But Morley hastens on his course with fun,
And listeners scarce believe the day is done.

Rumours have reached us of your dramatic fame.

[*Combe Florey*, 1840].

AN EPIGRAM.

I send Mrs. Murray my epigram on Professor Airey, of
Cambridge, the great astronomer and mathematician, and
his beautiful wife:

Airey alone has gain'd that double prize
    Which forced musicians to divide the crown:
His works have raised a mortal to the skies,
    His marriage vows have drawn an angel down.

A Liberal Person.

Do not imagine I am going to rat. I am a thoroughly honest, and, I will say, liberal person, but have never given way to that puritanical feeling of the Whigs against dining with Tories.

> Tory and Whig in turn shall be my host,
> I taste no politics in boiled and roast.

Poor Nick.

> Here lies poor Nick, an honest creature,
> Of faithful, gentle, courteous nature;
> A parlour pet unspoil'd by favour,
> A pattern of good dog behaviour.
> Without a wish, without a dream
> Beyond his home and friends at Cheam,
> Contentedly through life he trotted
> Along the path that fate allotted;
> Till time, his aged body wearing,
> Bereaved him of his sight and hearing,
> Then laid him down without a pain,
> To sleep, and never wake again.

On Mr. and Mrs. William Harcourt[1] passing their Honeymoon at the Lakes.

> 'Mid rocks and ringlets, specimens and sighs,
> On wings of rapture every moment flies,
> He views Matilda, lovely in her prime,
> Then finds sulphuric acid mix'd with lime!
> Guards from her lovely face the solar ray,
> And fills his pockets with alluvial clay.
> Science and Love distract his tortured heart,
> Now flints, now fondness, take the larger part,
> And now he breaks a stone, now feels a dart.

A Holocaust.

I am very glad, my dear Miss Fox, that you like my letter.[2] You see by the papers that the Great Western have given in, which on Friday last they positively refused to do. I

---

[1] Wm. Harcourt, geologist. [2] "On burning alive on railroads."

had another letter in store for them next week, in which I should have described them gazing with satisfaction on the burnt train of carriages and passengers.

1st Carriage. A stewed Duke.

2nd. Two Bishops done in their own gravy.

3rd. Three ladies of quality browned.

4th. Lawyers returning from sessions stewed in their own briefs à la Maintenon.

5th. First and second class. A grammar school returning home, legs out of window like a pigeon-pie.

6th. A fat woman much overdone.

7th. Two Scotchmen dead but raw, sulphuric acid perceptible.

God bless you, dear Fockey.

S. S.

ON JEFFREY'S THROAT.

How is Jeffrey's throat?—

> That throat, so vex'd by cackle and by cup,
> Where wine descends, and endless words come up.
> Much injured organ! Constant is thy toil;
> Spits turn to do thee harm, and coppers boil:
> Passion and punch, and toasted cheese and paste,
> And all that's said and swallow'd, lay thee waste!

TO LADY GREY.

As I know you are a good scholar, you may say to Lord Grey for me,—

> Precor ut hic annus tibi lætis auspiciis
> Ineat, lætioribus procedat, lætissimis exeat,
> Et sæpius recurrat semper felicior.

x

COMBE FLOREY, TAUNTON,
September 15, 1844.

MY DEAR LADY HOLLAND,

It is a sad scene, the last—the last act of life—to see beauty and eloquence, sense, mouldering away in pain and agony under terrible diseases, and hastening to the grave with sundry kinds of death—to witness the barren silence of him who charmed us with his exuberant fancy and gaiety never to be exhausted—to gaze upon wrinkles and yellowness and incurvations where we remember beautiful forms and smiles and smoothness and the blush of health and the bloom of desire, to see—but here I recollect I am not in the pulpit, so I stop.

Mrs. Stanhope, who is neither crooked nor yellow nor wrinkled, has been staying here for a fortnight.

DESPITE DR. JOHNSON.[1]

I doubt very much if I ever gained £1500 by my literary labours in the course of my life.

[*From a letter to Mrs. Grote on American Debts.*]

[1] Who said that nobody but a fool ever wrote except for money.

NOTES

The *Letters of Peter Plymley* appeared at first singly and were reprinted in sets of varying sizes. The complete set had run into numerous editions before the authorship was disclosed. The Rev. Richard King, Rector of Worthin, Salop, took upon himself the office of Brother Abraham, and wrote *Brother Abraham's Answer to Peter Plymley, Esq.*, and *The Patriot King, or Royal Rescue, being an invincible Refutation of the Letters of Peter Plymley*, in 1808. He did far less justice than Peter Plymley to the character of Brother Abraham and his replies were full of vulgar vituperation and gross calumny of Catholic saints. Sydney Smith appears to have ignored them.

Page 1. *Mr. Perceval.* Spencer Perceval (1762–1812) small, pale and pious Protestant, was Solicitor-General 1801, Attorney-General 1802. He was Chancellor of the Exchequer and nearly Chancellor of the Duchy of Lancaster for life under the Portland Administration in 1807 when George Canning was Foreign Secretary, and the *Letters of Peter Plymley* were written. Perceval was killed in the lobby of the House of Commons, when he was Prime Minister, in 1812. His assailant, though mad, was hanged for it.

Page 1. *Holland House.* The town house of Lord Holland, a social centre of the Whigs and advocates of Catholic emancipation.

Page 1. *Chancellor of the Exchequer.* Spencer Perceval.

Page 2. *Lord Mulgrave* (Sir Henry Phipps, First Earl of Mulgrave). Entered the army in 1775, and became General in 1809. He was First Lord of the Admiralty in the Portland Administration, 1807, and an incompetent.

Page 4. *Dr. Abraham Rees* (1743–1825). Cyclopædist. Tutor at the Hackney College and Pastor of the Old Jewry Congregation.

Page 4. *Dr. Andrew Kippis, D.D., F.S.A., F.R.S.* Nonconformist preacher and tutor in Hackney College for Dissenters.

Page 6. *His present Majesty.* George III, who strongly opposed Catholic emancipation.

Page 6. *Lord Howick.* Charles Grey, later 2nd Earl Grey. Foreign Secretary in Grenville's Ministry of "All the Talents," he resigned in the spring of 1807 when the king required a pledge that Catholic emancipation would not be re-introduced. He was a lifelong friend of Sydney Smith, and shared his strong opposition to repressive legislation.

Page 7. *London joker.* Canning.

Page 7. *Second-rate lawyer.* Perceval.

Page 9. *Baron Maseres* (1731–1824). Cursitor Baron of Exchequer, came of a Huguenot family, and was a zealous Protestant (Unitarian) and Whig.

Page 9. *Dr. Thomas Rennell*. Master of the Temple, and Dean of Winchester, scholar and divine, was, according to Sydney Smith, "a holy bully and an evangelical swaggerer who would kick and cuff men into Christians," and, fearful of Catholic machinations, a strenuous opponent of emancipation.

Page 9. *William Wilberforce*. M.P. for Hull and Yorkshire. Slave emancipator and leader of the Clapham Sect of Dissenters. Two of his four sons became Catholics, another was Bishop Wilberforce.

Page 9. *Dr. John Cockley Lettsom*. Quaker physician and philanthropist.

Page 9. *C——'s*. Canning's.

Page 10. *Human beings*. The Irish.

Page 10. *Dr. Patrick Duigenan*. Irish lawyer and politician, violently opposed to Catholic emancipation.

Page 10. *Mr. Thomas Newenham*. Member of Irish Parliament in 1798. Was a strong opponent of the Act of Union and endeavoured to promote the union of the Catholic and Protestant churches in Ireland. He wrote *Statistical and Historical Inquiry into the Population of Ireland* in 1805.

Page 12. *That man*. Perceval.

Page 14. *Lord Grenville* (William Wyndham, Baron Grenville) was Chief Secretary for Ireland 1782–3. Foreign Secretary 1791–1801, and resigned with Pitt on the Catholic question in 1801. He refused office because Fox was excluded from Pitt's second ministry in 1804. He was head of the Ministry of "All the Talents" which resigned on the Catholic question in 1807.

Page 14. *Thomas Killigrew*, the elder (1612–83) was a wit, writer of comedies and adventurer under Charles II.

Page 14. *Mr. Pitt* (William Pitt the younger) wished to complete his Irish policy, after achieving the Union, by granting Catholic emancipation in 1801, but George III was obdurate, so Pitt resigned.

Page 15. *Lord Hawkesbury* (Robert Banks Jenkinson, later second Earl of Liverpool) led the opposition to Grenville's ministry, and was Home Secretary for the second time from 1807–9. He was Secretary for War and Colonies under Perceval 1809–12, and an opponent of Catholic emancipation.

Page 16. *George Rose* was a close intimate and supporter of Pitt and held offices of profit under several governments. Lord Holland accused him of faking the account, which he presented to the House of Commons, of Pitt's last hours, and called him an "unscrupulous encomiast." His opponents said:

> *No rogue that goes*
> *Is like the Rose*
> *Or scatters such deceit.*

He and his sons derived large profits from their various offices. Sydney Smith attacked him in the *Edinburgh Review*, and Cobbett attacked him also.

Page 17. *Surveyor of the Meltings.* The sinecure of Clerk of the Irons and Surveyor of the Meltings was held by Perceval.

Page 18. *George Canning* refused office under Grenville, but was Foreign Secretary in 1807 under the Duke of Portland, the husband of his wife's sister. He was not intolerant—he retired with Pitt on the Catholic question. He wrote *The Needy Knife-grinder.*

Page 19. *Lord Castlereagh* (Robert Stewart, second Viscount) was Secretary for War under Portland in 1807. He had supported enfranchisement of Irish Catholics, but his methods in Ireland were ruthless and unscrupulous. His speeches, though well-informed, were long and tedious.

Page 21. *Terriers*=inventory or register of the property.

Page 25. *Jenkinsons.* Lord Hawkesbury and his father, Lord Liverpool.

Page 25. *Melvilles.* Henry Dundas, first Viscount Melville, impeached for malversation and found guilty of "negligence" in 1806; and Robert Dundas, his son, President of the Board of Control 1807.

Page 26. *John Hookham Frere.* Diplomatist and author, friend of Canning and Robert Smith (Sydney's brother), with whom he founded the *Microcosm* at Eton.

Page 28. *Sir William Hamilton, F.R.S., D.C.L.,* was Plenipotentiary at Naples from 1764 to 1800.

Page 28. *St. Januarius.* The patron saint of Naples.

Page 34. *Lord Amherst of Arracan.* Second earl, succeeded his uncle who was Commander-in-chief of Great Britain.

Page 34. *William Sturges Bourne.* Joint Secretary of the Treasury 1804–6, Lord of the Treasury 1807–9.

Page 37. *Henry Grattan.* Founder of the Dublin Whig Club, attacked parliamentary corruption and fought for Catholic emancipation. He was prominent as a member of the Irish and, later, Imperial Parliament.

Page 37. *Lord Redesdale* (John Freeman Mitford). Lord Chancellor of Ireland 1802, dismissed 1806. He was very unpopular in Ireland because he opposed Catholic emancipation, and the repeal of the Corporation and Test Acts. He had no sense of humour and a dull, drawling, tedious manner of speech.

Page 37. *Lord Eldon.* John Scott, first Earl of Eldon, was Lord Chancellor in the Portland Administration. He was an active opponent of Catholic emancipation and the Reform Bill. He could weep in public with facility, and did.

Page 39. *John Keogh* was the Irish Catholic leader instrumental in the passage of the Catholic Relief Act of 1793.

Page 39. *"Cardinal" Troy* was not a Cardinal, but Archbishop of Dublin from 1784 to 1823.

Page 43. *Poynings' Law.* Called after Sir Edward Poynings, Lord Deputy of Ireland. It was passed in 1494 and provided that no Act of the Irish Parliament should be valid unless previously submitted to the English Privy Council. This and several Acts restricting Irish independence were repealed in 1782.

Page 43. *Lord Auckland* (William Eden, first Baron). Member of Irish Privy Council and English Privy Council, President of the Board of Trade in Grenville's Ministry, 1806-7.

Page 44. *Hampstead Protestant.* Perceval.

Page 44. *Lord Henry Petty-Fitzmaurice.* Later third Marquis of Lansdowne, a very moderate Whig, met Sydney Smith at Dugald Stewart's lectures in Edinburgh. He was Chancellor of the Exchequer under Grenville in 1806, and a consistent supporter of liberal measures.

Page 44. *Samuel Whitbread.* The son of a brewer, was a close friend of Fox, and like him a vigorous defender of the oppressed, and an opponent of intolerance and maladministration.

Page 47. *Lesser of the two Jenkinsons.* Lord Hawkesbury, q.v.

Page 48. *Charles Rose Ellis.* First Baron Seaford, a friend of Canning, the Foreign Secretary.

Page 49. *George Augustus Selwyn* (1719-91). Wit and politician (a predecessor of Perceval in the office of Clerk of the Irons and Surveyor of the Meltings).

Page 49. *Richard Tickell* (1751-93). Barrister and pamphleteer, who obtained a pension for writing for the Government.

Page 56. *Porter.* Guinness, no doubt.

Page 56. *John Foster.* Later Baron Oriel, last Speaker of the Irish House of Commons, Chancellor of the Irish Exchequer, 1784, and again after the Union in 1804-6 and 1807-11. He opposed the Catholic Relief Bill of 1793, and opposed the Union.

Page 58. *Lord Sidmouth* (Henry Addington) was President of the Council in Perceval's ministry. He opposed the liberty of the Press and the Reform Bill, and his coercive measures were largely responsible for the Peterloo massacres.

Page 60. *Hanger.* A short sword, originally hung from the belt.

Page 60. *Mr. John Bannister.* A comedian.

Page 60. *Lord Fingall.* Arthur James, eighth Earl of Fingall, and later first Baron Fingall of the United Kingdom; a Catholic.

Page 63. *William Huskisson* was Secretary to the Treasury under Portland. He supported the Catholic Emancipation Act.

Page 65. *Lord Camden.* Sir John Jeffreys Pratt, second Earl and first Marquis of Camden, sometime Lord Lieutenant of Ireland. He was unpopular with the Irish because he opposed all remedial measures. He opposed Catholic emancipation until 1825.

Page 73. *Jesuits' Bark.* Quinine. Spencer Perceval secured the passing of the Jesuits' Bark Bill in 1807 to deprive the French of quinine and so embarrass Napoleon.

Page 77. *Trivial.* The schools of the three liberal arts—grammar, rhetoric, and logic.

Page 82. *Sir John Coxe Hippisley* was a diplomat who negotiated very successfully with the Vatican. He wrote *Observations on the Roman Catholics of Ireland* in 1806.

Page 82. *Sir Harry Englefield, F.S.A., F.R.S.,* was an antiquarian and scientific writer.

Page 84. *Lord Arden.* Charles George Perceval, first Baron Arden of Arden, Warwickshire, 1802.

Page 89. *Bentham on Fallacies.* A review of "The Book of Fallacies, from Unfinished Papers of Jeremy Bentham," *Edinburgh Review.* 1825.

Page 115. *Persecuting Bishops.* A review of five tracts on the subject of the eighty-seven questions proposed by Dr. Herbert Marsh, Lord Bishop of Peterborough, to candidates for Holy Orders and licences to preach in his diocese, from the *Edinburgh Review*, 1822. It was a common question whether Sydney Smith intended "Bishops" in the title to be in the nominative or accusative case.

Page 135. *Poor-Laws.* A review of four publications on the subject of the Poor Laws. The author wrote a further essay in the same strain on Scarlett's Poor Bill and other works on the Poor Laws, a topic on which he was always eloquent. The Poor Law Amendment Act of 1834 embodied many of Sydney Smith's proposals.

Page 137. *The Blue Coat School.* Christ's Hospital, more than once suffered from gross mismanagement. Sydney Smith much later propounded a theory that Blue Coat Boys were Quakers in chrysalis, see p. 279.

Page 156. *Game Laws.* A review of "A Letter to the Chairman of the Committee of the House of Commons, on the Game Laws: by the Hon. and Rev. William Herbert"; from the *Edinburgh Review*, 1823. Sydney Smith wrote several other vigorous essays on the same subject.

Page 156. *Spring guns.* For poachers, not game. There are two essays, "Spring Guns," and "Spring Guns and Man-Traps," in the *Collected Works*.

Page 170. *Characters of Fox.* A review, from the *Edinburgh Review*, 1809, of "Characters of the late Charles James Fox: by Philopatris Varvicencis" (i.e. Dr. Samuel Parr, a strong Whig and a friend of Bentham). Two other reviews on the subject of Fox and his historical work are printed in the *Collected Works*.

Page 178. *Chimney Sweepers.* From the *Edinburgh Review*, 1819, a review of an "Account of the Proceedings of the Society for superseding the Necessity of Climbing Boys."

Page 191. *The Society for the Suppression of Vice.* A review, from the *Edinburgh*, 1809, of two publications of the *Proceedings* of the Society for the Suppression of Vice. This provides an almost unique instance of the failure of Sydney Smith's propaganda. After over a hundred years, similar societies exist and flourish, and it is interesting to note that they behave exactly as Sydney Smith said they would.

Page 227. *Speech at Taunton.* The success of the Mrs. Partington speech was greatly enhanced, as were so many of Sydney Smith's speeches and witticisms, by his manner of delivery. R. A. Kinglake gives a vivid account in Stuart Reid's *Life and Times of Sydney Smith*, of how he demonstrated Mrs. Partington's actions with the mop.

Page 248. *Letter on the American Debts.* Printed in the *Morning Chronicle*. Sydney Smith had only a small pecuniary interest in America. This letter and others created a great sensation and much acrimony in America.

Page 252. *"Locking-in" on Railways.* These letters later had effect in the necessary legislation. They might well be written again in almost identical words to-day, substituting "the retention of gas lighting" for "locking-in," though gas was to Sydney Smith an innovation and a boon.